To Bill F
with
to my dear fr.
who introduc.
and thereby chang.
and to
the memory of my .
Meyer and Pauline L ,
who spent many sleepless nights
worrying about me
when I was "on the road."

Elvis Presley and Alan Fortas at Paramount Studios in 1958.

ELVIS

From Memphis to Hollywood

Alan Fortas and Alanna Nash

First published in Great Britain
2008 by Aurum Press Ltd
7 Greenland Street, London NW1 0ND
www.aurumpress.co.uk

Originally published by Popular Culture, Ink, 1992

A catalogue record for this book is available from the British Library.

ISBN 978 1 84513 322 1

1 3 5 7 9 10 8 6 4 2
2008 2010 2012 2011 2009

Printed in China

Contents

ACKNOWLEDGMENTS

The guys who made up the Memphis Mafia were, in almost all respects, like a family to me. We had great times together, we learned from each other (in retrospect, maybe some things we shouldn't have!), we stuck up for each other, and sometimes we threatened to shoot each other on the spot. But isn't that what all families do? I love you guys. Thanks for being there, not only in the fifties and sixties, but in the decades that followed. And thanks for helping me stretch my memory for this book, and for filling in details that had somehow escaped me.

Heartfelt thanks also goes to Priscilla Presley for continuing to be a friend. You're a class act--always were--and I'm thrilled to see all your success.

Thanks, too, to Colonel Tom Parker, for the memories--and for the recent phone calls. You made an old boy feel good.

And I'm especially grateful to Jerry Schilling and Elvis Presley Enterprises for allowing me to quote and reprint my letter from Elvis, which he wrote while he was in Germany in the army.

A number of other people deserve more than a mention. My son Miles, for example, was extremely supportive of the project, and never complained of the time it took away from whatever plans we might have had together.

I'd also like to thank Tom Schultheiss, my editor and publisher; Charlotte Sheedy, who acted as the agent on the project; Joanne Tingley, who waded through years of tape recordings and transcripts; Connie Lauridsen Burk and Lee Cotten, who read the manuscript for accuracy; and Alanna Nash, who gave unsparingly of her editorial assistance and advice. Alanna would like to thank Betty Williams, Gale Snyder, Richard H. Nash, Jr., Allan Nash, Emily Kay Nash, Elizabeth Bibb, and Judy F. May, who each played a part along the way.

Alan Fortas
Memphis, March 1992

EPIGRAPH

Is this

Grief? You pray
To God that this be grief, for
You want to grieve.

This, you reflect, is no doubt the typical syndrome.

But this will come later.
There will also be the dream of the eating of human flesh.

--Robert Penn Warren, "Tale of Time," 1960-1966

Prologue

The sweat streamed down the small of my back and gathered in heavy pools at my waistband. God, I was nervous! It was June 27, 1968, the scariest day of my life. I couldn't breathe, I couldn't talk, I couldn't do anything. The only time I'd ever been in front of a camera before this, I'd played a bit part, at best. Usually I was just an extra, a guy who threw a few punches in a fight scene, or sat at a table in a nightclub. And now, here I was, just an employee--not a musician, not even a songwriter--about to go on stage in front of a live audience for the most important concert of Elvis Presley's career, a concert that would later run on national TV for a viewing audience of millions.

I had been with Elvis for close to twelve years, eleven of them as part of what he jokingly referred to as his "Memphis Mafia." Like all the guys, I had several duties. I took care of his cars and made sure they got serviced when they needed it, I helped him buy his street clothes, and sometimes I drove his wife, Priscilla, or his manager and handler, Colonel Tom Parker, when they needed to go out of town. Currently, I was also the foreman for the Circle G Ranch that Elvis had bought down in Mississippi. Mainly, though, my job was just to hang around and keep Elvis company, and to keep him amused. Sometimes I was pretty good at it.

Music, however, was another matter. You could put all my knowledge of music inside the world's smallest thimble and still have plenty of room. And now I was about to go out and show everyone on the face of the earth how much I didn't know.

1

We were in Burbank, California, at the studios of NBC-TV, where Elvis was taping his first television special, "Elvis," now generally known as "The Singer Special," for the sewing machine company that sponsored the show. The special, which was scheduled to run the following December, would last an hour, and consist of various performance segments. The taping that day called for two hour-long evening concerts, one at six o'clock, and one at eight, which would be edited together into one of the segments--the one that opened the show.

Shortly before the first concert, panic gripped me around the throat and delivered a one-two punch to my head and stomach. I felt as though I were spinning somewhere out in space, clutching frantically for something solid, something familiar. Suddenly, I heard Elvis's voice.

"Alan," he said. "Come here."

"What?"

"I know you're nervous, man. I know you're scared."

I swallowed hard. My palms were sweating, I had a terminal case of dry mouth, and my heart was pounding to beat the band. I looked down at my hands. They were strangers, shaking at the end of my arms. "Nervous ain't the word for it," I rasped. "I'm backing out of this deal, man. Forget it."

"Look," he said. "Just act like we're in the living room at home, with nobody around but us. Don't worry about it. Be yourself."

I shook my head.

"I promise, man," he said. "You'll be okay."

What Elvis didn't understand was that I was as nervous for him as I was for myself. What if I acted like a fool and messed up? I wasn't qualified to be there, and it was hard enough for Elvis to take care of his own part, much less worry about me, too. But Elvis had a hell of a lot more riding on this deal than I had. And I'd already seen him sweating in make-up.

In June of 1968, Elvis was thirty-three years old and at his physical peak. Lean and lithe--he'd recently traveled to Hawaii to trim off the results of his cheeseburger attacks--he looked like some kind of mythological god, especially in the tight black leather outfit that costume designer Bill Belew had

created for the show. But Elvis had been more or less seques-
tered in Hollywood for the last eight years, making twenty-
eight motion pictures, most of them embarrassing throwaways.
None of them lost money, but his movies weren't turning the
profits they used to, and the reviews seemed to get worse with
each one. It wasn't that Elvis wasn't a good actor--a lot of the
critics thought he showed real flair, especially in his dramatic
roles. But the scripts were terrible, the songs were worse, and
Elvis really didn't care about his movie career much anymore.
He knew it wasn't going to get better.

Understandably, he was anxious about the TV special. He
hadn't made a television appearance since 1960, when Frank
Sinatra, Sammy Davis, Jr., and other establishment show-biz
heavies welcomed him home from the army. On top of it, he
hadn't done a live concert since 1961, and his records hadn't
topped the charts with any consistency for six years. The
Beatles and the psychedelic era had knocked the wind out of
his sails, and the movies had made him seem passe, a kind of
pathetic caricature of himself.

Elvis knew that he was no longer the rebellious teen-idol
rocker of old. After all, his daughter, Lisa Marie, had been
born earlier in the year. And recognizing that he was more like
Dean Martin, an early idol, than the rough-and-ready Hillbilly
Cat, he told producer-director Steve Binder that he felt "sheer
terror" at the possibility that the public might not like him
anymore.

As it turned out, that was exactly what Binder wanted to
hear. Binder was cool. He'd done a Petula Clark special before
this one--the one in which Harry Belafonte touched Petula on
the arm and all of up-tight white America went crazy--and he
had a gift for sizing up a performer and psyching him out.
Binder was a Presley fan. And on this particular special, he
wanted people to see the real Elvis, not the Elvis that the
Colonel wanted people to see.

Colonel Parker is one of the sharpest individuals I've ever
known in my life, bar none. But Colonel wanted this to be a
Christmas special, one of those wholesome shows for the little,
old, blue-rinse ladies who hung out at the Singer Sewing

Machine centers. There was talk that Colonel had cut this deal as a TV special *and* a movie, so that he could get his usual million dollars. The way he saw it, Elvis would come out and sing a few Christmas songs on a stage full of plastic snowflakes, there'd be some kind of corny exchange with a guy in a Santa Claus suit--probably Colonel himself, since he always played Santa on Elvis's Christmas cards. And after a homey scene with a pretty girl and a roaring fire, Elvis would be out of there with a "Ho, ho, ho" and an "Auld Lang Syne," no doubt a couple of elves in tow.

Binder, though, tapped into Elvis's soul. He saw that he was ashamed of some of the songs he'd recorded, particularly a lot of the stuff on the soundtrack albums--junk like "Do the Clam," and "(There's) No Room to Rhumba in a Sports Car." He sat Elvis down and found out he was hip to a lot of the changes in contemporary music, that he loved "MacArthur Park," for example, and that he would have cut it if he'd had the chance.

He also convinced Elvis that this Christmas theme was kind of like doing another of his nowhere movies, and that this was his moment of truth--that he could either recapture the magnificent essence he once was, or he could return to grinding out mass-production hack movies. Elvis was fast becoming a musical joke, as irrelevant to the music of the sixties as Bing Crosby. The special was his last chance to turn that around. If it was done right...well, nobody in Elvis's camp used the word "comeback," but everybody knew that's what it meant.

It took a long time to turn Colonel around on this Christmas deal, and it didn't help matters that he kept calling Binder "Bindle." Finally, however, Steve got him to accept the idea of presenting the adventures of a young man leaving home and making his way in the world. Elvis was still pretty freaked about all of this, though, and Colonel demanded a damn meeting anytime anybody looked cross-eyed. As a result, executive producer Bob Finkel made it his business to make Colonel happy on the set, and Binder started looking for ways that Elvis could chill out during rehearsals.

Elvis was basically a hyper guy, and the only time he ever

really felt comfortable was when he was performing or hanging out with Joe Esposito, Charlie Hodge, Red West and all the rest of us who made up his so-called "bodyguards." Binder knew this, so he suggested that I get together with Charlie and Scotty Moore and D.J. Fontana, Elvis's long-time guitar player and drummer, and the five of us use whatever methods we could to get Elvis to relax and cut up before he went on camera. I didn't know it then, but Binder watched to see how well this experiment went down. If Elvis loosened up enough, sitting around talking to the guys he knew and trusted, Binder wanted to work it into the show.

We spent about a week sitting around together at night in Elvis's dressing room, trying to relax at the end of a long day that started at noon and ended around midnight. Scotty brought in a couple of guitars, and he and Elvis and Charlie banged around a little, while D.J. kept time. Mostly, they just played the old songs, like "Love Me," or "Are You Lonesome To-night?"--stuff they were comfortable with. In between, we'd tell stories on each other, remembering the old days, like the time I went through Elvis's fan mail and found all those pictures of naked girls who had written in asking for autographs, or funny and weird things that happened on the road. This went on for four or five hours a night. We laughed a lot, and we had a ball.

Binder kept a tape recorder going during all this, and when he listened back, he liked what he heard. The jam sessions took the edge off Elvis's anxiety, and they showed him to be the witty guy that he really was, something that rarely came through in his concerts or movies. In the end, Binder decided to open the special with the five of us up on stage--joined by Lance LeGault, a former L.A. disc jockey, blues singer and Elvis's double in the movies--to recreate the informal guitar-pullings we'd had in the dressing room.

By now, Colonel was certain that this wasn't going to be any Christmas special, even though Elvis would sing two bluesy Christmas songs in the show. So, in relaliation, he managed to get in a couple of good licks. The first came before the taping of our first jam session. For each of our concerts, we were to have

5

a different audience, and Colonel insisted that he personally give out the tickets for the first show. But, for reasons known only to Colonel--maybe just to prove who was really the boss-- he stashed the tickets in his pocket instead of giving them away.

Just before show time, then, when the studio was still half empty, the producers ran around as nervous as a pack of politicians on primary day. Where was the goddamn audience? Finally, they just ran out into the streets of Burbank, pulling people into the studio any way they could, seating them on the bleachers set up around the fifteen-by-fifteen-foot stage.

Then, at the last minute, Colonel, who's as shrewd as they come, suggested putting the best-looking girls closest to the stage, even seating a couple of them *on* the stage near Elvis. This was Colonel at his carnival-barker best, moving through the crowd asking, "Who here really loves Elvis?" and picking the prettiest faces.

When Elvis came out on stage that night, the girls reacted just like Colonel knew they would--some crying, some shriek-ing--the way they had since 1955, when the lightning bolt from Tupelo split the Rock of Ages. Elvis, however, strumming a big shiny electric guitar, was still so nervous that his hand shook when he reached for the mike. Lance sat closest to him, down on the stage, rather than on a chair, and played tambourine when he wasn't helping Elvis position the microphone stand. The rest of us, Charlie, Scotty and D.J., and me, dressed in red suits that matched the trim on the stage--Christmas, you know--tried to pretend we were in Elvis's living room at Graceland, picking out a rough accompaniment.

I don't remember much about how we finally got started. I just remember a floor director pointing straight at my heart, after which I frantically tried to keep time on the back of a turned-around guitar. After about ten minutes, it really did feel like we were at home, with the music taking us places only music can take you. Elvis seemed rattled for a long time--he forgot the words to "Santa Claus is Back in Town"--but then we were laughing and cutting up as usual, teasing Elvis about his tough leather suit, and echoing one of his favorite expressions,

"Random memories. Good times."
Wall-to-wall fans--some of the best times that I can recall.

"My boy, my boy, my boy!"

Eventually, Elvis relaxed and got into it, too. He joked about the time in the early days when the cops came out in Florida to make sure he didn't do anything obscene on stage ("I couldn't move anything but my little finger"), a situation that still clearly hurt his feelings. Then, when he felt steadier, he delivered a mock serious rendition of "Are You Lonesome To-night?" And in both sets, he jumped into a few impromptu bars of "MacArthur Park," probably as a message to Binder that the music that was going down that evening was far more real and roots-oriented than the stuff that was hitting the charts those days.

Everybody there that night knew it, too. Elvis ripped it up as he hadn't done in a decade. He gave it everything he had that night, and he proved that he still had the passion and the muscle to do it right, moving through the early hits--"That's All Right (Mama)," "Blue Suede Shoes," "Tryin' to Get to You," "One Night"--not as some sweetly amusing nostalgia act, but with the vengeance of a wild animal that's been caged too long. By the end of the second set, he was so exhausted we almost had to carry him to his dressing room. But hissing, sweating and strutting across that stage that night in his solo segments, his hair the color of blue-black ink and his body coiled like some sexual python, Elvis was the most potent rock star of all time, the biggest surprise of sound ever to ride the train. Those girls got as hot as the tip of a sparkler on the Fourth of July. You'd have thought Elvis had slipped his hand right into their undies.

When the show aired on December 3, it received an enormous reception, becoming one of the top-rated specials of the season, and more important, setting the standard for rock performances on the small screen. Critic Jon Landau wrote that there was "something magical about watching a man who has lost himself find his way back home."

But as Elvis enjoyed the finest and most important moment of his life, renewing his self-respect and giving him the confidence to return to the performance stage, I knew that my days with Elvis were numbered. For just an average kid from

Memphis, my dozen years with Elvis had often seemed like a dream. They taught me a lot of things I wouldn't have learned in books or in the business world. But in 1968, I was thirty-two years old. For a long time now, I'd felt the need to move on. I knew that the older you get in life without a real career, the harder it is to find one.

And there were other reasons. Being with Elvis wasn't much fun anymore, partly because of his rapidly growing drug habit, and partly because of my own. Somehow, things had gotten wildly out of control, and I didn't know how to stop it. Elvis had popped megadoses of stay-awake and sleeping pills for years, but nothing like what he'd been doing in 1967-68. And I had done so many uppers and downers for so long that I knew I was in big trouble, caught in a narcotic web of my own making. But I couldn't do much about it as long as I stayed with a boss who was, in effect, a benevolent enabler.

Finally, in 1969, I looked up from my hospital bed and saw the face of Elvis Presley staring down at me. Days before, I had damn near died of an overdose. Working for Elvis was the best and the worst thing that ever happened to me. I wouldn't trade the experience for anything in the world. But I also wouldn't repeat it for all the prayers in heaven.

####

Elvis with our buddy George Klein, January 1958.

Chapter 1

Donkeys In The Pool
Graceland And The Boppin' Hillbilly

The summer of 1957 seemed like one of the steamiest on record. It was especially sweltering in Memphis, my hometown, and the place I'd come back to after I'd quit Vanderbilt. I hadn't exactly been the school's top honor student. I lasted a year-and-a-half over there in Nashville, but then they asked me to leave, temporarily, of course, because of my grades. I could have re-entered, but it was just too hard of a school, and if the truth's told, I never studied. Hell, I hadn't gone to Vandy to set any records for scholarship. I'd gone to play football.

Anyway, I was home in Memphis. I'd gone to local Southwestern College for a quarter, but it was harder than Vanderbilt. I'd leaped from the frying pan into the fire, so I quit and started working at my father's scrapyard. I'd just turned twenty-one, and, like a lot of twenty-one-year-olds, I wasn't sure what I was going to do with my life. I'd planned on majoring in business administration if I'd ever gotten past my sophomore year. Instead, my college career had ended, and I wasn't particularly eager to think about things like that just now. Besides, summer was the season for fun, for meeting girls and having a good time.

One night I got a call from George Klein, a guy I'd known during high school through the local Jewish organizations, even though George had gone to Humes, a technical and vocational school, and I had gone to Central, one of the largest high schools in Memphis. George was a popular guy in high school. He'd been president of his class, and voted the student "Most Likely to Succeed." Afterwards, he'd gotten into the radio business a little bit, a job that behooved him to stay in contact with Elvis Presley, the most famous guy to ever come out of Memphis. In fact, George traveled with Elvis when his schedule permitted.

My freshman year at Vanderbilt University no mystery why Elvis dubbed me "Hog Ears

The imposing facade of Humes High today (Humes is now a Junior High).
(Photo: Alanna Nash)

George had never learned to drive, and he said if I'd carry him out to Graceland, Elvis's mansion in the Whitehaven section of Memphis, he'd introduce me to him. George even pumped me up a little when he told me what an avid football fan Elvis was, and how he'd like to meet *me*.

Elvis was just a year older than I was, and back in his days at Humes High, where he was, believe it or not, a *library* worker, he went to a lot of football games, particularly whenever Central played. Central had one of the top teams in the state, along with Southside, the other big giant in Memphis high school football. It was nothing for us to have thirty thousand people at our games--you could get in for $1.50--and on Thanksgiving Day, we'd sell the stadium out. We took football seriously enough to have college-type coaching, and we were one of the only high schools in the state that sent its players away to football camp every year.

By the time I was in the eleventh grade, I was offered scholarships to what seemed like every college in the country. As an All-Memphis player and Central's defensive guard, I'd gotten my share of newspaper clippings then, since the *Commercial Appeal* wrote up the games every Saturday. We lost maybe two or three games the whole three years I was there. Little did I know that Elvis, who hadn't played for Humes for various reasons--Coach Rube Boyce decided he didn't make the cut when he went out for the team in 1951, and his mother was afraid he'd get hurt anyway--was following every one of them.

When George and I arrived at Graceland that night, passing through the ornate wrought-iron music gates that Elvis had just had installed a couple of months earlier--he'd only bought Graceland in March of that year--I had mixed emotions.

I was excited, and a little scared, because here was a wild-eyed kid with wicked good looks who'd set the universe ablaze with his music and the way he moved. The first time I heard his early Sun records on radio, I said, "This guy's got something." I didn't even know he was from Memphis until I saw him perform at the Overton Park Shell in July of 1954.

It was basically a country show with Slim Whitman, Billy

14

Walker, and some folks I'd never heard of, and Elvis did about three songs--Arthur Crudup's "That's All Right (Mama)," a flying blues with a country beat, "Blue Moon of Kentucky," a souped-up version of the Bill Monroe classic, and "Good Rockin' Tonight," the Wynonie Harris blues tune. I'll never forget it, because the crowd just about did a collective back flip. They kept screaming and clapping even after he was offstage. He came back out, looking bashful and like he was trying to find some place to put his hands, and managed a crooked smile. "Uh, I'd like to do some more songs," he stammered, "but I don't know any more."

I knew then that Elvis was like a comet, straight out of the heavens, a meteor just passing through. He was too original. But I didn't dream of how big he would get because, hell, nobody'd ever gotten that big before. By 1957, the year George took me out to Graceland, Elvis had made three movies, "Love Me Tender," "Loving You" and "Jailhouse Rock," and his singles were selling like thousand-dollar bills for a quarter--fifty thousand copies a day. *Life* and *Look* had written stories about him, how the son of a small-time Southern farmer (nobody actually printed the term "white trash," but that's the idea that some people got), sang in his parents' First Assembly of God church, made note of how those rag-tag preachers moved and jumped all over the piano, cut a little record for his mama, and somehow parlayed that into nationwide fame.

Steve Allen and Ed Sullivan had put him on their national TV shows, too, where he'd looked pimple-faced, clumsy and unsophisticated--even a little hayseed--and ready to spontaneously combust. And his new friends included Natalie Wood and Nick Adams, who'd come to Memphis all the way from Hollywood to see him.

On top of it, everybody, everywhere, was talking about Elvis Presley. The funniest part was that parents and school officials were going back and forth about whether his act was obscene. "We do not tolerate Elvis Presley's records at our dances, or blue jeans, or ducktail haircuts," said a school principal in Wichita Falls, Texas. Even Billy Graham stepped into the pulpit to declare that, "Elvis isn't the kind of boy I'd like

Elvis had pretty much been a regular on the "Louisiana Hayride" from October 16, 1954 to April 7, 1956.

my children to see." And when two high school girls from San Francisco, a so-called "liberal" part of the country, won a "Why I Love Elvis" contest and were flown to Hollywood to collect a kiss, their principal *expelled* them, declaring, "We don't need that kind of publicity."

Of course, in decades to come, such indignation would do a royal turnabout. The Smithsonian Institution, for starters, would call Elvis "the single greatest event in the 200-year history of American music." But in the wildest stretch of my imagination, I wouldn't have been able to guess that Elvis would transform American music, American life, and American culture. How could an uneducated Southern boy do that? Especially a little cracker who sounded black, a boy who sang for the segment of lower-class society that had been refused even the slightest privilege? I saw only that he had become a millionaire traveling around the country, shaking an invitational hip, getting the girls, and having the time of his life.

So I was thrilled to be meeting Elvis Presley, yes sir! And nervous about what I was going to say. But I was proud that my ability to play football had made me a little special to Elvis, too.

The Elvis Presley I met that night was about as jovial a guy as you'd ever hope to find. Handsome, well-dressed, with his trademark pompadour greased with Royal Crown Pomade and gleaming like a new Cadillac (Elvis called it his "Tony Curtis Cut"), he was friendly and accommodating--none of that "big shot" stuff. He tried to make me feel at ease, told me to take a load off. We talked about football a lot, and I saw that if he got interested in something, he did it 190 percent. I figured he could play football for twelve hours straight.

In fact, he said that he and his buddies played tackle there at Graceland all the time. The previous Christmas, he and Red West, his old pal who'd helped him fight his battles in high school, staged a rough game at Elvis's old house on Audubon Drive. Later I found out that Elvis was a pretty good player. He didn't mind getting tackled at all, but since he was making movies, everybody pretty much left his face alone.

Even though I knew that George went out to Graceland all

The marquee of the old Rialto Theatre, Louisville, Kentucky, December 8, 1955. Elvis is second on the bill to the Hank Snow Jamboree. (Photo: Univ. of Louisville Photographic Archives, Lin Caulfield Collection)

the time, I was surprised to find that Elvis had a kind of "inner circle," a group of guys who either lived there with him or went everywhere he did, a sort of fraternity of bodyguards. It made sense, of course--Elvis was becoming so famous, and aside from the fact that he just needed help looking after his affairs at home and on the road, he couldn't go anywhere by himself. Girls had attacked him in the showers after a show in Jacksonville in May of 1955, and it just seemed to snowball.

The funny thing was that male fans were getting about as bad now, and Elvis needed somebody to keep them away when he didn't want to be bothered. And then there were the guys who got jealous when their girlfriends carried Elvis's picture in their wallets. Elvis had gotten into more than one fist fight in a situation like that. And before long, he would make me a present of the ring--a horseshoe of diamonds spanning a gold horse's head--he'd broken in a bar in Toledo in exactly that kind of scramble, when a steelworker doubled up his fist, saying his ex-wife's love for Elvis had broken up their marriage.

But I also knew that Elvis thought a lot of Frank Sinatra, and I wondered if Elvis's entourage was a way of emulating his hero. Then, too, I had the feeling, even that first night, that Elvis was kind of a lonely guy, that he didn't like to be by himself, and that he just needed companionship. It was something he'd always had, first with his mother when he was a child, then with Scotty Moore and Bill Black when he started working on the road, when they were the "Blue Moon Boys" and Elvis was the "Boppin' Hillbilly" (soon to be the "Hillbilly Cat").

In decades to come, Elvis's girlfriend Linda Thompson would say that he needed more care than anybody she'd ever met, both because of where he came from and what he became, and because his parents, though poor, had spoiled him and catered to him from the time he was born. He craved that love all his life.

As the years went on, Elvis would stay in his room for days on end and never come out. But in these early days, in spite of a restless quality about him, he wanted people around him at all times. And when they were there, he usually seemed like one of the happiest human beings in the world. Stuff was always going on at Graceland--people playing games, listening to records, drinking Pepsi and watching TV, riding motor-cycles, shooting off fireworks. The more stuff going on, the happier he was. He loved to play tricks on people, and he was as big a joker as anybody.

I also came to realize that Elvis wanted friends who talked like him, who were from the South, who shared his love of Southern cooking, and who knew his ways and were easy to be around. Especially since he was spending more and more time out in Los Angeles, a place where you can lose your way and get taken advantage of pretty quickly. Elvis may have been happy, but he wasn't always the most secure person. And nothing in his background could possibly have prepared him for what lay ahead.

I've forgotten exactly who was there that first night, but it was likely Lamar Fike, Elvis's cousins Gene and Billy Smith, and Cliff Gleaves, who did a little of everything, including part-time disc jockey work. As time went by, the guys who traveled with Elvis would have a fast turn-over rate, and some would come and go as many as three or four times. George Klein would have loved to have traveled with him full-time, but his radio job pretty much kept him grounded in Memphis.

George was fairly close to Elvis, and Elvis's affinity for him seemed to go beyond the camaraderie of two guys who went to school together. Part of it, I think, was that George was Jewish, same as me. In time, Elvis would ask a handful of Jews to join the inner circle, including Marty Lacker and Larry Geller. I loved being Jewish, and when I was growing up, most of my friends were Jewish. But I had friends who weren't Jewish, too.

Elvis told us once that there was a little Jewish blood in his family, from way back on his mother's side somewhere, but we always surmised that Elvis's fondness for Jews sprang from two situations. When the Presleys first moved to Memphis from Mississippi and couldn't find anywhere to stay, a rabbi let them live in the basement apartment of his house. Even as a

A shot of me and George Klein (right) taken at Graceland, hamming it up with none other than Miss Canada.

grown-up, Elvis never forgot the night he came in and turned on the lights and the rabbi fussed at him, saying, "Don't turn the lights on during the Sabbath, Elvis! We don't do that in the Jewish religion."

But Elvis also never forgot the people who were nice to him when he didn't have anything, and he always remembered the Jewish merchants who extended him credit when no one else would. That included the Lansky Brothers, Bernard and Guy, who serviced the black pimps and hustlers of Beale Street with outlandish clothing (Elvis would also hang out in the Beale Street blues joints), and who sold Elvis his bodacious pink-and-black Hep-Cat combinations and clear plastic shoes. Scotty Moore remembers that the first time the duck-tailed Elvis came to his house wearing a pink suit and white shoes, his wife almost went out the back door.

And it also included Harry Levitch, a local jeweler and wholesaler who had helped feed and clothe the underprivileged Red West when he was in high school. Elvis was astonished that anyone would be that kind-hearted, and so he went to Levitch when he wanted to buy a mixer for his mother, paying for it with the money he earned from his first record. Later, Elvis would become a regular customer, going back to buy a second Mixmaster "so we can put one at each end of the counter, and cut down on all the walking my mama has to do."

In contrast to Elvis and Red and some of the other guys, though, I came from a solid middle-class environment. Actually, my family was upper middle-class. We lived at the corner of Linden and Orleans, which was a prestigious address until people started moving east and the neighborhood went down. Urban renewal eventually got it, and we lived about two blocks from where they parked the city buses. Anyway, I'd never known what it was like to want for anything, much less struggle for the essentials of life. I went to camp in the summer, bought my clothes at the "right" shop, Julius Lewis, down on Union, and there were always plenty of cars to drive when I got old enough. I had everything I wanted, although, of course, at the time I didn't see it that way.

My family had been Memphians for generations. My mother's

parents ran a bakery down off of Main Street, and at the time I popped into the world on April 6, 1936, my father, Meyer Fortas, was in the grocery business. This was in the days before the big supermarkets, when every neighborhood had its corner store. He stayed in the grocery trade until I was in about the ninth or tenth grade, when he sold the store to my cousin and partnered up with my uncle Izzy Bloom to go into the scrap paper business. They called it the Dixie Wastepaper Company. It was like a junkyard, except people brought old waste paper and cardboard, rather than scrap iron or metal. He had taken a chance, and my mother, Pauline--everybody called her Midge--was proud of him.

My father was fairly successful, then, but his brother was the real star of the family. Abe Fortas almost went all the way from being just a local Memphis lawyer to becoming Chief Justice of the Supreme Court. As it turned out, he made it only to Associate Justice. President Lyndon Johnson had named him to succeed Earl Warren in 1968, but Abe pulled out from nomination when Congress accused him of "lacking propriety" because he accepted $15,000 for some lectures he'd given, and because he continued to advise Johnson--he'd always been his man--while serving on the high bench.

He resigned from the court altogether the next year, again over what they called "an ethics matter." Uncle Abe had collected a yearly fee of $20,000 for services to the family foundation of Louis E. Wolfson, who went to prison for selling unregistered securities. By this time, Nixon was in office, and power shifted from the Democrats to the Republicans. I always thought the charges were just a ruse to get my uncle out of the way. The Republicans had already jumped on his back for voting with the liberal Warren Court on issues such as obscenity and criminal defendants' rights. Compared to Watergate or some of the scandals of today, it was nothing. But Uncle Abe emerged as one of the most controversial figures of the Johnson administration.

I wasn't ashamed when it happened. I thought it was admirable that he had been a justice--LBJ had appointed him to replace Arthur Goldberg in 1965--and I was proud that he had always been so liberal. But I was never that close to him. He had come to the house only a few times when I was growing up, especially when my father was sick, or during traditional Jewish holidays.

I had an older brother, Billy, who, unlike me, was more of a student than an athlete. He was always small, very astute, and very smart, a Phi Beta Kappa. He grew up to become an attorney, specializing in real estate. When we were kids, teachers compared me to him all the time, although not very favorably. Usually they said, "There's no way you could be Billy's brother, not with the grades you make."

And so I became something of the Class Clown, always cutting up and making jokes. I was a sensitive kid, and I read a lot, mostly books about sports or animals. But I knew I couldn't make the Dean's List or the Honor Society, so I attracted attention some other way. You know the type: If three guys stood around and one started acting goofy, I was the one. Anytime anything happened, I always got the blame. But basically, I was a good kid, kind of sweet-natured and easygoing. I got into things like any other boy, but I didn't have any real bad problems.

That is unless you consider being overweight a problem. A few years ago, I went on a strict weight loss program, and now people tell me I look pretty trim. Before that, though, I'd been big all my life, from Day One. Nobody else in the family was big, but I guess I just ate too much. I was the apple of my father's eye, and I was very spoiled, because my father thought I could do no wrong. I was closer to him than I was to my mother, who was a lot stricter than he. If I wanted something and my mother said no, my father would either sneak it to me, or make sure I got it some other way.

That included food. He used to bring me all kinds of treats from his grocery, and of course, I'd just gobble them right down. By the time I was thirteen, I was buying my clothes in the stout shop or the men's department. That didn't stop me from having girlfriends in high school, though. In fact, I had several, maybe because I was a football star. All of a sudden, girls seemed more important than sports.

My childhood, then, was pretty normal. I remember learning only one really hard lesson, and that was the time I got the stuffing beat out of me when I was about fourteen. I'd gone to the movies with a friend, and we ended up at the corner of Parkway and Central. I had to catch a bus going toward town, and he had to catch one going east.

We were standing there waiting, when a car pulled up and five strange guys got out. At first they just stood around talking. Then my friend got on his bus and left me alone with these fellas, who must have been seventeen or eighteen years old.

To kind of get away from them, I went over and sat down on the steps of Fairview Junior High School. One of the guys came over and asked me where I went to school. I said, "I go to Bellevue." Well, Bellevue and Fairview were big rivals at the time. His voice was rough and razory. "Do you play football?"

"I'm in the seventh grade," I said. "I don't play very much, but I try."

"How tall are you?"

I told him.

Suddenly, his tone changed, and I knew I was in trouble. "Aw, I don't believe you're that tall."

"Yeah, I'm that tall."

He shook a thatch of unmanageable dark hair. "You don't look that tall to me. Why don't you stand up and let me see how tall you are?"

I was a little scared of this guy, but I didn't know any better, so I stood up. Next thing I knew one of the guys hit me from behind, and another knocked me in the face. In a heartbeat, my eye puffed up, and a knot the size of a plum grew out of the back of my head. I looked as though I'd been through some kind of sadistic fraternity hazing. When I got home, I went straight to bed. My brother, who was about seventeen, told my parents, and my father took me to the hospital and had me X-rayed.

I'm not sure what that taught me--not to stand up, for one thing--except that there are a lot of bullies around who'll do something like that for no reason at all. We hadn't hollered at

them or provoked them in any way, and then, in a flash, five guys came up and jumped me. I couldn't believe it, because I'd never experienced anything like that in my life. After that, I believed in safety in numbers. And I knew I wanted to run with the right pack.

Being with "the right pack" was probably one of the reasons I liked going over to Graceland that summer. Hanging around Elvis Presley was about the coolest thing a guy could do in Memphis, or anyplace else, for that matter. It made you feel like you could do anything--jump over the clouds, if you wanted to--like you were immortal. It was kind of like a dream, and sometimes a bizarre one. When I first started going out there, for example, Elvis had three or four live donkeys--a gift from Colonel Parker--living in the new swimming pool. Those were only temporary quarters until the fence was completed all the way around the property, but I loved the oddity of it. I also liked going out there because it gave me something on my brother, Billy, who was on his way to becoming a lawyer while I was recycling trash at my daddy's junkyard.

I was still working at the Dixie Wastepaper Company, when one day a Board of Education truck came in with a ton of paper to dump. I looked through some of it, and saw that it was a bunch of old school records for the Memphis area. For some reason, I thought, "God, wouldn't it be funny if I found Elvis's report card?" And, I swear, about the next one I pulled out was his. It wasn't just his report card, but a transcript of all of his grades from the eighth grade through the twelfth. I looked at one of the first entries and cracked up: Elvis got a "C" in music.

That night, I was back out at Graceland, and I told Elvis what I'd found. "Do you want it?" I asked. "No, man," he said. "I'd probably just lose it. You keep it." And so I did. I have it to this day, in a safety deposit box at the bank.

I took Elvis's reaction to mean that he thought I was an okay guy. This was apparently one situation where my Class Clown antics were finally appreciated. Aside from the fact that Elvis was a big football fan, and we had that in common, he liked humor. I could keep him laughing, or I would get on the

Form 8   STANDARD TEST RECORD

NAME OF TEST	Form	Date Given	School Grade	Proper Grade According to Test	Chronological Age	Educational Age	Mental Age	Total Score or Grade Equivalent	Standard Median
Iowa Silent		5/9	8	7.6	Yr.	Yr.	Yr.		8-8
Reading		1949			Mo.	Mo.	Mo.		
Hundred Problem	✓	6/14		✓	Yr.	Yr.	Yr.	192	90
Arithmetic Test		1949			Mo.	Mo.	Mo.		
Metropolitan Achiev.	T	1949	8	10-1	Yr.	Yr.	Yr.	10-1	8-7
		19			Mo.	Mo.	Mo.		
					Yr.	Yr.	Yr.		
		19			Mo.	Mo.	Mo.		
					Yr.	Yr.	Yr.		
		19			Mo.	Mo.	Mo.		

ACCUMULATIVE RECORD CARD

MEMPHIS CITY SCHOOLS

The Accumulative Record Card is designed to furnish definite information which will assist teachers and principals in classifying a child as he passes from grade to grade or from school to school, and when he is promoted from the elementary school to the junior high school, or from junior high school to the senior high school, his Accumulative Record Card is to follow him.

When a pupil enters the Memphis City Schools for the first time, all the required data under I, II, and III should be carefully supplied. If the pupil has previously attended the Memphis City Schools, do not start a new Accumulative Record Card; his original card should be located.

The State Compulsory Attendance Law requires that the date of birth be correct.

The surname of parent and child must be written first.

When a pupil withdraws to make his home elsewhere his new address should be obtained by the teacher and recorded under IV, and the Accumulative Record Card sent immediately to the Central office.

When a pupil's Accumulative Record Card is requested by a Memphis City School all data asked for under V should be given. "Date of Transfer" should be interpreted as the date the Accumulative Record Card is sent from a school. Children who change schools during the first month should not be discharged or received as transfer pupils.

It is very important that the results of all standard tests be recorded on the Accumulative Record Card.

Elvis's Humes High report card. His middle name is here spelled correctly (Aaron), as it is on his grave, scant support for those who claim that Elvis Aron Presley lives on. (Photo: John Nation)

I Name of Pupil
Presley, Elvis Aaron

	Sex	Birth Date
	M	1/8/35

II Place of Birth
Tupelo, Miss.

Occupation

III Name of Parent or Guardian
Mr. & Mrs. Vernon Presley

If Recently Moved to Memphis
Former Address

Home Address: 370 Washington

Business Address

School Last Attended

IV Date of first entry in Memphis Schools NOV. 8. 1949

Age: 13 Years. Months. Placed in 8 Grade

Withdrawn: Date JUN 3 1953 Reason GRADUATED

185 Winchester

4 & Alabama

Telephone Number: 37-7961

When pupil moves from city give new address.

Record Data

V Transfer Data

From	To	Attendance This Year Present	Absent	Date of Last Attendance	Date of Transfer	Grade	Principal	Teacher
Humes	Co	157	28	6-13-53	6-10-53	12	Brindley	Scrivener

ELEMENTARY SCHOOL RECORD

		Gr.__	Gr. 8	Gr.__	Gr.__	Gr.__	Gr.__	Gr.__	Gr.__	Gr.__	Gr.
Attendance	Days Present		165								
	Days Absent		15								
	Times Tardy		0								
Health	Good										
	Poor										
SCHOLASTIC RECORD	Conduct										
	Arithmetic		C								
	Language		A								
	Reading										
	Spelling		B								
	Geography										
	History		B								
	Health										
	Music		C								
	Art										
	Physical Ed.		B								
	Science		C								
UNUSUAL ABILITIES OR HANDICAPS	Teacher										
	School										
	Date										

Elvis's report card for grades 8-12 reveals him to have been a fairly
average student, not the dumb "hillbilly" of biographers who allege
that he excelled only in subjects like woodshop. (Photo: John Nation)

HIGH SCHOOL RECORD

	Gr. 9	Cr.	Gr. 10	Cr.	Gr. 11	Cr.	Gr. 12	Cr.	Gr. ___	Cr.
Days Present	84		81		78		79			
Days Absent	1	9	4	9	1	12	13	15		
Times Tardy	1	3	2	5		3	9	14		
Good										
Poor										
Conduct			3		5		1			
English	B	B	A	C	1	C	C	1	C C	1		4
Civics										
Gen. Math.	B	C	1							1
Mathematics										
Social Science					C	C	1			1
Science	B	B	1				C C	1		2
Art	C	C	1							1
Speech			C C	1	C C	1				2
Typing										
Wood Shop			B B	1	B B	1	C C	1		3
Am. Problems							C C	1		1
Physical Ed.	B	B	¼							1¼
R.O.T.C.				4¼	C B	½	C C	½		4	1¼
Graduated										16¼
In Cl.										
Standing										
of Boys										
of Girls										
ding Among B										
G										
a-Curricular itles										

	Teacher	School	Date
	Henry Johnson	Henry Johnson	1-20-57
	Eugene J. Johnson	Eugene J. Johnson	6-2-50
	Henry Williams	Henry Williams	1-19-51
	Eugene Williams	Eugene Williams	6-5-51
	Henry Alexander	Henry Alexander	1-26-52
	Henry Alexander	Henry Alexander	6-4-52
	Henry Scranton	Henry Scranton	1-30-53
	Henry Scranton	Henry Scranton	6-3-53

other guys' cases and kid them a little bit, and Elvis just loved that. He didn't want us to get mad about it, but if we did, he wanted us to forget it and be friends again. You could pick up on Elvis's mood the minute he walked into the room. If he was real serious, it was time for everyone else to get serious. Or if he had a bad night, it was time to cheer him up. He'd look at me and say, "Get something going here. It's too quiet."

No matter what happened, though, Elvis wanted it known that he was both the boss and the center of attention. Sam Phillips, who first recorded Elvis at Sun Records, says Elvis tried not to show it, but he felt very inferior. Sam said Elvis was probably the most introverted person who ever came to the studio, since he never played with bands, and he didn't go to some little club and pick and grin. He only sat with his beat-up guitar on the side of his bed at home--didn't even play on the front porch. Sam was speaking about the nineteen-year-old Elvis, of course, but in some ways, Elvis never got beyond that.

For example, I'll never forget the night that Jerry Lee Lewis came to the house. Jerry had just made a sensation with "Whole Lot of Shakin' Going On" and "Great Balls of Fire." There must have been thirty or forty people there, and after awhile, we all ended up in the music room by Elvis's piano. Elvis sat on one side of the piano bench, and Jerry Lee sat on the other. They sang together for a little while, and then Elvis played his version of "Whole Lot of Shakin' Going On," and Jerry Lee played his. Then Elvis played "Hound Dog," and Jerry Lee played it, too.

This went on until the small hours of the morning, and, of course, George Klein and I were really loving it, telling Jerry Lee how good he was. Finally, when everybody left, Elvis came up to George and me and said, "Hey, y'all think Jerry Lee was good tonight?" And we said, "Yeah, Elvis, he's fantastic!" He said, "Good. Why don't y'all go see if he'll hire you?" And he turned around and went to bed. Of course, he was kidding, but sometimes he meant it, and sometimes he didn't. Elvis was one unpredictable character.

It hadn't been that long, after all, since Grand Ole Opry

manager Jim Denny had told Elvis he'd better go back to driving a truck, a sting, along with his rejection from "Arthur Godfrey's Talent Scouts," that never quite went away.

By January of 1958, I'd been going out to Graceland almost every night for six or seven months, and each time I was about to leave, Elvis would look at me and say, "See you tomorrow." In some ways, it seemed more like an order than a request or a way to end a conversation. But maybe that's because I knew the guys who traveled with him were on call twenty-four hours a day, seven days a week, and I was beginning to feel like one of the gang. Then, on January 12, he asked me what I was up to these days.

"I'm still just working for my father, Elvis."

"Can you get off for a little while?"

"Sure," I said. "When you work for your father, you can do whatever you want."

I was well aware that Elvis was set to do "King Creole" soon, and that he'd gotten a deferment from the draft to make it. But for some reason, I wasn't prepared for what came next.

"Good," Elvis said. "We leave tomorrow for California."

A begloved Elvis with friend Cliff Gleaves at Graceland, Christmas 1957.

Chapter 2

"King Creole,"
Hot Watermelons
And The Colonel

On January 13, 1958, Elvis boarded the train from Memphis to Hollywood, where he would begin filming "King Creole" for Hal Wallis and Paramount Pictures. This was his second movie on a three-picture contract, with fees that started at $100,000. With him were his cousin Gene Smith, Cliff Gleaves, Freddy Bienstock, who collected songs for Elvis to record, especially for the soundtrack albums, Tom Diskin, one of Colonel Parker's lieutenants, and me.

I'd hardly ever been out of Tennessee, and to me, this was *something*. The last time Elvis had been out to Los Angeles, that past October, he'd played the Pan Pacific Auditorium for two days, and just about anybody who was anybody in Hollywood--Sammy Davis, Jr., Nick Adams, Ricky Nelson, Carol Channing, and Tommy Sands--either came to the concert or to the open house afterward at Elvis's suite in the Beverly Wilshire Hotel. When the guys told me about it, I wanted to be able to say I'd met people like that, too.

First, though, there was this train trip to negotiate. Seemed like every little watering hole we passed through, a thousand girls were lined up and waiting for a glimpse of Elvis. Hell, the whole town would be there--people just everywhere. I wondered how they knew, but later I found out that Colonel Parker had planted the information so the people *would* turn out. Colonel figured that if Elvis passed through a town and nobody was there, he'd think his popularity was slipping.

Of course, Colonel knew the value of publicity like Proctor & Gamble knew soap. In years to come, when the reporters and photographers showed up, Colonel would always get a

mock scowl on his face, slide his cigar to the side of his mouth, and declare, "There must be a leak in our organization somewhere!"

Publicity was especially important on this picture for a number of reasons, several of which had to do with Elvis's imminent rendezvous with Uncle Sam. In two months, Elvis would report to the Memphis draft board, and both he and Colonel were plenty worried about whether the public would forget him during his tour of duty. Colonel probably could have kept him out--Colonel could do anything--but he figured it was more important to portray Elvis as the all-American boy.

Meanwhile, the task at hand was to keep him in the American consciousness through records and movies. That meant that "King Creole" had to be something special, a truth that echoed in every clack of the train wheels. Laying in his berth with a teddy bear from a lathered fan, his hooded eyes fixed on the ceiling, Elvis was snared in a whirlpool of emotion and doubt. At night, as the towns blurred by in the moonlight, he studied a game plan in his head.

Aside from how the army might derail his million-dollar sideshow, Elvis was concerned about something else. He'd done all right with the movies, especially "Love Me Tender" and "Jailhouse Rock." But he wanted to be known as a serious actor, in his view, "like Frank Sinatra or Dean Martin," or more to the point, the late James Dean. After Elvis's screen test, Hal Wallis compared him to Errol Flynn, saying he had "exactly the same power, virility, and sexual drive." But it was Dean whom Elvis wanted to replace. He revered Dean to the point that he could recite whole pages of dialogue from "Rebel Without a Cause." And in 1956, when he heard that Robert Altman, then an unknown director, was set to make a film about Dean's life and was looking for an actor to play him (Altman eventually decided to do a documentary), Elvis wanted to audition.

In fact, Elvis never smiled in a lot of his early photographs because Dean had looked so dark and brooding in his. And the James Dean connection was one reason Elvis got to be friends

To prove to my friends that I was *actually making movies with Elvis Presley*, I had wallet-sized pictures like these made up from shots taken at promotional photo sessions for "King Creole" held at Paramount Studios in 1958.

with Nick Adams and Natalie Wood, both of whom had been in "Rebel...." Just the same, I believe that Adams, who introduced Elvis to Natalie, sought out Elvis's friendship, rather than the other way around.

Elvis's career, after all, had blossomed right after Dean got killed in a car crash in September of 1955. As the new symbol of teenage rebellion, he doubtless inherited part of Dean's audience. Nothing could have thrilled him more. In her book, *Dennis Hopper: A Madness to His Method*, Elena Rodriguez quotes Hopper as saying, "When Elvis Presley first came to Hollywood to make a movie, he came to see me. He was twenty-one and a millionaire. He had seen James Dean in 'Rebel Without a Cause' and he wanted to know more about Jimmy."

When our California-bound train stopped at the major cities, reporters clamored for a few words with Elvis, wanting to know if he thought the army would render him washed-up with the American teens.

They scratched down every word Elvis uttered, even his usual nervous mumbling. They also rubbed it in about how much money the draft had cost him in terms of cancelled personal appearances, recording schedules, and movie commitments: $200,000 for a film for 20th Century-Fox, scheduled to have been shot that year, and $250,000, plus 50 percent of the profits, for MGM's bio-pic of Hank Williams. Elvis, ever the diplomat with the press, said he didn't know much about that, because he'd been learning his lines for "King Creole."

Based on Harold Robbins' best-selling novel, *A Stone for Danny Fisher*, "King Creole" co-starred Carolyn Jones, Dolores Hart (who'd been in "Loving You"), Dean Jagger, Walter Matthau, who would spend his spare time on the set playing poker with Colonel Parker, Vic Morrow, and Lilliane Montevecchi. Elvis played Danny, a beleaguered high school kid who worked two jobs and couldn't seem to graduate, and who wound up trapped in the New Orleans underworld of racketeers and hoodlums.

It seemed preposterous that Dean Jagger, the very essence of Yankee reserve, was cast as Elvis's Southern father, and that no one in the film but Elvis had a Southern drawl. There

were other credibility problems, as well. Why would any of the women in the picture be attracted to the men that the screenwriters had paired them with? And how could the figure of Danny possibly be the son of a pharmacist?

To the people who controlled the purse strings, and that included Colonel, it didn't matter. "King Creole" was essentially a star vehicle, and like all of the movies that Elvis made before he went into the army, "King Creole" mines the "poor-boy-makes-good" fairy tale that surrounded Elvis himself. As with the earlier films, "King Creole" preaches that the rebel can make it in society, but only if he sticks to the status quo.

Elvis's audience was supposed to not only applaud this, but apply it to their own lives. And those who had originally despised the rough-necked singer were now presumed to accept and even admire him for toning down his revolutionary image. As proof of Elvis's transformation in each of these films, he is attracted to a woman who is usually older, richer, and infinitely higher-classed. All the way around, it took an amazing willingness to suspend belief to pull this off.

We'd been in California a matter of hours when I got my first gander at Colonel Parker, who insisted that he be given "Technical Adviser" credit on every film. Later, I found out the title was mostly a perk Colonel negotiated into the contract, although he was also there to keep an eye on the production schedule. If anything cost Elvis Presley money, it cost Colonel, too. The only time I ever saw Colonel when he wasn't in a good mood was when things weren't running right. That meant the meter was ticking off dollar signs.

In those days, everybody knew Colonel as Thomas Andrew Parker, the "Colonel" designation an honorary title bestowed by the governor of Louisiana, country singer Jimmy Davis, in 1948, then seconded by the governor of Tennessee in 1953. Now, of course, it's come out that Colonel is really a Dutch national, born Andreas Cornelis van Kuijk above a livery stable in Breda, Holland, in 1909. It seems the Colonel entered the United States illegally in 1929, easily assimilating himself into the American culture, even allegedly serving a stint as the dogcatcher of Tampa, Florida, before the war.

In 1939, Colonel signed on as advance man for singer Gene Austin, traveling the backwater towns of the South. As a result, in the mid-forties, the Grand Ole Opry hired him to do advance publicity for their shows, starting in Tampa, and later in other Southern cities. That's when he became Eddy Arnold's manager, patterning his Southern "good ol' boy" persona after Arnold's former manager, Joe Frank. Colonel built the relatively unknown singer to national fame, and then took on country veteran Hank Snow when Arnold fired Colonel in '53, ostensibly for constantly meddling in Arnold's private life. For a time, so I heard, Colonel even moved in with Arnold and his family.

Some people say Colonel is a cross between W.C. Fields and P.T. Barnum. They also say he's the shrewdest huckster ever to walk down the pike, and that he's the con artist's con man. I say he's a genius. To reporters, Colonel would insist he was born to carney parents in West Virginia, and that he learned to trod the sawdust during his childhood, going to work for his uncle's pony circus when he was orphaned at the age of ten. Later, he supposedly joined the Johnny J. Jones Exposition, a respected outfit, going on to serve his real apprenticeship with the Royal American Show, the biggest and best collection of midgets, bearded ladies, two-headed calves and fire-eaters in the land.

Whatever the story on that, Colonel has pulled some of the most outrageous stunts in the history of show business--heck, his own masquerade is proof of that. I guess everybody's heard the story of how he painted sparrows yellow and sold them as canaries, and how he promoted "dancing chickens," by setting the poor peckers down on a hidden hotplate.

Marty Robbins used to tell a tale about how Colonel went down to a real small town in Mississippi, buying the big billboard at each end of town. Both billboards displayed only two words, "It's coming." Ten days later, he changed them to read, "I'll be here--December 4." By the time the date was announced, everybody got to wondering, "What *is* it? What's going to be here?"

Finally, the time came for *it* to be on stage. The theater

was packed, the money had already been put in the black bag, the back door was open, and the driver was in the car. And Colonel went in and pulled back the curtain, revealing only a big sign that said, "It's gone." Marty always said he didn't think the story was true, but that it was a perfect example of how far people thought Colonel would go to get something done. He knows every angle.

In other words, Colonel is as good in his field as Elvis was in his, and neither one of them would have been nearly as big without the other. Elvis was the talent, and Colonel knew how to sell it.

I'd get to spend a fair amount of time with Colonel in the years to come, since Colonel didn't like to drive, and I'd chauffeur him between Los Angeles and his home in Palm Springs. But here on my first visit to California, I could have sat and listened to him tell stories until Ft. Knox ran out of gold.

One of the funniest had to do with the days when Colonel promoted country shows down in Florida, before he became a personal manager to Arnold and Snow. Colonel, who had a reputation for squeezing a buck so hard you could hear George Washington yell, took a tent show into a town that immediately slapped a big amusement tax on him.

"I don't understand this," Colonel said.

"That's the way it is," came the reply.

Later, Colonel was driving along pondering the situation when he saw a big truckload of watermelons by the side of the road. Watermelons cost, let's say, fifty cents a piece back then. Whatever it was, it was a whole lot cheaper than the amusement tax. Colonel stopped and said, "Tell me, son, is there a tax on watermelons in the state of Florida?"

"No, sir."

That night, when people arrived for the show, they saw a makeshift watermelon stand set up next to the tent, with a big sign that read: FREE ADMISSION WITH PURCHASE OF WATERMELON. Colonel had just bought the whole damn truckload, and marked 'em up to the price of admission. He saved his tax, all right, but the only problem was, nobody could clap during the show because they were all sitting out there

with damn watermelons on their laps. Colonel said he looked out, and as far as he could see, there was nothin' but rows and rows of watermelons.

Who knows whether it's true? Knowing Colonel, I'd say it probably happened. But Colonel is a great storyteller, and when Colonel's in a good mood, there's nobody funnier in the world.

Elvis recorded the soundtrack album for "King Creole" almost as soon as we got out to California, cutting at Radio Recorders with L.A. studio musicians, the regular members of his band, and the Jordanaires, the vocal group that backed him on most of his RCA recordings.

Scotty Moore and Bill Black had quit traveling the road with him in September, but both would continue to play on records, Bill sticking around until Elvis went into the army, and Scotty until 1969. The way I understand it, Scotty and Bill had a long-standing gripe about what Elvis paid them. Despite the fact that he had become richer and more famous than even his most decadent dreams could have summoned in 1954, Elvis was still paying Scotty and Bill $150 a week at home, and $250 on the road, plus a $1,000 bonus at Christmas. That wasn't Elvis's idea, I'm sure. Elvis didn't really think about money--it didn't mean anything to him.

This was the first time I'd seen Elvis in the studio, and I was surprised at what a perfectionist he was, during this session and at every other one I would attend for years to come. The Hollywood recording sessions were always more rigid than the Nashville sessions, because they took place in the daytime, as opposed to nighttime sessions in Nashville, and the film company executives usually pushed to get the project finished.

Elvis took a long time to get settled into the mood of recording, and he'd usually prepare by sitting down at the piano and singing spirituals and religious songs with the Jordanaires. It seemed to relax him and stoke him up at the same time. The movie brass didn't understand this, though, and thought their young star was just wasting time and money.

During one of these sessions, the MGM honchos went over to the Jordanaires during a break and told them to cut this gospel crap, that they had to get on with the session.

When Elvis went back to the piano and the Jordanaires stayed behind, a wave of surprise rolled across his face. "What's wrong with you guys?" he asked. Their leader, Gordon Stoker, explained. Elvis's upper lip curled into a snarl, and, sap rising, he flew into a huff.

"If I want to bring you guys to Hollywood to sing spirituals all day long, that's what we'll do," he bellowed. And then he left. That was the last time anybody tried to alter his routine. When Elvis finally got down to business, he would sometimes cut a song in one take. But more often than not, he'd want to record it again and again, putting the musicians through eight, ten, or maybe fifteen takes. In 1956, he'd insisted on thirty-one takes on "Hound Dog." Apparently, he knew his stuff--the single sold six million copies in its first year of release.

The soundtrack to "King Creole" had a Dixieland influence rumbling through it, as well as some ballads and uncategorizable "filler." Some of the sting and raw energy had already begun to fade from the kind of music Elvis recorded--something that would especially prevail with Elvis's Hollywood sessions. But when he cut loose on the rocking "Hard Headed Woman" that day, he ate it alive.

Where did Elvis's real impulse come from? It's too easy to quote Sam Phillips' notion of "a white man who had the Negro sound and the Negro feel." Or even writer Lucian K. Truscott IV, who called it "an elegant hybrid of nigger and 'neck." Aside from instinct, I don't think anybody knew where it came from, not even Elvis. He couldn't read music, but he knew the sound he wanted ("Let's get real, real gone," as he said in the Sun days), and he would stop the session and say something like, "Scotty, could you try playing something with a little more space in the break?"

Scotty, a former dry cleaner--he was a hat specialist--had the fastest hands I'd ever seen. He'd answer with a bent note from a wailing guitar. Elvis would smile or frown, and they'd take it from there. If he flubbed the vocal, Elvis would turn

away from the microphone as if from a gun. He'd say, "Wait a minute, man, I don't like it. We gotta do it again."

Then he'd walk over and prop his left hand up against the studio wall and bounce on his toes, and then maybe chew his nails. Next he'd run his fingers through his hair, pull out his comb, close his eyes and roll his head, and crouch in the corner --listening to the music in his head. "Okay, guys," he'd say, his face a knot of determination. "Let's try it once more." He'd go again, then, pacing back and forth while he sang, giving the engineers fits trying to keep him on mike. Sometimes they'd have to put up two or three microphones just to catch his words, since he didn't like his voice to be too prominent on his records, preferring to sound only part of the whole. And so he often stood five or six feet from the mike, and when the engineer protested he was having difficulty picking up Elvis's voice, Elvis simply told him to turn up the volume.

Whatever they ended up with, Elvis wasn't about to short-change his merchandise--he had to be satisfied. And yet there were times when I think he doubted that he'd ever get it right. When that happened, unadulterated panic crossed his face.

We'd only been in California a few days when I found I'd already grown accustomed to the treatment afforded a member of Elvis's touring party. It was like a fantasy, traveling with one of the most famous people in the world, living in luxury at the Beverly Wilshire Hotel, signing for my cigarettes and cleaning --anything I wanted--and being around movie stars and studios. Elvis wasn't paying me a salary--we all worked for expenses then--but heck, if I had to, I would have paid *him* just to be there.

Elvis knew that, of course, and he got a certain pleasure from it, partly because he still thought of himself as just an average guy from Memphis who lucked into an incredible situation. But he loved to see the reactions of the guys the first time he took them out to Hollywood, and he'd watch our faces when we saw the celebrities that we'd always watched in the movies. I admit that it had a kind of "Twilight Zone" quality to it. One day I was working at my father's junkyard, and the next day I was sitting at the same dining room table with Carolyn Jones.

After Elvis's death, there was a lot of talk that he was such an unhappy guy, that he hated what his success had done to him, and that he wanted to just end it all. If the years finally took their toll, the Elvis I knew in the early days was a very different guy. He loved being around people, and he loved to see how people reacted to him. During "King Creole," for example, we left the studio one day in a chauffeur-driven limousine, when a kid, a young boy, came up to the car, all excited, panting, "Can I have your autograph, Mr. Presley?"

Elvis said, "Yeah." He leaned out the window to scribble his signature, when the kid suddenly said, "I've written a song, and I'd like to sing it to you, if that's okay!" Then the kid started rockin'. We listened patiently for a minute, and then we told the driver to pull out slowly. Well, the kid ran alongside the car, singing his lungs out. We just egged him on, saying, "Gee, the song's great, Elvis. Isn't it great?" And Elvis just laughed. Meanwhile, the kid was getting a little out of breath, but he must have sung for five blocks. Elvis loved it.

Naturally, I wanted to do a good job for Elvis, even if he really didn't make many demands on me. Mainly, I was there as a traveling companion. Elvis clearly would rather have been with us guys than with all those movie people. Some of them made fun of him behind his back--the way he talked, his hair, his music, the way he moved, his still burgeoning acting skills. He was as serious as a heart attack when it came to his career. And when he caught on to what they were doing, it cut him to the bone. He shied away from them after that, except when he had to be on the set.

One night I stayed up real late, and Elvis never liked us to sleep at the studio while he was working, because his routine was completely turned around from the schedule he kept at Graceland. There, he stayed up all night and partied, and slept in the day. But here he had to look sharp by the time the cock crowed, so we all tried to keep regular hours.

This particular day, I was so tired, I said, "Godalmighty, I have to take a nap someplace."

At the studio, each of the stars had a portable dressing room that went from sound stage to sound stage, and a permanent dressing room like a bungalow, with a kitchen and a shower. While Elvis was filming, I decided to sneak over to the permanent dressing room and lay down for thirty minutes.

When I finally woke up, I made the horrible discovery that it was seven o'clock at night. I sprang up and saw that it was completely dark outside. My heart raced like a Lotus. "Oh, God," I thought. "Elvis is gonna kill me!" I ran over to the sound stage where he'd been working. No Elvis. Then I panicked. Here I was at Paramount Studios in Hollywood, California, I didn't know a soul, and I didn't even know how to get back to the hotel. Finally, I had the sense to call transportation. Elvis had left at five. I was still trying to figure out what to do when a studio car pulled up, and the driver said he'd take me to the hotel.

I was nervous as hell when I walked into that place. But when Elvis saw me, he just started laughing.

"Gosh, Elvis, I'm sorry. I gotta admit it. I just slipped off and went to sleep."

But he didn't get angry, because he was too busy eating and sleeping this movie. He knew "King Creole" was a better-than-average story, that he was surrounded by top actors, and so he studied his lines every minute he could. Elvis was a very nervous person, so much so that he was frequently hot and perspiring. He always had an air conditioner on blasting cold air, no matter what the temperature outside. Reading and learning of any kind calmed him down. From as early as the days he traveled the blue highways doing one-nighters for Bob Neal, he'd declared his intentions of becoming a respectable actor. Bob remembered that Elvis would pump his wife, Helen, with, "Do you think I can make it? I've *got* to make it!"

Besides, now with his army hitch hanging over him, "I'm gonna be gone two years," he'd say. "I've gotta do a good job on this one." And yet after he'd see the dailies--the scenes filmed the previous day--he'd never watch the whole movie. He said he couldn't stand to--that he didn't like that fast-talking Southern boy up there on the screen. He mumbled so much that he

couldn't understand the words that came out of his own mouth.

Of course, it's an understatement to say that not everything that came out of Elvis's mouth was golden. The first time he met the actor who would play the role of Dummy--the kid who couldn't talk plain--Elvis tried to pay him a compliment. "Man, you really look the part!" he said. Elvis was mortified when he realized how it sounded. But after awhile, it got funny, and we ribbed him about it a lot, especially when we got bored waiting between scenes.

Boredom is pretty commonplace on a movie set, and we'd do all sorts of thing to alleviate it. I remember we got stuck on one line of dialogue--"You beat up my brother in school the other day, and I believe in an eye for an eye"--and we repeated it among ourselves like a broken record. We also imitated the director, Michael Curtiz, who was Hungarian.

Curtiz was always jumping on Vic Morrow for sounding too much like Marlon Brando. Heck, everybody tried to sound like Brando--James Dean had made a career out of it--but Curtiz would stop the action and say, "Cut, cut! Vicky, if vee vanted Brando for dees movie vee vould have hired Brando!"

The irony of the situation came full circle a few days later, when we found out that Lilliane Montevecchi was a good friend of Brando. As the movie progressed and we got to know her better, we pumped her for Brando stories more and more. Elvis, after all, had gone to see "The Wild One" in 1954, and immediately flipped out, later posing for pictures on his Harley-Davidson with his motorcycle cap pulled down low on his forehead.

After a couple of weeks of this, it got to the point where Elvis was dying to meet Brando. And when Lilliane mentioned it to Brando, she found out that Brando wanted to meet Elvis, too. The problem was, neither one would go to the other.

Gene and I went crazy over this, saying, "C'mon, Elvis, let's go see him!" But Elvis, a novice actor who would have given a lifetime of record royalties to be thought of in the same category as Brando, steadfastly balked. "If it ever happens, it'll just happen," he said.

Finally, we were having lunch at the studio one day, and

the commissary was packed. All of a sudden a hush fell over the place. The stars eat in a back room, but even in there, we could hear the sound of knives and forks dropping. Then a kind of silence moved toward us with the weight of a freight train.

Nobody could figure out what it was, but then we looked up, and there stood Marlon Brando. Lilliane happened to be eating at our table that day, and as Brando walked by, she turned around and unceremoniously said, "Marlon Brando, Elvis Presley." It was just a nod, or maybe a hello. I don't think they even shook hands. Brando just kept walking, and Elvis kept eating.

Secretly, I'm sure they were both thrilled to the marrow. Two years later, Brando would make a film called "The Fugitive Kind," based on Tennessee Williams' "Orpheus Descending." The play had, as its central character, a small-town Mississippi hero named Val Xavier, a beautiful and innocent guitar player destroyed by the corruption around him.

CHAPTER 3

"Toadies, Stooges, Buffoons,
Yes-Men, Gold-Diggers,
And Dull Thugs"

In February, everyone concerned with "King Creole" climbed aboard a Southern streamer en route to New Orleans for location shooting. I'd spent more time on trains in the last two months than I had in my whole life put together. But this time out, we had another star companion, Elvis's friend Nick Adams. Adams was a great guy, very colorful and fun to be with. He did a lot of impersonations--I especially remember his Jimmy Cagney. But when Nick met Elvis in 1956, Nick was out of work. He usually played neurotic types, and though he'd done both "Rebel Without a Cause" and "Mister Roberts" in 1955, he wouldn't have another picture out until later in 1958, when he played a very funny role in "No Time for Sergeants."

Nick was an exceptionally talented guy, but somehow he never quite made the big time. When he got down on his luck, Elvis gave him money to keep the repo guys off his '57 Thunderbird, and invited him to travel on the road. He'd gone down to Tupelo in 1956 for Elvis's return to the Mississippi-Alabama Fair and Dairy Show, giving a radio interview about how humble Elvis was, and bragging on Gladys's Southern cooking--"Elvis, what's the name of those things your mother fixed me up? Oker? [okra] I like oker." Then in 1958, he stayed with us for two or three months.

In years to come, Nick was always welcome at the house, but he was kind of a quicksilvery guy. We'd say, "You coming back tomorrow, Nick?" And he'd say, "Yeah, tomorrow," and then we wouldn't see him for six months to a year.

Another of James Dean's friends would come around, too, Jack Simmons, who'd been Dean's roommate for awhile, and

49

played the minor role of "Moose" in "Rebel...." But he was a strange guy--real quiet, a loner. If there were fifty people in the room talking, Jack would be over in a corner by himself. Turns out that Nick was the troubled one, though. He finally got a taste of mainstream fame with his TV series, "The Rebel," but he died on February 1, 1968--the day that Lisa Marie was born--at the age of thirty-six. Suicide, they said. An overdose of drugs, paraldehyde and tranquilizers.

We stayed in New Orleans for about a month, filming around the French Quarter and Lake Ponchartrain, and taking up the whole tenth floor of the Roosevelt Hotel, half a block from the French Quarter. Whenever Elvis went into a town to do a movie on location, Colonel played advance man, showing up six months ahead of time, checking out hotels to see which one was best-suited for Elvis and his merry pranksters. It had to be a place with isolated quarters or some large area that could be sealed off from the rest of the building, so that only one or two policemen could keep guard.

At the Roosevelt, they told the elevator operator not to let anybody off on the tenth floor, which worked wonders. Except for the night we dragged back there half-dead after a full day's shoot, and asked to be taken to the tenth floor. The elevator operator wasn't the sharpest guy.

"Tenth floor, please."

"I'm sorry, I can't stop on the tenth floor. Mr. Elvis Presley's party is staying on that floor, and no one else is permitted entrance."

"Yeah, I know," Elvis said. "I'm Mr. Presley."

The guy looked right at Elvis and said, "Yes, sir, but I can't stop on that floor for anybody."

We got off on the eleventh floor and walked down.

Getting Elvis to and from the hotel could also prove a problem. So could security on location. When Colonel talked to Hal Wallis about the New Orleans shoot, Wallis explained everything he had in mind, and calmly told Colonel how smoothly things would go. "That's fine, Mr. Wallis," Colonel began, "But what kind of security do you have?"

"We have two of the finest policemen in New Orleans."

Colonel said two cops just wouldn't get it. Hal Wallis, who in the future would declare that "a Presley picture is the only sure thing in show business," was probably under the impression that Colonel was just some big, fat, ordinary carnival rube.

"Colonel Parker, I just don't believe that," he said. "We had Dean Martin and Jerry Lewis under contract at the height of their careers."

Colonel chomped on his cigar. "I don't care who you had, you didn't have Elvis Presley. You're going to be in a lot of trouble here."

Next day, we had a bunch more policemen. The only problem was, the people in New Orleans weren't as blase about having celebrities around as the citizens of Los Angeles, and on the day that the mayor declared it "Elvis Presley Day" and let the kids out of school, it led to one shit-scary time.

Looking back, the guys who worked for Elvis knew how to move. If we were someplace and there were a thousand people cornering him for autographs, he signed them, but he scribbled as he walked. We never stopped. We just presented ourselves as a traveling wedge of flesh, escorting Elvis through a building and out the door. Here in New Orleans, though, we ran into a different kind of situation. "Elvis Presley Day" brought out more people than I'd ever seen in my life. Coming out of the French Quarter, we managed to maneuver Elvis through the crowd to a cab. But once we got inside the taxi, we lost control. People started shaking that cab like a coconut on a tree.

"Drive!" we yelled.

The cabby froze. Poor bastard didn't know what to do.

"Start driving! They'll move!"

"I can't! I'll run over 'em!"

He did it, but he was scared half to death. Tell the truth, we were, too.

But what was mostly on my mind during that time was making my movie debut. I was no thespian, of course, but I was dying to be in a movie, because George Klein and all the other guys had been in "Jailhouse Rock," although they were just part of the crowd scenes. None of us were in the Screen Extras Guild at this point, and we wouldn't be until Elvis got back from the service. We didn't care about that, though. We just wanted to be able to point at some fleeting figure on the screen and yell, "There I am!"

While we were still in California, I went up to Mickey Moore, the assistant director, and said, "Just put me in a movie. I don't care if I get paid." Mickey shrugged his shoulders and said, "Okay." Just like that! I couldn't believe it.

Except that days went by, and they were filming and filming, and nobody ever called me to be in a scene. I went to Mickey.

"When are you going to use me?"

"Any day now, any day."

Every day, I got stoked and primed, waiting for my break. Then, next thing I knew, they were through!

"Mickey, you didn't use me!"

"Don't worry," Mickey said. "We're going to use you in New Orleans."

I thought about it all the way down on the train, wondering what kind of scene they'd put me in, hoping I might see some real action. But a couple of days into the New Orleans shoot, I was still standing on one foot and then the other.

"What about me?"

"Any day now, Alan."

We got closer and closer to the end of the movie, and still no Alan. So I went back up to Mickey and said as emphatically as I knew how, "You told me you were going to use me in this movie. People write books in shorter time than this! When's that gonna happen?"

"Right now, Alan," he said. "Go to make-up."

I was stunned. Make-up? They never put make-up on extras. The only people who get make-up are the stars, or the people who get filmed in close-up. My heart was pounding like a scared rabbit's. I went to make-up, and they put tissues around my collar and rubbed pancake all over my face. Then somebody else did my hair. I thought, "Godalmighty, this is gonna be fantastic! I'm gonna be right up there with Elvis! This is a close-up!"

I reported back to Mickey.

"What's next?"

"When Elvis works, you'll work. Follow Elvis, and don't let him out of your sight."

I was like white on rice. If Elvis went to the bathroom, I was standing at the door. If he went to eat, I was closer than his plate. I was a damned bloodhound, following his every step. Every couple of hours, somebody would come and check to make sure I hadn't smudged my make-up, and I walked around the set with tissues around my collar.

I was a pro.

Finally, we stood there for what seemed like ample time for hell to freeze over, and next thing I knew Michael Curtiz called, "It's a wrap."

Movie's finished.

My jaw sank. I ran around and found Mickey, and I said, "You haven't used me yet! I'm still not in the movie!"

Mickey slapped me on the shoulder and grinned. "Don't worry, we're going to pay you anyway. See you in Hollywood."

I'd been conned! I don't know if Elvis and Colonel had put him up to it or what, because that's the kind of humor Elvis liked, especially with the guys. It kept us from feeling self-important. Elvis and I laughed about it years later, but at the time, I was ready to jump off a goddam bridge.

On March 10, we took the train back to Los Angeles so Elvis could get his release from Hal Wallis. That done, we headed back to the station and began the long trip home to Memphis. We traveled by train because, two years earlier, Elvis's entourage had been on a small airplane that developed engine trouble and nearly crashed. He remembered that the pilot told them to take everything sharp out of their pockets, and to rest their heads on pillows placed between their knees. The worst part was that he knew that even the crew was scared--the pilot was soaked with sweat when they got back on the ground. Ever since, Elvis had been afraid to fly. And his mother, who worried about him all the time anyway, made him promise to take the train or travel by motorhome whenever he could.

As usual, girls seemed to line the entire train route, something I still couldn't quite get over. Most of them were nothing special to look at--no trip to Hawaii, that's for sure--but I had to admire the way they got into it. At times it was overwhelming, girls screaming and shrieking and vying for just a wave or a nod--some acknowledgment of their existence on the planet.

Train travel was as slow as a government check, and being the antsy guy he was, Elvis decided we'd get off the coach in Dallas and rent a fleet of Cadillac limos to take us into Memphis. Renting cars wasn't any faster, of course, but it made Elvis feel in control. Photographers from the newspapers seemed to be everywhere when we stepped off the train, and the *Fort Worth Daily Star* snapped a picture of Elvis kissing a pretty dark-haired girl on the cheek. When it ran in the paper, I was surprised to see myself standing behind them.

Everyone was sure glad to be home in Memphis, but, of course, when we told our tales of high glamour in the Hollywood hills, we made it sound like we never wanted to come back to this lazy river town. In some ways, it now looked better than ever.

The day after we got home, Elvis gave two shows at Russwood Baseball Park, drawing fourteen thousand fans. They were his last live performances before his induction into the army later that month, and for that reason, there was something enormously exciting and poignant about them. I think Elvis sensed he'd come back from the service a different guy, and he was desperate to hold on to the moment. For the next eight nights, he rented the Rainbow Roller Skating Rink for one long, final party.

I didn't stay out at Graceland when we got back in town, because I wanted a little breather from it all, and because my parents' house was nearby, at 381 North Highland. Somebody like Lamar Fike, though, stayed at Graceland all the time.

Lamar, or "Lamoine," as I called him, was originally from Memphis, but his parents had moved to Texas. He met Elvis through Cliff Gleaves in 1956--they were both staying at the YMCA--when the Presleys lived on Audubon Drive. Then he drifted away to Waco and worked in radio in Jacksonville,

Texas, but he remembered Elvis's invitation to keep in touch. He was still down in Texas when he read an item in the paper that said that Elvis was making a picture called "Jailhouse Rock," and that he'd swallowed a cap off his tooth during the filming. Lamar gave him a call in Los Angeles, and about the next day Elvis looked up and there was Lamar--three hundred pounds of ectoplasm in yellow cowboy boots and a black-and-white '57 Chevy.

Lamar was kind of a go-fer, but he was also a joke-teller and fall guy for a lot of pranks, even though he was no dummy. I think Elvis felt sorry for him--he called him "Mr. Bull," and later "Lardass" and "The Wrestler." The guys called him "The Great Speckled Bird." But then Elvis often picked guys to join the group who were not exactly misfits, but underdogs. Often, he'd choose somebody nobody liked. If everybody talked bad about somebody who came out to the house, that's the first person Elvis would hire.

Through the years, there were a lot of them. Once they were in the group, they usually fit pretty well. But I really never understood Elvis's reasoning. The more the rest of us would team up on a guy or try to backstab him, the more Elvis seemed to like him. Maybe that was Elvis's private litmus test.

I think trust played a big part in Elvis's decision to hire someone. That, plus family loyalty. Four of Elvis's cousins worked for him at one time or another, all Smith boys, kin on his mother's side. When they all lived in Tupelo, they were tight as ticks, and then when Elvis and Vernon and Gladys moved to Memphis, they followed. After Elvis became famous, he figured he'd been close to them all his life, and he trusted them. In fact, Travis Smith, his wife Lorraine, and their son Billy lived in a tiny house on the back of Graceland for awhile, Travis working as a gatekeeper on the property. Then later, when Elvis started going to Hollywood, he didn't want to go by himself, so he took his cousins along to have someone to talk to. He also figured he'd give the kids a chance.

If Elvis had a best friend, he never told anybody. He was, after all, an enigma to almost everybody during his short time on this earth--what writer Steve Simels, in an allusion to the film classic "Citizen Kane," called "the Rosebud of our popular culture." But if anybody was really close to Elvis at the end of his life it was Billy Smith. I have a tendency to always say "Little" Billy Smith, because he was the baby of the entourage, as well as Elvis's baby cousin. He was also short. Because he was the youngest one who joined us on the road--and he was *very* young when he started, and only thirteen when I met him --he was always called "Little Billy." He didn't care for that much.

In contrast to some of the guys through the years who more or less fit the unflattering labels that the media often gave the Memphis Mafia--"toadies, stooges, buffoons, yes-men, gold-diggers and dull thugs," as journalist Dave Marsh put it--Billy was pretty sharp. He was also the best of the whole Smith lot. In the early days, he helped take care of Elvis's wardrobe, but later Elvis trusted him with a lot more, because he could. He was a good kid. Elvis could have left $10 million in small change scattered around his room, and I guarantee you Billy wouldn't have touched a penny. Elvis pretty much raised him. The other three Smith cousins were an odd lot. The closest one who traveled with Elvis at the time I worked for him was Gene. Gene was a character. Sometimes I'd talk to Gene and it was almost like talking to a retarded person. I didn't know if he was acting or whether he was really that dumb.

Elvis had a weird sense of humor, and at first Gene was the one who was supposed to keep Elvis in a good mood. But Elvis would get so mad at him half the time you could hardly say that Gene was doing his duty. One time after Elvis started paying us a little salary, he said, "Gene, I don't believe this. Here I am paying you good money to make me laugh, and I ain't cracked a smile in two years." When we'd be away from home, Gene would get on the telephone and talk to his wife, Louise, in Memphis for five hours at a time. But I'd never hear anything except grunting. It was just, "Uh, uh, uh." Never any talk.

Gene was the one who first started calling Elvis "E." Elvis didn't mind that coming from Gene, but then a lot of guys who wanted to fit in would call him "E," or "El," or some variation, like "Big E" or "Big El," and he didn't go for that at all. He didn't like being called "Presley," either. I called him Presley a lot, but then he called me "Hog Ears," partly because my ears were larger than most people's, and partly because he wanted to give me a kind of football player's nickname--like "Night Train" Lane or "Refrigerator" Perry. Elvis had some kind of pet name for almost everybody who spent any time around him, an outgrowth of the baby talk routine he'd gotten into with his mother years before. Sometimes it got to be too much.

Unlike some of the guys who traveled with us, Gene never really cared about the Hollywood glamour. He wanted to be home in Memphis with a beer in his hand and his feet propped up. He mostly hung out with Elvis because they'd worked together at the Precision Tool Company before Elvis started working for Crown Electric, and because Gladys had asked Gene to look out for Elvis when his show business career picked up. Finally, around 1962, after some kind of altercation with Elvis, he stopped going on the road with us. He ended up driving a cookie truck.

The Smith cousins also had an unbelievable run of bad luck. Take Junior Smith, for example. By the time I went to work for Elvis, Junior, who was a year older than Elvis, had quit traveling with the group. But he would come by once in a while, and he was a nice guy. He was kind of a combination of Elvis and James Dean. If Junior liked you, he was your best friend. There was a story about him, that he'd gone off to the Korean War and come back battle-crazy, a little bit psycho, and that he'd shot a whole family of Korean allies for no good reason. God knows he looked the part, but I thought he was straight as a string.

Then one night three or four years after I started going to Graceland, Junior went to bed stinking drunk. It made him sick, and when he started throwing up, he suffocated in his own vomit. Some people say he died of a seizure of some kind. I don't know. I only know that Junior was dead by his mid-twenties.

Another Smith boy, Bobby--Billy's brother--bit the dust by

downing rat poison. But then Bobby had always been a mixed-up kid. He swallowed razor blades to get out of the army. There was also another cousin who drowned. It was getting to where I figured it was kind of dangerous to be part of the Smith family.

When we first got back from Hollywood, I'd go out to Graceland about four or five o'clock in the afternoon. I never knew who or what was going to be there. There could be fifty brand new Cadillacs, because every day was like Christmas. And, of course, things were completely turned around, because Elvis reversed day for night--he partied until dawn and slept most of the day, until about two in the afternoon. If any construction needed to be done on the grounds, the workmen had to wait until Elvis was out of town.

Any business matters were taken care of in the afternoon, because the night was meant for parties. Things started popping around half past seven or eight o'clock. The gang would sit around talking, or shooting pool, or watching television for awhile, and then Elvis's uncle Vester would start calling up from the gate, saying so-and-so was there.

Elvis would let them come up, and then after midnight, when the places shut down to the public, we'd usually go to the Rainbow Skating Rink, or to the fairgrounds and ride the roller coaster. Sometimes we'd take in a movie at the Memphian Theatre, which Elvis would rent out the same way he did the roller rink. The owner would borrow films from the local storage depot, and most of the time, we'd get to see first-run movies that weren't even playing yet.

We didn't always see a movie all the way through, though, because if Elvis got bored, he'd yell out for the projectionist to run something else. Sometimes there'd be as many as two hundred of us, and the owner would keep the concession stand open, even though we'd slip in pizzas, and leave the greasy boxes on the floor. That wasn't the worst of it. Food fights broke out almost every night. It's a wonder the owner let us in, no matter how much Elvis was paying, or who he was.

It never got wild at Graceland, though. In fact, everybody left the house by two in the morning, partly because they respected Graceland as Elvis's home, and partly because his mother was still alive. And the language never got rough around there, either, because Elvis didn't allow any cursing. Occasionally, he uttered the same epithets as any other normal American, but not very often. When he used that language, we knew he was double-barrel mad. But if anybody said, "goddamn," he erupted in a rage.

"Don't ever say that in front of me!" he'd scream. "You can use any other word you want to, but don't use the Lord's name in vain!" A religious man reacting to a blasphemous act? I don't think so. Elvis wanted you to know his mama raised him right.

As such, nobody drank at Graceland, either. That was Elvis's rule. There was plenty of Pepsi for everyone, and the soda fountain in the basement turned out an endless supply of milk shakes. The basement was really the center of all the action. Elvis had a record player built into the wall--it wasn't a jukebox, although it played records like one. It must have had two hundred songs on it. Sometimes Elvis sang along with his own records, producing a kind of early stereo effect.

About the wildest we got there in those days was going through the fan mail. Sometimes we'd crumple it up and start a fire and roast marshmallows, but we read it first. Girls would send in incredible pictures of themselves in swim suits, in pajamas, in the semi-nude, and even in the buff, in every possible pose. Or they'd write, "Please call me. My measurements are 42-19-34."

That was pretty racy back in the fifties. One of the secretaries made a photo album of the cleaner shots, and put the naked ones in the bottom drawer of her desk. We'd go through 'em every chance we got, of course, and if we saw somebody really sharp, we'd pocket the damn thing, and then show the picture to Elvis. Who knew? We might be traveling through her little town sometime. Actually, Elvis didn't get off on pictures like that. They were too crude for him. Vernon had a hissyfit when he found out we rifled through "the dirty file," as he called it. Finally, Vernon laid down the law: "Y'all stay out of the office!"

There were always girls of every kind and description hanging out at Graceland, but Elvis was almost exclusively dating Anita Wood. Anita was twenty years old, and the hostess of the "Top Ten Dance Party," a local TV show with Wink Martindale. George Klein had introduced them, and Elvis had his first date with her in July of 1957, when he took her to watch the construction of a special theatre front for the Memphis premiere of "Loving You." The following month, by which time he was already calling her "Little," or "Little Beady Eyes," he bought her a diamond and sapphire ring. Elvis was impulsive in matters of love.

Anita was a good gal, and Elvis knew it. She was the all-American girl, blond, petite, with a great, bubbly personality that just didn't stop. Everybody was crazy about her because she was so damn much fun, and nice as hell. I think their relationship was a healthy one. They laughed a lot, and he could be himself around her. But that didn't mean that Anita was immune to his practical jokes. She usually went along on the outings to the movies and the all-night roller parties at the Rainbow Skating Rink, and one night when they first started dating, Elvis pulled a good one on her.

It was about five or six in the morning when we left the Rainbow and started back to Graceland in a limo. These skating parties often got pretty ferocious, since we played tag and roller derby, identifying our teams by colored bandanas we wore in our hip pockets. And this particular night, Elvis was keyed up more than usual. Lamar and I climbed in the front seat, and Elvis and Anita sat in the back. We were just tooling along, when all of a sudden Anita announced in a loud voice, "My cunt hurts!"

What? My mouth dropped down to my ankles. Maybe I misunderstood. I cleared my throat, Lamar did the same, and we drove on a little farther. Then Anita burst out again. "Did y'all hear me? I said, 'My cunt really hurts!'"

I about fell out of the seat, and Lamar damn near wrecked the car.

It wasn't until we got back to Graceland that I found out that Elvis had told Anita the whopping lie that "my cunt hurts" is a Hollywood expression for "my rear's sore." And every time she'd yelled it out, it was only because Elvis nudged her and told her to say it. She had no idea what it meant. She only knew her rear *was* sore from falling down on the skating rink. Here was this beautiful thing, on television, sitting back there yelling, "My cunt hurts." In retrospect, it was funny as hell.

Mostly, though, Elvis treated Anita with respect. She wasn't overly impressed with him because she was, in effect, in the business. In their private moments, she and Elvis went for a spin on his motorcycle, or piled into his old panel truck and drove around the Lauderdale Courts, the government-subsidized housing complex where the Presleys used to live.

One day back in the summer, Elvis took Anita to McKellar Lake here in Memphis, and I snapped a photo of them sitting on a blanket (reproduced below). Elvis, holding Anita's hand, looked into my camera and curled his full lips into a sneer. Elvis wasn't stupid, by any means. Rather, he was complicated in his simplicity. But he was, in many ways, an inarticulate man, scarcely able to share the thoughts that started in his gut and worked their way up to his brain. On top of it, he was hardly introspective. But the look on his face was the reaction of a man who is at once loathe to share his territory, but powerless to save himself in the landslide of his success. Elvis was well on his way to discovering that fame has a way of devouring its worshippers.

Fifteen-year-old Elvis with girlfriend Betty McMann.

Chapter 4

GLADYS AND VERNON

Of course, no matter how much Elvis cared for Anita, the real woman in his life was Gladys, and it was Gladys who shaped his life. There's a photograph of Elvis, taken perhaps in his very early teens, long before his days of sideburns, ducktails and Sun Records, that offers an intimate look at their relationship. In it, Elvis sits on the street curb with one of his first girlfriends, a pinch-faced Southern lass in rolled dungarees, white socks, and loafers. The girl sits with her elbow on her knee, with her chin nestled in the meat of her palm. Smiling, she looks into the camera in a relaxed and amiable pose.

But Elvis has placed some distance between himself and his friend--they do not touch--and he has raised his eyebrows with the anxiety of a young man who is unsure of himself and his actions. His gaze is directed not at his young companion, but toward the shadow of the photographer, a shadow cast wide and long in the Memphis sun. It is Gladys, a hovering specter whose ghostly presence would forever illuminate--and darken--Elvis's world.

So much so that after Natalie Wood returned to Hollywood following her visit at Graceland, she complained to family and friends that while he was "constantly hiding from fans," she was "constantly hiding from Mama Presley." As a result, Natalie cut her visit short--from a week to two days--making a frantic phone call to her mother to invent some family emergency so she could get out of Memphis on the next plane. Furthermore, she reported, Elvis could sing, "but he can't do much else."

Such indiscretions would have hurt Elvis to the core. He was caught between wanting to present himself as a Southern gentleman--his shyness and insecurity masquerading as good

The shotgun house where Elvis was born--306 Old Saltillo Road, Tupelo, Mississippi--is today an historic site open to the public. (Photo: Alanna Nash)

manners--and needing to react to Natalie the way any red-blooded young man would, while still proving to his mother that he had not abandoned her.

Gladys had been abandoned before, of course, both by an infant son who had not survived a trip through the birth canal --Elvis's own twin, Jessie Garon--and, according to Elaine Dundy in *Elvis & Gladys*, by another child, miscarried when Elvis was seven. Elvis had seen the suffering on his mother's face on that second awful occasion, and he had shared her bitter loss that there would be no other children in the Presley household. But even that did not carry the sting and disgrace of another abandonment, this one brought on by the desperation and thoughtlessness of his father.

In November of 1937, when Elvis was nearing his third birthday and the family still lived in Mississippi, Vernon, along with Gladys' brother Travis Smith and a man named Lether Gable, were indicted for forgery. Earlier, Vernon, whose neighbors thought him weak and work-shy, sold a hog to a local dairy farmer named Orville Bean, who had also loaned Vernon the money to build the family's modest home. In return, he received a check for the sum of four dollars. Four dollars! Vernon felt not only cheated, but insulted. With his pride flying like a cowlick--and with a fondness for hooch perhaps clouding his judgment--he, Travis and Lether made it up to alter the check to a greater amount, either to $14 or $40. Allegedly, according to Vernon's friend Aron Kennedy, it was Vernon and Travis who traced a new check over the old one, holding both pieces of paper to the windowpane.

The judge took a dim view of such activity, and sentenced Vernon to three years in Parchman, the state penitentiary. Gladys took in laundry to survive. At first, young Elvis couldn't quite comprehend what had happened, but when he found out his daddy wasn't coming home, he nearly lost his mind. He bawled so hard he couldn't catch his breath, and the neighbor women would later say that he broke their hearts with every sob.

As it turned out, in January of 1941, Vernon was released seven months shy of his full three-year sentence, largely because of his good behavior and the letters Gladys wrote tire-lessly in his defense. But in his short absence, something profound had happened. Instead of becoming the "little man" of the house, Elvis had become the parent, and Gladys the child. Her sister, Lillian, would later tell Elaine Dundy that the young tot would pat his mother on the head and console her with tender and soothing language: "There, there, my little baby." And he would see to her needs--"Mama, do you need anything?"-- as if he were her guardian.

Eventually, they came up with a language of their own, a vocabulary of baby talk in which "little sooties," for example, referred to women's feet. Milk was "butch," water was "duck-ling," ice cream was "iddytream," and "soaks" were slabs of cornbread sopped in buttermilk. The neighbors in Tupelo recall seeing them on the front porch of their two-room shot-gun home on the Old Saltillo Road, Gladys in the swing, and Elvis sitting at her feet, his arm on her knee. It was not so much the action of a young son clinging to his mother, as it was that of a boy protecting her. Now he would call her his "Sattnin." In years to come, Elvis would say that his mother had never let him out of her sight when he was a boy, that he couldn't even go down to the creek like all the other kids. Maybe it was really the other way around.

In Elvis's eyes, Gladys was his ward, and when Vernon returned from the shameful Parchman, his son saw his father, too, as someone to cuddle and coddle, if only figuratively. Vernon found permanent jobs had a way of slipping through his fingers, both through his own shiftlessness and the unsinkable prison record. Not even a WPA project job, at the Pascagoula, Mississippi, shipyard worked out, although the family relo-cated there for some eight months. In 1948, the Presleys--who now included Vernon's mother, Minnie Mae, whose philander-ing husband, Jessie, had run off in 1946--packed everything they owned in a '39 Plymouth and moved to Memphis to try their luck in a larger town.

Vernon would never really make a success, however, and at nineteen, Elvis would "retire" his father and become his par-ents' sole support, calling them his "babies," even though he

Elvis in 1956: Mobbed at L.A. airport when he arrived to begin work on "Love Me Tender" in August. . .

himself was still in need of the attention and affection afforded a young boy. This had come to a head years before, when Elvis and Gladys--and, one presumes, Vernon--nestled each night in the same bed for a period much longer than most mothers and sons would ever think of doing, until Elvis was thirteen.

In 1956, at the Mississippi-Alabama Fair and Dairy Show in Tupelo, to which native son Elvis would make a triumphal return, drawing 20,000 people to a town of 22,000, a radio reporter asked Gladys which of Elvis's songs was her favorite. Gladys hesitated not a moment, but offered in the plaintive, high-pitched tone of a woman who was clearly not prepared for her moment in the sun, "Baby, Let's Play House." It was a song that perhaps reflected not only her musical taste, but to some extent, the domestic and dysfunctional intimacy she enjoyed with her watchful son.

When Elvis became the most popular and successful entertainer in the world, details of the Presleys' modest circumstances in Tupelo worked their way into the headlines, fueling the notion Northerners already had of the Presleys as "poor white trash" or, at the very least, vulgar "rednecks." Just because a family is poor doesn't mean they're trash, but although the just-famous Elvis continued to unconsciously offend polite society by appearing in photos in his undershirt (at his girlfriend's house, in pictures for *Life* magazine, no less), he became even more resolute in his intention to shield his parents from mental and physical harm.

In part, that's why Elvis bought Graceland. For generations, country people had come out and sat on the front porch after supper, both to get out of the heat of an airless home and enjoy the night breeze, and to engage in social repartee. The Presleys' $40,000 house at 1034 Audubon Drive, built after the war in typical American ranch style, with pastel green siding and red brick trim, had been snug on the street, and Vernon and Gladys couldn't see a minute's peace for the fans. At first, Elvis's admirers just stole the wash right off the line. But then they started worrying the water out of the Presleys when the couple took their evening's respite. Finally, the fans began snatching even the chairs, and when the Presleys put up a

Graceland today, a place "like a picture from a coffee-table magazine."
(Photo: Alanna Nash)

brick and iron barricade, the fans simply figured a way to get over it.

Elvis was determined to find his mother a house that sat back from the road, a place where she could sit in solitude and gather her thoughts, a place that suggested the rural South that Gladys loved. But it also had to be a home of such elegance that it spoke of her stature in Elvis's world. This mother and son had once spent three weeks in the charity ward of the Tupelo hospital when Gladys began to hemorrhage after the burial of Jessie Garon, and her surviving son seemed undersized and weak. Elvis wanted to show his mother how far he had brought them from all that.

Once, when the family first moved to Memphis and Gladys found work as a nurse's aide at St. Joseph's Hospital, impressing both the patients and staff alike, she had not been able to accept the hospital's recommendation that she become a full nurse. Her lack of education and her financial impoverishment held her back. It had been her life's opportunity, and she had missed it. Elvis, never wanting her to miss anything again, would try to make it up to her in every way he could.

When Elvis first showed Gladys the thirteen-room, neo-antebellum mansion at 3764 South Bellevue Boulevard (U.S. Highway 51 South), she could not believe her eyes. Never had she seen such splendor! Two stories of reddish-brown Tennessee limestone, trimmed with painted white wood and dark-green shutters, like a picture from a coffee table magazine. Apart from the structure, the estate included thirteen acres of rolling grassland. Elvis's purchase was about turf, after all.

The house was perfect, even to the fact that Whitehaven, the section of Memphis in which it was situated, was still so rural that when Elvis returned from a tour in 1956, he got off the train at a stop that was mostly a grass field, posted with a sign that said only "White." As the train made a rheumatic turn out of the station, photographer Alfred Wertheimer looked back to see the solitary figure of Elvis, dressed in a suit and white knit tie, making his way through the burrs and foxtails, finally asking directions of a black woman standing on a sidewalk at the edge of the field. Today, Whitehaven looks quite

different, with its busy thoroughfares of convenience stores and fast-food restaurants. But, in a sense, it's only traded its rural exterior for a blue-collar state of mind.

Elvis had so adored the look on Gladys's face when she first saw Graceland that he immediately arranged to pay $100,000 --outbidding the local YMCA, which had offered $35,000--to the widow of Dr. Thomas Moore, the original owner who had built the home in the late thirties. Dr. Moore had named it for his wife's Aunt Grace Toof, who had willed the couple the land. For the past few years, the mansion had been used by the Graceland Christian Church for services. Elvis, it seems, had bought his mother a temple, using the Aububon Drive home as a down-payment.

But then, when he spent $20,000 or $30,000--a sobering amount of money at the time--to erect the large white pillars, the stone fence and the black iron music gates, Elvis effectively turned Gladys's monument into a museum, or perhaps, as has been suggested, her mausoleum. Elvis had bought the house for her--he even installed a few chickens and peacocks, who took up roost in the back yard, to make Gladys feel as if she were back in the country. Nevertheless, it was still his house, and for the most part, he controlled what went on within its walls.

What that meant, precisely, was that soon Elvis would not have the time to do the caretaking that had been the staple of his relationship with both of his parents, but particularly with Gladys. In fact, Elvis had not really had the time in several years, and Gladys had suffered it as a cruel blow. She was proud of him--desperately proud that he had made something of himself, and that her moral tutelage had paid off. But she herself was paying a terrible personal price in the process.

In all of 1956, for example, Elvis had been home only five or six times. And when he was back in Memphis, he scarcely resembled the boy with whom she had shared her every thought and dream. He was preoccupied--planning for trips, rehearsing for shows, learning movie scripts (he had even arranged for Vernon and Gladys to be on camera in "Loving You," as part of a theatre audience), and making new friends.

He was also hanging on to every word that slid out of the mouth of Colonel Parker, a man Gladys distrusted and disliked, even if he *had* been Eddy Arnold's manager. To Gladys's way of thinking, hadn't Arnold found reason to fire Parker in '53? And hadn't Hank Snow been shocked and appalled to find that even though Parker signed Elvis as an agent for Hank Snow Jamboree Attractions, Snow had no financial stake in the act? Gladys had liked the kindly Bob Neal, Elvis's manager after Scotty Moore, much better. As Gladys's sister, Lillian, would later say about Colonel, "He didn't look like our kind of people...he didn't act like our kind of people, either."

Part of Gladys's reaction was instinct, although Elvis and Vernon had tried to assure her she was wrong. And the remainder of her derision stemmed from the contract Colonel talked her boy into signing, a document that funneled 25 percent of Elvis's income to his manager. Gladys knew nothing about professional show business, but she knew this insufferable man, whom she felt had insinuated his presence into every facet of her son's life, was taking too much of Elvis's money.

Worse, in Gladys's view, Colonel seemed to have Elvis under a kind of spell, to where he followed his every command like some hypnotized lackey. She may have suspected that Colonel held the threat of exposing the secret of Vernon's ancient imprisonment over the young singer's head--or promised he could keep the news from the press if Elvis jumped every time he cracked the whip. But Gladys saw only that it was no longer she to whom Elvis went for advice, but to Colonel, who was now, unquestionably, the boss.

Soon Gladys got to where she could not bear to hear his name uttered in her presence. She was a woman who had gone her entire forty-five years without feeling powerful even for a day, except for the personal power she knew with Elvis. Now even that seemed in question.

Gladys, then, felt as if she were losing Elvis--to the Colonel, to the road, to the big cities of New York and Los Angeles, to the young men who hung around the house and accompanied him on his trips, to the thousands of girls who screamed his name, and the dozens who had made a play for him. It was apparent in her every act and move, although now I know that only in hindsight.

My memories of Gladys are few. I remember Vernon a lot better from that period, mainly because while I think he liked us, he was always leery of anyone who spent a lot of time around Elvis: He was afraid we were after his money. At this point, of course, we still weren't getting a salary--we were really just traveling companions. But Elvis's famed generosity was real, and Vernon, who managed his son's finances, tried to keep him in line, especially since some of the guys would borrow money and never pay it back. Vernon watched every dime. He was hard to get along with--hard to joke with, even. And Vernon wasn't a genius. But I think he did the best he could.

I remember those press clippings that, soon after Elvis's death, trotted out the question of the forged check and the disputed hog. But at least when I knew Vernon, I never thought he was shady. He liked to wheel and deal, and if he bought a used car he'd argue for three days over twenty-five dollars. But I don't think he was a crook. Some of the guys were scared of Vernon, because he was tough sometimes. I thought he was fair--hard, but fair. He had to be hard, though. There's no telling how many people came up and begged or borrowed money from him, especially his own relatives. He had to draw the line somewhere. And because people couldn't always get to Elvis, they'd hit on Vernon.

I especially remember one of the early Christmases. Elvis decided to give everyone who worked for him a thousand-dollar bill as a bonus. Vernon went to the bank and got the money, and then even though it was cold as a witch's tit that December, Elvis got on his motorcycle and took the envelopes to every one of his uncles and cousins--Vester Presley, Travis Smith, Johnny Smith--who worked for him guarding the front gates. That was probably the most money that they'd had in their pocket at one time in their life, and the next day, every one of them quit. Nobody saw them again until the money was gone.

Vernon wasn't about to hire them back, especially his brother

Vester, who was my favorite of the lot. Vester may have shown Elvis his first chords on the guitar, but he wasn't the brightest guy. We used to play jokes on him all the time when he worked the gate, usually concerning one set of girls going in and another coming out. Vester had a way of pulling rank, though, like the time he said he thought he should have a more responsible position than taking care of the gate and the yard. Not only was he Vernon's brother, but he'd married Gladys's sister, Clettes, which made him, in his view, double family. (His daughter, Patsy, was indeed Elvis's double first cousin.) Vester said, "I've bucked that gate long enough." And Vernon said, "If you don't like buckin' that gate, you can just get on somethin' buckin' the other way." Finally, Elvis said, "C'mon, Daddy, you've gotta hire him back. You've gotta hire 'em all back." And Vernon did.

But while I always thought that Vernon looked at us guys a little funny, Gladys seemed to appreciate us, even though she resented the fact that Elvis always had us around. She was nice, and she was quiet. And even though Elvis and Vernon had shanghaied her about signing that contract with Colonel, I had the feeling that of the two parents, she really ruled the roost, maybe because of Vernon's aversion to work in the early days, or because she was four years older than he.

Anyway you look at it, though, Gladys wasn't a sophisticated woman. She hurled a frying pan at Vernon whenever he got her dander up--calling him "steercotted," a fancy term for "castrated," which probably revealed her true attitude toward him. And she liked her black-eyed peas and cornbread, never caring about going out to social events or restaurants, or even staying in luxury hotels. Gladys padded around the house in her big, floral mumus, and she almost never wore jewelry or make-up, which just accentuated her dark eyes--eyes which gave away her Cherokee Indian heritage.

But Gladys also had a lot of heart, and love beyond all reason. Whenever we started to leave the house with Elvis, she'd tell us, "Take care of my baby, and be careful." And Elvis would call her at least a couple of times while we were out, no matter if we only went to a movie, just to let her know he was all right.

Nobody in the group teased him about it--you always worry a little more about the mother--but I did think it was extraordinary that he still changed clothes in her presence, something borne out in the photos in books like *Elvis '56: In the Beginning*. This wasn't just a situation where a boy was under his mother's thumb all the time. Gladys had attended a fair amount of Elvis's concerts, and it unnerved her to see her son caught up in a swirl of grabbing hands and stampeding bodies. The mobs scared her, and she was terrified that Elvis, who was still in many ways her protector, would get hurt.

Once, in the very early days, Elvis played a high-school dance somewhere around Memphis, and Gladys had been horrified to see the girls rush the stage. Before Vernon had a chance to stop her, she threw herself into the throng, and collared the girl nearest her son, demanding in a shrill, excited voice, "Why are you trying to kill my boy?" The astonished girl responded, "I'm not trying to kill him! I just love him! I want to touch him!" Gladys flung her aside like a weightless toy, and with Vernon's help, hoisted Elvis off the bandstand and carried him to safety.

Gladys saw that Elvis's inner circle played a necessary role, then, and I'm sure that she kept Vernon from giving us a harder way to go than he did. But at the same time that she was grateful to us for "taking care" of her boy, she lumped us into the category of the "enemies" who robbed her of the only true joy in her labored existence. She hated the way Elvis looked on his brief visits home, how pale he seemed from lack of sleep and overwork, how hyperexcited he seemed all the time, and how edgy and nervous. "You're puttin' too much energy into your singin'," she told him. "Keep that up and you won't live to be thirty!"

Most of all, though, she hated the trappings of his success.

Gladys's sister told writer Elaine Dundy that after Elvis became famous, his mother was never happy another day, that after he started going to Hollywood and playing the road between pictures, she never had another moment's peace. And, indeed, it was during this time that Gladys was telling her

Gladys's pink Cadillac still parked--until recently--at Graceland. Gladys never got a driver's license, and couldn't operate a car. (Photos: Alanna Nash)

friends back in Mississippi that she wished that she and her family "could just go back to being poor again."

I can still see her to this day, sitting at home by the window in the kitchen, daydreaming, or looking out in the backyard at her chickens. Sometimes she sat out in front of Graceland, safe from the fans who had tormented her on Audubon Drive. On rare occasion, Vernon would take her for a drive in the pink Cadillac Elvis bought her, something she'd coveted ever since her nurse's aide days, when she saw a wealthy patient drive up to the hospital in one. Actually, that was Gladys's second pink car. The first one was a Ford.

The irony, of course, was that Gladys never got her driver's license. Elvis had learned to drive at the age of ten--not unusual for country boys--and, as something of the family chauffeur, he always took her where she wanted to go. In fact, Gladys couldn't even operate a car. And so she hardly ever left the house. Exactly what she did with her time is yet another question. Elvis had once bragged about what a good cook she was, but I don't remember her ever fixing a meal, since the maid, Alberta (Elvis called her "VO5") took care of everything, something Gladys might also have resented. I just remember passing through the kitchen on my way out to the pool or into the den, and she'd always be there.

"Hello, Miz Presley, how you doin'?"

"Fine, Alan."

That was it. She was a nice, simple woman who never pretended to be more than she was. She dipped her snuff, she watched TV in her room, and she worried about her boy. That was her life.

Or at least, that's what I *thought* constituted her life. Elvis always said that she stayed the same throughout his brilliant blaze of fame, and I, too, thought she was unaffected by it. I see now that Elvis called her every time we left the house not just to reassure her that *he* was all right, but so that he could also check on *her* well-being. If Gladys had perceived great changes in Elvis, he noticed shocking transformations in her. And someone--Colonel maybe?-- had been telling Elvis that his mother's looks and increasingly erratic behavior weren't good

for his image. It would be better if they kept her under wraps for awhile. And so Gladys became a virtual prisoner in her dreamhouse.

At first, Gladys's trouble was difficult to ascertain. It wasn't just that her liquid eyes had looked increasingly bruised and raccoon-ringed in recent years. And it wasn't that she seemed not to care about the material things Elvis bought her, not even the decorator-selected furniture, with the fifteen-foot couch dominating the living room. She didn't seem to care about anything, except maybe her toy dog, Sweet Pea, which she cuddled like a baby.

Once, when Elvis was on the road with Scotty and Bill, Elvis traveling separately with a date in his first pink Cadillac (actually, a used '54 Cadillac that he'd had painted pink), a wheel-bearing locked up, and the Caddy caught fire just outside of Texarkana, Arkansas. Elvis was lucky to escape with his life. At that moment, Gladys, sound asleep back in Memphis, suddenly bolted upright in her bed and screamed his name, so intuitive was the bond between them. Now when Elvis came home, he could hardly reach her, a situation that must have shattered his heart.

Photographs taken of the family when Elvis was eight or nine years old show a relatively slim Gladys. In the early days, when she was a young woman, Gladys loved to dance, and from the stories people tell, she was good at it--the kind of dancer people would stop and watch, leaving Gladys to shine alone in the spotlight. But whatever motivated Gladys's spirit in those days was long gone, and her son had watched her put on a great deal of weight since about his seventeenth summer.

Although she tried to melt away the pounds through the hyperactive jolt of diet pills, she seemed only to get bigger. Losing weight became a real priority for her once Elvis became the darling of photographers 'round the world, since a number of them--particularly Alfred Wertheimer--wanted to profile Elvis at home with his family. It wasn't so much that Gladys was vain, but that she wanted to look good for her son, and she didn't want to embarrass him by an appearance that spoke of sad poverty fat. The diet pills soon became the mainstay of her

intake, a dangerous practice by itself, but a potentially lethal one when coupled with the beer she now shared with Vernon.

For Elvis, who'd had the evils of drink drilled into him from babyhood, it was impossible to think that his own Assembly of God mother was often awash in an alcoholic and amphetamine haze, especially since she never drank in his presence. Elvis, after all, wouldn't even allow any of us to bring beer in the house.

But even though he had long known about her "medication," he was mystified by her mood swings, since she was deliriously happy one moment and plumbing the depths of depression the next--seeming too often to be weepy, and for no real apparent reason. He couldn't understand why her bloat began to look so unnatural, as if she would instantly deflate if pricked with a pin. Each time he came home from a movie or a road trip, she seemed more distant, withdrawn, and despondent, less like the woman who had been the center of his universe. And when he implored of her--"Sattnin, what's wrong? Why do you seem so tired all the time?"--she repeatedly told him that she was all right.

But Gladys was far from all right. Her lower left side ached almost constantly, and she hadn't the energy that it took to merely maneuver through the day. Her doctor, who had no knowledge of Gladys's regular nips, recommended that she enter the hospital for tests. Gladys would have nothing of it. Elvis was home, and not just resting before another movie or tour. Soon he would report for duty for the "war thing," as she called it, and he wouldn't be coming home for two years.

Two years! It might as well have been forever. Clearly, it was more than Gladys could stand, even though she knew she would be seeing Elvis whenever the army allowed it. No, she would not enter the hospital now. She would stay at Graceland and savor every second that her beloved boy was at home, even if they had almost no time alone, and the laughter of dozens of interlopers filled the house. At that moment, Gladys Presley would have traded Graceland and every dollar that her son would generate his whole life long, for only an hour back at the little house on Tupelo's Old Saltillo Road. There, with his arm

81

on her knee, Elvis was hers, and hers alone. And if she closed her swollen eyes, she could feel him in her arms, and cradle him into eternity.

CHAPTER 5

"Everything I Have Is Gone!"

March 24, 1958. The day the sky fell. Clear across the country, girls were weeping, wailing, tearing their hair out. Elvis was finally going into the army.

Private Elvis Presley, serial number 553-1076-1, ten-hut. It never occurred to Elvis to have Colonel Parker buy him out of the service. He'd rejected special offers from the navy and the marines to enlist, even when the navy said he could have his own company made up of the Memphis Mafia and other local boys. Now that the army had delivered old-fashioned conscription on him, he even refused to take the white glove treatment as an entertainer in the special forces. Elvis would never have understood the Yippies and other political radicals of the sixties and seventies. He was a cultural rebel, but that had come naturally.

It also wasn't his style: Elvis wanted to be liked, and if he'd stayed out of the draft--even legitimately claiming he was an only child with dependents--the negative publicity might have ruined him. Down deep, he hated confrontation, something that would increasingly appear as a tragic flaw. He'd already recorded dozens of songs he despised rather than make waves. This passivity--which would reach a new level of numbness after the army--lay in what he told *Life* writer/photographer Lloyd Shearer: "We Presleys--we been poor as far back as I can remember."

No, if Elvis had to record songs (and later make movies) that robbed him of his self-respect, or if he had to go to the army to pacify that faction of the country that despised his every victory, he would do it, and do it gladly, however much he might grumble in private. It was all part of the job.

And Elvis, who had his humble act down pretty good, knew instinctively just what the public wanted to hear.

"I might have been in uniform before this if my mother hadn't wanted me to wait for the draft," Elvis told the newspapers. He went even farther on the morning of his induction, declaring, "I am looking forward to it as a great experience...The army can do anything it wants with me. Millions of other guys have been drafted, and I don't want to be different from anyone else."

With me, though, he talked a different story, especially when he thought I might just join up anyway and go with him. "I gotta go," he said, "and I'm goin'. But I'll tell you one thing. Make 'em come get you. Don't join anything. Take your chances."

There was a lot of talk at the time that Elvis was drafted to teach the youth of America a lesson--that "race music" and the moral laxity it supposedly fostered would not be tolerated in middle-class white society. The government and the right-wing majority of this country, the theory went, wanted to cut him down to size. But Elvis's popularity was not confined just to America anymore. He was an international figure. And as crazy as it seems now, there were people--and a lot of them--who thought he had to be *stopped*. Behind his humble facade, they reckoned, he was too arrogant, too dangerous.

Locally, of course, jealousy played as big a role in the draft board's eagerness to put him in uniform as any perceived knife that Elvis held against the throat of the American Dream. "After all," sniffed the head of the Memphis Draft Board, "when you take him out of the entertainment business, what have you got left? A truck driver."

The night before his induction, Elvis threw an all-night party at Graceland, which included a final spin around the Rainbow Roller Rink, Elvis bugging out his eyes and making faces as if he hadn't a care in the world. He was, of course, as frightened as a puppy in a lion's den. What would happen to him in the army? How would his officers and fellow recruits react to him? Could he cut the physical demands? Would his fans forget him? Would someone else on the American music horizon usurp him while he was gone? And how would Gladys cope while he was away?

That night, after a horde of photographers went home, Elvis asked me to sleep in his room at Graceland. In the early days, someone always slept in his room, because he had a tendency to sleepwalk, one of the myriad of reasons Gladys constantly worried about her son. Gladys was a sleepwalker, too, which may have predisposed Elvis to the condition, although psychiatrists believe it stems from an emotional disturbance. That makes sense in Elvis's case, since it started about the time his father packed off to prison. The army would cure him of it, but for now, nobody knew what he would get into.

Usually Lamar performed sleepwalking duty, curling up on a pallet on the floor. But for some reason, I got tapped. The funny thing was, I was probably the worst person to ask, because I was a sleepwalker, too! When I was thirteen or fouteen, and my Aunt Florence was visiting and staying over on the living room couch, I had a dream that I was playing football. I jumped up and ran through the house, and when I saw Aunt Florence move, I tackled her and broke her leg. Poor Aunt Florence didn't know what in the hell was happening. One minute she's half-asleep, and the next some crazy bastard's got her pinned to the floor.

I can't remember if I ever told Elvis that story, but I imagine he asked me to stay over because, unlike some of the other guys who were already figuring on meeting up with Elvis wherever he was stationed after basic training, I'd planned to stick around Memphis and work construction. Anyway, Elvis didn't have to worry about sleepwalking that evening. We sat and talked all night long, Elvis venting his fears about how things would be when he got back.

At 6:35 that Monday morning--a half-hour early--Elvis, wearing a striped shirt under a loud plaid sports jacket, and carrying exactly what the induction notice said for him to bring--a razor, a toothbrush, a comb, and enough money to hold him for two weeks--reported to the local draft board, number 86. Vernon and Gladys, who'd taken to her bed unusually early the night before, went with him. So did Lamar, Anita Wood, and Uncle Vester and his family. Colonel was there, too, palming off balloons stamped "King Creole!" And even Judy Spreckles, president of Elvis's national fan club, came, along with every photographer in Memphis.

The army of the fifties was typically made up of rednecks and ne'er-do-wells, country boys and urban trash, and poor whites and luckless blacks. Elvis's fellow recruits fit that bill-- goony-faced boys whose facial features seemed a hopeless mismatch. Shortly after seven, they all piled onto a bus for Kennedy Veteran's Hospital for physicals and in-processing. When they arrived back at the draft board around four, Elvis raised his right hand and swore the words that marched him into the United States Army. Somewhere in the room stood Sgt. Walter Alden, whose two-year old daughter, Ginger, would have her own appointment with Elvis nearly twenty years later.

Afterwards, Elvis, who was put in charge of the other fourteen recruits, dutifully led them out to an army bus bound for Fort Chaffee, Arkansas. Then he approached his parents for a final good-bye, trying to put a humorous spin on the situation with lame one-liners about soldier life, and promising to call home as soon as he could. As Elvis and the others boarded the bus, Vernon, fighting back emotion, screwed up his face and knitted his eyebrows. Gladys dabbed at her puffy eyes, tears streaming uncontrollably as she waved at the government vehicle wheeling out of sight. Elvis would be home on leave in a matter of months, but their life together as she had known it was gone forever.

In Arkansas, Colonel Parker, wearing a long, floppy and ridiculous polka-dot string tie, would be on hand to juggle the seventy reporters and photographers who turned out to chronicle Elvis's first real taste of military life. On Tuesday, Elvis's first full day in the army, he would take a five-hour aptitude test. Later, he'd meet civilian barber James B. Peterson, who, for the price of sixty-five cents, would shear his swept-back bristle cut into a regulation G.I. flattop. And he would receive part of his first month's pay--$7.00 out of $83.20. The next day, with Colonel straining to see what the reporters scratched down in their notebooks, Elvis modeled his new uniform, obligingly buttoning his shirt on and taking it off again to the clicking buzz of Nikons.

In the next several days, Elvis reported to Fort Hood, Texas, for his eight weeks of basic training and advanced tank preparation. He was assigned to Company A, Second Medium Tank Battalion, Thirty-seventh Armor, Second Armored Division, whose motto was "Hell on Wheels." Although hundreds of fans tried to telephone him at the base, and his mail call was some two thousand fan letters a week, he and Colonel took pains to see that he fit in with the rest of the company. Elvis slept in the barracks and refused all interviews with the press.

From a public relations standpoint, the strategy paid off. On April 1, RCA released "Wear My Ring Around Your Neck," an obvious song of farewell for Elvis's fans, backed with "Don'cha' Think It's Time." The record entered the *Billboard* Top 100 charts at number 7, the first of his singles to debut that high. People were starved for anything Elvis.

Typically, Elvis never talked about it, but those first days of basic training must have swirled him into inexplicable anxiety. Not only was he thrown into a completely new situation, with men who both revered him and wanted to see him broken down in the discipline of the military. But it was, after all, the first time he had ever been really alone, without the protective seal of the Memphis Mafia, or Scotty and Bill, or Gladys, or even Colonel.

To most people, that freedom would have been exhilarating. But Elvis, who at his emotional core was still a small boy, needed people around him almost constantly. Even if the Memphis Mafia was, as writer Dave Marsh has assessed, "the most small-time sidekicks that any great man has known," Elvis chose us for a reason. At heart, he was a big kid trying to get a grip on his manhood, and if we protected him from the world a little bit while he did that, what harm could it do?

Even with his new freedom, certainly Elvis knew that he was now so trapped in *adult* expectations--of pleasing his fans as well as the establishment he secretly wanted to join, of realizing his own dream of becoming an accomplished actor-- that there would never be any true freedom again. His music had galvanized a generation, but his life was beginning to grow beyond him and spin out of control. The most he could do was make the best of things every day.

As part of that, Elvis was determined to be the model soldier, just as he'd been a teacher's pet in school. That first day, he was up making his bed when reveille came at 5:30 a.m. He must have indulged in a bit more apple polishing in the next few months, because the last week of May, he was named assistant squad leader for a fourteen-mile, full-pack march.

It was strange to be in Memphis and not be going out to Graceland every night, but I was keeping busy. I'd gone to work for some distant relatives in the construction business, and they'd made me a foreman overseeing the building of houses and apartments and shopping centers. Basically, I made sure the sub-contractors showed up, and checked to see that the jobs were running smoothly. After a while, I started selling houses on Sunday. I was also dating a little Memphis girl, and I thought I was in love.

This wasn't nearly as glamourous as traveling with Elvis, something my parents and brother had supported wholeheartedly. After all, it made me the talk of the local Jewish population. But I knew that Elvis would be out of uniform in almost no time, and we'd be back to making movies again. I figured that I'd travel with him for a couple more years, and then I'd take over my father's scrap business. It looked like a pretty easy life.

I didn't see Elvis again until June, when he got a two-week leave after basic training. Anita Wood picked him up in a convertible outside Fort Hood on June 1, and together, with the heat of the summer sun on their faces, they drove the 400 miles home to Memphis. Elvis's hair was a lot shorter, and he had a lot more stories to tell, but that was about the only difference I saw in him. He rented the Rainbow rink as usual --something that now seemed fairly adolescent for an army man--and we stayed up most nights and partied, except when he went to Nashville for two days to record a session that would yield a string of hits: "A Fool Such as I," "I Need Your Love Tonight," "A Big Hunk O' Love," and "I Got Stung." He also found the time to take his parents to a local theater to

preview "King Creole," which was set to open nationwide the following month.

Elvis had shown steady improvement as an actor since "Love Me Tender," his first crack at films, when *Time* magazine sneered, "Is it a sausage? It certainly is smooth and damp-looking, but whoever heard of a 172-lb. sausage, six feet tall?" But I don't think anyone expected him to be as good in "King Creole" as he was. For as long as he lived, it was his favorite, and his best. Even the *New York Times* declared that the film was "a surprisingly colorful and lively drama," with Elvis doing some "surprisingly credible acting." If he had continued his film career in this dramatic vein, and been allowed to develop into the kind of actor he yearned to be, the ultimate story of Elvis Presley's fate would likely have been far different.

Elvis's two-week leave, then, was a perfect, triumphal homecoming except for one disturbing matter: Gladys's escalated decline. Elvis couldn't stop thinking about it, and when he returned to Fort Hood for eight weeks of advanced training as an armor crewman, and six more weeks of training with his unit, he made a request. After basic training, soldiers who had dependents were allowed to move off the base and live with their families. Would Vernon and Gladys come to Texas?

By now, Gladys was gravely ill with alcohol-aggravated hepatitis, a condition that could have been reversed had she admitted to her addiction long before. Still, she continued to tell her son that nothing was wrong, and Elvis, refusing out of denial to realize just how sick she was, did not insist that she see a physician. In the middle of June, with her life quickly ebbing away, she joined her husband, her mother-in-law Minnie Mae, and Lamar Fike in the long journey to Fort Hood.

Yet Gladys's reunion with her son was anything but sweet. When the Presleys moved into a rented trailer parked just outside the base, Elvis's fans besieged them at all hours of the day and night, disturbing Gladys's peace and robbing her of rest. Once more the family was uprooted, this time to a rented house at 609 Oak Hill Drive, in the nearby town of Killeen. Elvis moved into one of its three bedrooms.

If Gladys had labored under the impression that she would finally have Elvis to herself again, now that she had only weeks to live, it is impossible to gauge her disappointment in realizing that things would be only marginally better than they'd been at Graceland. Soon Anita Wood would come from Memphis to visit, and Elvis spent many of his weekends at the Waco home of Eddie Fadal, a disc jockey whom Elvis had met while on tour in Texas in 1956. Often, as on the Fourth of July, the entire Presley clan traveled the forty-five miles to eat hamburgers with Fadal's family. Gladys, who suffered constant pain, massaging her left side at every opportunity, continued to downplay her condition.

Finally, her fortitude gave out during the first week of August, when she began to lose her motor coordination. Her mental faculties also seemed impaired. Elvis and Vernon drove her to a doctor in Temple, who insisted she immediately fly to her own physician in Memphis. But Gladys held fast to her fear of flying, and on Friday, August 8, Elvis, who had been denied a weekend pass, put his parents on the train. The next day, Gladys was examined by her family doctor, who promptly admitted her to Methodist Hospital. There, four specialists diagnosed her as suffering from acute hepatitis and severe liver damage.

When the frantic Elvis got the news from his father, he immediately asked for emergency leave, only to have his request denied. Finally, on August 12, with the threat of going AWOL and the intervention of Gladys's doctors, Elvis received his leave. He drove to Waco at breakneck speed and caught a plane for Memphis, arriving late that afternoon.

Gladys was critical. And yet when Elvis, still in uniform, entered her room just before eight that night, she mustered the strength for an emotional reunion: "Oh, my son, my son!" Elvis stayed at the hospital until after ten o'clock, talking to Gladys in their special language, caressing her hands, and praying for her recovery.

The next day, Wednesday, August 13, Gladys grew worse. Elvis, crazy with anxiety, visited her during the afternoon hours and then again that evening. In between visits, Lamar,

George Klein, Billy Smith, a new member of the entourage, Louis Harris, and I, sat around a table with Elvis in a hospital conference room, waiting for news of his mother's condition. Around midnight, when Elvis's face sagged with fatigue, both Gladys and Vernon insisted he go back to Graceland to rest. Elvis kissed his mother good night. Gladys knew she was fading, and wanted to spare Elvis the agony of watching the final struggle. "Son," she said weakly, "when you get here tomorrow, I want you to see that all these flowers are given to other patients."

Whether he fully grasped what she was telling him, the exhausted Elvis went home and fell into a deep sleep. Shortly after 3:15 a.m., Vernon telephoned Graceland, relaying the news to Billy Smith, who had the awful task of telling Elvis that his Sattnin was gone.

Elvis rushed to the hospital, hoping that there had been some terrible mistake, that Gladys had faltered for a moment, but that she had revived, and that she would regain her strength and eventually come home. But when he saw his father's face engulfed in grief he knew that it was true. "She woke me up struggling," Vernon cried. "She was suffering for breath. I got to her as quick as I could, and the nurse and doctor put her in an oxygen tent. But it was too late." Gladys had apparently suffered a heart attack.

Elvis's anguish filled him with the force of a raging river. He felt such emptiness--such gnawing sickness--that he could barely stand. How could they not have saved her, she who had more heart than anyone he ever knew, and so much less happiness than she deserved? The hospital staff would later report that Vernon and Elvis tore the nighttime quiet with mournful cries and wailing, at once praying for their loved one and trying to shake off their despair. That afternoon, Gladys was brought home to Graceland to lay in state, the hearse snaking its way through the music gates and up the Graceland drive like a mystery train of Elvis's own design. Then the family members and Elvis's close friends were invited to pay their respects.

When I arrived at Graceland, Elvis was in a daze. His voice

was small and strained. "My baby's gone, Alan, she's gone!" he rasped. "I know, Elvis," I said. "I'm sorry. She was a nice lady." Then he took me over to view the body, as he did everyone who came in the house. Gladys lay in a silver casket, clad in her pretty baby blue dress.

I wasn't there when he supposedly flung himself on the corpse, hugging and kissing her and crying out to her to come back, using that baby talk of theirs. And I wasn't there when he pulled out his comb and rearranged her hair, or began rubbing her feet, her "sooties," massaging them the way he had when he was a youngster and his mother had come home from a long day working at the hospital. But it doesn't sound out of character for Elvis--he loved her like no one on this earth--and he was out of his mind with grief. Except when he got up to greet visitors, he just sat there with her, almost as if they were the host and hostess of their own little party. It was a pitiful thing to watch. He must have sat there all night long.

On Friday, August 15, the Graceland gates opened a last time for Gladys, as her body was transferred to the Memphis Funeral Home for the one o'clock afternoon service. Nick Adams, who had loved Gladys's okra, flew in for the funeral, as did the Blackwood Brothers gospel group, who came from North Carolina to sing "Precious Memories" and "Rock of Ages." Anita Wood was there, too, as were four hundred other invited guests. And then there were Elvis's fans, some three thousand of them, who stood outside the funeral home and gave the affair a kind of circus atmosphere.

The Reverend James E. Hamill, pastor of the First Assembly of God Church, had known the Presleys almost since they moved to Memphis, and it was he who preached the service, remembering how earnest Gladys had been about her son's religious teaching, and recalling Elvis when he was a boy of thirteen, a kid with trousers too short and hair too long. The remembrance plunged Elvis into an abyss of pain, and he was heard to sob, "Oh, God, everything I have is gone!" Reverend Hamill paused to let Elvis collect himself, but before long he would know him as a troubled man who would come into his office and say, "Pastor, I am the most miserable young man you've ever seen. I'm doing the things you taught me not to, and I'm not doing the things you said I should do." Tears would stream down his face, and he would ask the pastor to pray for his soul.

When the hearse carried Gladys to Forest Hill Cemetery, Elvis, his eyelids swollen from days of weeping, looked out the car window and saw the streets clogged with fans. Couldn't they see this was private? Hadn't they worried Gladys enough while she was alive? Hadn't they helped put her where she was today? But for decades to come, Gladys's sister, Lillian, would insist that it was Elvis who killed Gladys, not his fans.

As Gladys's casket was lowered into the grave, Elvis could not contain himself. "I lived my whole life for you!" he cried. But, of course, a good case could be made that it was precisely the other way around. Rarely have two people wounded each other so deeply out of love, although, of course, neither one of them would ever have realized it. "She was very close, more than a mother," Elvis would publicly say. "She was a friend who would let me talk to her any hour of the day or night if I had a problem. I would get mad sometimes when she wouldn't let me do something. But I found out she was right about almost everything."

Gladys's death seemed surreal to me. One day she was there at Graceland, staring out the window--at what? And the next time I saw her, she lay dreamlike in her casket. How could none of us have known how ill she was? In many ways, Gladys was a woman of mystery, and her son took after her.

The unreal quality of Gladys's passing was strengthened by the odd fact that Red West's father died the same day, also in Memphis. Red, who had been Elvis's friend since high school, had joined the marines before Elvis was drafted. He was on emergency leave, trying to get home from Norfolk, Virginia, when his father slipped away. The day after Elvis put his mother in the ground, he and I, Lamar and Gene Smith paid our respects to Mr. West. The funeral home was getting to be a regular hangout, and I didn't care for it much.

For the remainder of his leave, Elvis stayed at Graceland. In the day, he traveled the local countryside in a new van, trying to find some perspective in what had happened. At night, we all gathered to take in a movie and blitz the skating rink, thinking Elvis needed to do something besides ramble through that big house. Even the Tennessee Highway Patrol obliged in helping Elvis through his grief, inviting him on their morning helicopter rides, and teaching him how to take off and land. But I don't think Elvis's heart was in it. When he reported back to Fort Hood on August 25, he was glad to get away from Graceland and the memories that lurked like ghosts in every room.

Some people say that Elvis found out in June that he was soon to be sent to Europe, but I've always believed that it was no accident that the army assigned Elvis to Germany the following month. Even at Fort Hood, Elvis was so depressed that he could barely function. He walked around as if he weren't really there. Beneath the soldier's uniform was a man who had suddenly, and terrifyingly, been hurled back to childhood. Only now there was no Gladys to share it, no Gladys to love him, no Gladys to protect him, or for him to protect, either physically or morally. Elvis was Little Boy Lost.

In my view, it was Colonel who arranged for him to go to Germany as a truck driver with the 3rd Armored Division. There, Colonel hoped, Elvis would be too overwhelmed with the new culture and the new girls to mourn the way things used to be when Gladys was alive. He would come back a new man, Colonel thought. But I don't think any of us were prepared for the Elvis who would return. The image was reversed in some great, perverted mirror somewhere. He would go away an innocent, posing to the world at large as a defiant provocateur, an image based somewhat on the early Tony Curtis movies that still played daily in Elvis's head. Yet the Elvis who would come back--cleaned up in looks, dress and manner to fit the all-American, establishment mold--would submerge himself in a life-style that was far more sordid than the darkest secrets that his critics had ever imagined.

CHAPTER 6

Private Elvis
Frauleins And Frolics

On September 22, 1958, Elvis sat for a farewell press conference the likes of which were usually reserved for war-time generals and heads of state. As usual, his revelations were hardly earth-shaking: He said he was most looking forward to seeing Paris--"and I'd like to look up Brigitte Bardot." The reporters laughed and wrote it down, and flashbulbs went off with the pop! pop! pop! of fireworks.

Three days alter, Elvis had boarded a troop train bound for the Military Ocean Terminal in Brooklyn, N.Y. Vernon, Red West, Lamar, Anita Wood, and Elvis's grandmother Minnie Mae Presley--he called her "Dodger" because he'd once thrown a baseball that had missed her head by inches--saw him off, with a promise to meet him in a few days in the land of the kraut and the beer.

"One of the last things Mom said was that Dad and I should always be together...Wherever they send me, Dad will go, too," Elvis had told the reporters. He was in no shape to be alone--when had he ever been? But especially not now. With Gladys gone, he would build a thicker wall around himself, a wall of people who would insulate him from harm, a wall of people he could trust, and better still, control.

Elvis found an addition to that group right on the train speeding to New York. His name was Charlie Hodge. A musician himself, Charlie had been a singer with Red Foley's Foggy River Boys, one of the most popular country acts of the forties and fifties. He'd also played back-up for Roy Rogers and Gene Autry. Like Elvis, Charlie was a Southerner--he hailed from Alabama--and he knew how to have a good time.

When their ship, the USS General Randall, weighed anchor with 1,400 soldiers aboard, Elvis and Charlie arranged to be

95

roommates. Some say Charlie was assigned to keep Elvis company, since he was clearly still distraught over his mother's death. Whatever, they had enough in common to hit it off, both taking part in the serviceman's variety show at sea, which Elvis produced. Charlie, five-feet-three-inches tall and a born ham, did a stand-up comedy routine and served as master of ceremonies. Elvis played piano. Charlie would prove indispensable to Elvis as the years went on, helping him on stage (Charlie would become the keeper of the scarves), and off, as a kind of valet.

Elvis would meet someone else during his army days who would become an important part of his entourage--Joe Esposito. Joe was a Chicago boy, with a dark-complexion and deep, Mafia eyes. Rumors would abound in years to come that Joe actually *was* part of the Mafia, but I imagine the only Mafia he truly belonged to was that of the Memphis variety. Joe was a good businessman, something Vernon immediately saw and put to use, asking Joe to handle some of Elvis's accounting. Even so, I don't know how smart it was to allow Elvis to keep more than a million dollars in his checking account at Memphis Bank of Commerce, an account that drew no interest during Elvis's lifetime.

For now, though, fifteen hundred fans were waiting for Elvis when the ship docked at Bremerhaven, West Germany, on October 1. That was a good sign, as far as Elvis was concerned. Back home, for the first time in two years, he failed to place a single on the *Billboard* charts, a situation that wouldn't change for five weeks.

The U.S. Seventh Army was based at Ray Caserne, Friedberg, about twenty miles north of Frankfurt. Shortly after Elvis's arrival there, the base held an open house for the media. The press was told that Elvis would be joining Company "D," First Medium Tank Battalion, Thirty-second Armor, Third Armored Division of the Seventh Army, and assigned to drive a jeep for Lt. Col. Henry Grimm. It was hardly grueling work, but Elvis still insisted he didn't want special treatment. Indeed, as a scout jeep driver, he would go on field training exercises and weather the same discomforts as everyone else.

My draft board classification--4-F, the result of a football injury--left me back in Memphis while Elvis was away in the army. Nonetheless, we kept in touch with Elvis's pals. Here we are at a Memphis hotel--that's me on the left in the white shirt and skinny tie, with George Klein mugging for the camera down front--with Tommy Sands, in town on a record promotional tour.

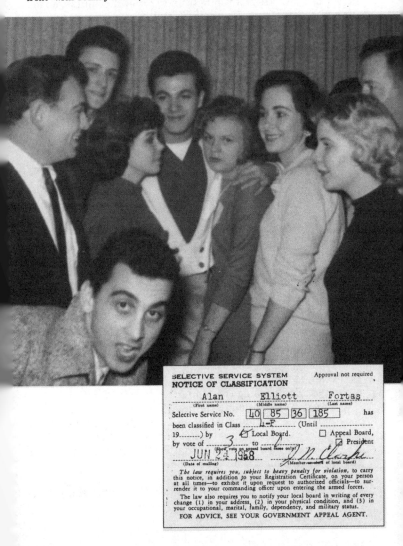

"He doesn't want to entertain," announced Major General Thomas F. Van Natta. "We've asked him and he said, 'I'd rather not, sir.' He just wants to mind his own business, do his job and be left alone. He's a good soldier."

Elvis may have been a good soldier, but he wasn't exactly a run-of-the-mill soldier. He would get promoted often--to private first class by November ("I'm proud to have a stripe," he said)--and newsmen would follow him every time he stepped off base. Elvis would actually be spending a great deal of time off base, for early in October, Vernon and Grandma Minnie Mae arrived in Germany, as did Lamar and Red. Soon, Cliff Gleaves would join them. They moved into a three-bedroom apartment in the Hotel Gruenwald in Bad Homburg for a little while, and eventually settled into a four-bedroom house at 14 Goethestrasse in Bad Nauheim. There Elvis, who paid the $800-a-month rent, also stayed when he wasn't on duty. They put a sign on the gate in German, which translated as: AUTOGRAPHS BETWEEN 7:00 AND 8:00 P.M. ONLY. At home, the press was reporting the erroneous news that Elvis was looking to buy a castle, or maybe a medieval mansion.

While he was still stateside, Elvis had invited me to come to Germany, too. But I was torn between staying with Elvis and moving on, because I knew that sooner or later it would all end, and I'd have no qualifications to do anything in life. Now I'd been rejected by the army--a knee injury from my football days had rendered me 4-F--and I was satisfied to be working construction. One day the phone rang. Elvis was on the line from Germany.

"You still happy?" he asked.

"Yeah," I said. "We're doin' real good, puttin' up a lot of buildings. I'm learning something."

"Why don't you come to Germany?"

I hesitated a minute, but then I thought, "Alan Fortas, a Jewish kid in Germany...I'd better stay where I am."

I'd already heard from Red that Elvis still wasn't paying a salary. I mentioned it on the phone.

"I'll pay you," he countered.

"It's not really that, Elvis," I said. "I'm doing something

98

that I enjoy. I feel like I'm accomplishing something."

Elvis was a little ticked about that, but I think he understood. I wanted to learn something about business. Sooner or later, I'd take over my father's scrap paper yard, and I wanted to know how business worked.

Now, of course, I wish I'd gone to Germany. It would have been a good chance to see the country. Instead, every so often George Klein and I got together and made tapes--"talking letters"--for Elvis. I think he appreciated them. They were funny and upbeat, the same kind of humor we used when the guys were all together.

I wrote notes to Elvis, too, because I liked to stay in touch. But I didn't expect a letter back because I'd never known him to write one. He'd just pick up the telephone and call. I was surprised as heck one day when George called and said, "Guess what? I got a letter from Elvis!" Then I found out Anita got one, too. But no one else.

In November, 1958, Elvis joined the Thirty-second Tank Battalion at Grafenwohr, West Germany, for several weeks of maneuvers near the Czechoslovakian border, during which time he learned to handle every kind of weapon, from a pistol to a 90mm gun. This would, in part, inspire his later love of firearms. But, at the time, I felt sorry for him, because I figured he was camping out a lot in terrible weather. I also wondered what the snake population was over there, and if snakes hibernate in the winter in Europe the same as they do over here. When Elvis was a kid, snakes got into the Presleys' house in Mississippi right often. As long as he lived, Elvis had an inordinate fear of snakes, especially of turning back the bed sheets and finding one of those cold-blooded babies coiled between the covers. He could tell you more about snakes than you really wanted to know.

Anyway, he was on my mind a lot. And then one day, this turned up in my mailbox:

Dear "Hog Ears":

Got your letter and was glad to hear from you. Well, you know I am bound to be pretty lonely or I wouldn't be writing a letter.

We are up at a training area for 50 days and believe me it's miserable. It's cold and there is nothing at all to do up here. I am about 200 miles from Friedberg and won't be back until the 20th of December. It will sure be a *great* Christmas this year ("ha").

I would give almost anything to be home. You know it will be March of 1960 before I return to the States. Man, I hate to think about it. Of course, don't say anything about it, because a miracle may happen.

Boy, it will be great getting out. I will probably scream so loud they'll make me stay two more years (ha). I can hardly wait to start singing, traveling, making movies, and above all seeing the old gang and old Graceland. All I do is sit and count the days.

Well, it'll be over in about 15 months and as Gen. MacArthur said, "I shall return." Tell D.J. [disc jockey, George Klein] uh, and Lewis [Louis Harris] I said hello and to hold down the fort till I get back. If you see cous [Gene Smith], tell him I said ap skep skep skep [a nonsense phrase they used with each other]. I have been dating this little German "chuckaloid" by the name of Margrit. She looks a lot like B.B. [Brigitte Bardot]. It's *Grind City*. Well, I gotta go wade in the mud.

Your Pal,

Elvis Presley

On the back, he had scribbled, "Eri Viar Ditchi," an attempt at "arrivederci."

It was so rare for Elvis to write a letter that, at first, I didn't really think it was from him, even though I knew his handwriting. That was the only letter I'd ever get from him. Today, I keep it in the safety deposit box with the transcript of

Dear "Hog Ears" (1)

Got your letter and was glad to hear from you. Well you know I am bound to be pretty lonely or I wouldn't be writing a letter. We are up at a training area for 50 days and believe me it's miserable. It's cold and there is nothing at all to do up here. I am about 200 miles from Friedberg and won't be back until the 20th of Dec. It will sure be a *great* Christmas this year. I would give almost anything to be home. you know it will be March of 1960 before I return to the States. Man I hate to think about it. Of course don't say anything about it because a miracle may happen. Boy it will be great getting out. I will

Elvis's only handwritten letter to me, November 1958, reproduced with the kind permission of Elvis Presley Enterprises. (Photo: John Nation)

probably scream so loud they'll make me stay 2 more years. ha.

I can hardly wait to start singing, traveling making movies, and above all seeing ~~the~~ the old gang and old Graceland. All I do is sit and count the days. well it'll be over in about 15 months and as Gen. MacArthur said, "I shall return". Tell D. J. uh, and Lewis I said hello and to hold down the fort till I get back. If you see cous. tell him I said ge shep shep shep. I have been dating this little German "Chuckaloid" by the name of Margrit. She looks alot like B. B. 20's Grind City. well I gotta go wade in the mud.

"over"   your Pal Elvis Presley

Second page. (Photo: John Nation)

Back of second back and envelope. (Photo: John Nation)

his grades.

As it turned out, Elvis may have been lonely, but he was hardly at a loss for companionship. I knew that Elvis was still telephoning Anita Wood in Memphis, and he was still writing her letters, too. But I also knew from the guys that in addition to sixteen-year-old Margrit Buergin, he was dating a pretty eighteen-year-old named Elisabeth Stefaniak, and Vera Tschechowa, a German actress.

In October, RCA had released "One Night," Elvis's steamy song of sexual yearning and delayed gratification. In reality, though, Elvis wasn't denying himself much of anything. From the Rudolf Paulini photographs that later emerged in the book *Private Elvis*, edited by Diego Cortez and published in 1978, Elvis appeared to have plenty of opportunity to sample Germany's fabled showgirls and prostitutes. These photographs, taken at the Moulin Rouge in Munich on three occasions in early 1959, were totally at odds with Elvis's wholesome, all-American image. They probably would have finished him in the States had they appeared here then.

Elvis had been photographed in intimate situations with girls before. Alfred Wertheimer had captured him French-kissing a groupie in a stairwell, and close-dancing *sans* shirt with former high school sweetheart Barbara Hearn in 1956. But those photos had a playful, innocent quality to them. You knew nothing really went beyond them.

By contrast, the German images were unsettling, strange, and sordid, Elvis hanging on to a parade of European hookers, B-girls, and strippers. A couple of them were mildly attractive, but most of them looked like your worst nightmare from Hell. They either held him provocatively with full-body hugs, or pecked at him in the lewdest, most lascivious manner imaginable. Only rarely is Elvis smiling in these photos. He looks transfixed, dazed, like he's watching a scummy movie in his mind. Critic Dave Marsh says they look like "the answer to a question no one thought to ask." To me, they look like the answer to a question no one *wanted* to ask.

After that, Elvis began spending more and more time in places and in situations he hadn't dared to go before. That summer, he took a two-week furlough in Paris with several of the guys. They checked into the somber Hotel Prince de Galles, and then scampered off for the Champs-Elysees and a famous nightclub called the Lido. One night, Elvis sat at the piano and sang "Willow Weep for Me," and noodled around with some classic supperclub standards, drawing applause from the Lido's regular musicians. But the main reason Elvis was there was to ogle the club's legendary chorus line, the Bluebelle Girls. Each night, Elvis and the guys would eat dinner at the Lido, and then after the first show, trek the entire company of showgirls back to the hotel, where they would remain until the manager of the club called and implored them to return for the second performance. Elvis watched that show, too, and then everyone headed back to the Hotel Prince, where Elvis, the entourage, and the girls dallied until dawn.

What was Elvis up to? There had always been girls on the road, of course, but this kind of orgiastic behavior was new and heretofore out of character. My own feeling is that Elvis had lived his life basically as he'd been told. He had honored and obeyed his parents, he had attended church and prayed for salvation and direction, and he had shown respect for his elders. More recently, he had reported to Uncle Sam, been a good soldier, and donated a sizable hunk of money to charity.

In short, he had towed the line for twenty-four years. And what had it brought him? Fame? Fortune? That didn't really mean anything. All he knew was that his mother, his centeredness, and his sense of self had been yanked out from under him, leaving him empty, embittered, and exposed. Now he would do his best to suspend himself from his suffocating misery. If it took a constant and shameless round of parties to blot out his memories, then he would indulge until the ache was gone, until he couldn't tell the difference between wrong and right, past and present.

However Elvis was spending his nights, his days often included public relations stunts that benefited both himself and the army. In April of 1959, he served as host when the Friedberg base held an open house. And while on leave, he campaigned for the Salk polio vaccine by receiving an inoculation in front of photographers, just as he had publicly given blood four months before. He also supervised a unit of soldiers sent to Steinfurth to help the town move its large World War I memorial statue.

But according to Charlie Hodge, Elvis drew the line at one P.R. junket, when he was asked to tour a handful of European cities and take time for a meeting with the pope. The pope! What a picture that would have been, especially in view of Elvis's new sexual tenor! Elvis declined, noting that the tour was scheduled for the exact time he was supposed to be on his maneuvers. "There's fifteen thousand men out there sleeping in the snow," Elvis told his colonel. "For me to leave and go to a nice, warm, comfortable place, and then to come back and work with the guys, well, I just couldn't face them. I think I'll just stay here."

How much of this dance Colonel was orchestrating from the States, I don't know. But that was a smart move all around, one that helped insure Elvis's popularity with the guys in his outfit. He may have now gotten fifteen thousand letters a week, lived off the post and driven a $7,160 BMW 507 (which was totaled on the autobahn on the first day of 1959), but whenever he got packages of candy and cake, he passed them around. He also took the time to talk to the guys one-on-one, something that promoted his image as a "regular fellow." None of the guys seemed to resent it, then, when Elvis was promoted to specialist fourth class in the summer of 1959, a rank which raised his salary to $99.37 a month.

"We hope nobody complains that Elvis was promoted before other soldiers in his unit," a citation from his battalion went, "but he really tries hard to be a good soldier and he deserves it." Six months later, he got still another promotion, to acting sergeant and squad leader, becoming a full sergeant shortly thereafter. Now he was earning the princely pay of $122.31.

The irony, of course, was that in February 1960, *Billboard* magazine would announce that Elvis had sold $50 million dollars worth of records to date. For a time during his army hitch, his sales had slumped, but in the spring of '59, Colonel stirred up interest in "the Boy" when he negotiated with the

television networks for an Elvis special upon his discharge. And things got *really* jumpin' when an RCA executive announced at a November press conference that Elvis would probably change his singing style when he came home. So many fans telephoned Colonel's office in protest that they jammed the long distance lines.

With his promotions and the news that his career was heating up again, Elvis must have felt good about himself in the fall of '59, when he met fourteen-year-old Priscilla Ann Beaulieu, the step-daughter of an air force officer who had just been transferred to Weisbaden, near Friedberg. The two were introduced by Currie Grant, an American in his twenties who was serving in the air force. Grant and his wife had often visited Elvis's white-stucco, three-story house at 14 Goethestrasse.

Currie knew that Elvis's taste in women ran to small-featured, soft-talking brunettes with blue eyes, and he'd spotted Priscilla at the Eagles Club, a place where service families often went for dinner and entertainment. Grant was in a habit of inviting comely teenage fans to join Elvis's gatherings, and one day he simply walked over to Priscilla and introduced himself. He asked her where she was from, how she liked Germany, and what she thought of Elvis Presley. From there, he invited her to go along the next time he and his wife paid the Presleys a visit. The teenager could hardly believe it! Elvis was almost as popular in West Germany as he was in America.

Priscilla, who was exceptionally pretty even at fourteen, probably didn't classify herself as an Elvis Presley fan, even though she'd bought a little book about him for twenty-five cents, and she'd been attracted to him when she saw him on Jimmy and Tommy Dorsey's "Stage Show." Her father had stood in line at the PX to buy his first album for her, but her mother had reacted to Elvis pretty much the same as the high school principal from California, vowing that he was a "bad influence" on teenage girls. If there was ever a mothers' march against him, she'd remarked, she'd be the first in line.

Nonetheless, Priscilla's parents allowed her to go to Elvis's home, which Currie assured her was well-chaperoned. When they arrived, as Priscilla remembered it, Elvis was in the living room, smoking a cigar and mixing it up with a knot of people that included Red and Lamar and their dates. As soon as Currie led her in, Elvis stood up and smiled. "Well," he drawled, "what have we here?"

Priscilla may have been young, but she was a dignified girl, and she didn't particularly like Elvis's tone. At first, she was too overwhelmed to say much of anything, but when Elvis expressed surprise at the news that she was only in the ninth grade--he'd guessed she was a junior or senior in high school--she let him know she didn't appreciate his laughter. Elvis liked that kind of spunk, and with that, he walked over to the piano and began an impromptu performance of "Rags to Riches," inviting his friends to join in on "The End," by Earl Grant.

When Elvis Presley wanted to be charming, there wasn't a man, woman, or child who could resist him, and now Elvis concentrated all his attention on this shy, little American girl. He liked the fact that she was dark-haired and kittenish, and that she had spent most of her youth in the South, in Texas. On Priscilla's second visit to Bad Nauheim, Elvis invited her to his bedroom, a request that understandably scared the whey out of her.

But Priscilla needn't have been frightened. As it turned out, she was precisely the age that three of Elvis's friends at home--Gloria Mowell, Heidi Heissen, and Frances Forbes--had been when they first started coming to Graceland. Since 1956, when the Presleys lived on Audubon Drive, the trio had been part of Elvis's personal traveling show, accompanying him on his all-night roller skating parties and movie rentals, spending the last days before Elvis's army induction at the house, and even going down to Fort Hood for a visit.

No one thought anything unusual about this, except that they were junior high students, and that their parents allowed them to stay out until the wee hours, when Lamar would drive them home. What *was* unusual about the relationship was that Elvis took such an interest in them. When they were at the house, Elvis seemed totally involved in their world, as if he, too, were fourteen. Nothing they had to say was too juvenile, none of their life's experiences too limited, none of their opinions too ill-informed. It was as if he identified with them. And so Elvis, who could have had his pick of some of the world's most desirable women, spent a considerable amount of time with these fourteen-year-olds--throwing them in the pool, challenging them in watermelon-seed spitting contests, engaging them in pillow fights, roughhousing with them, tickling them, and rolling around on the bed with them. On and on it went, until one of them declared that Elvis had gone "too far," and he would stop. But Elvis would tell Gloria that he had a rule: "I'll never break a virgin. There's too many prostitutes walking around."

Incredibly, they settled for "pajama parties," during which Elvis would allow them to wash and dry his hair, and he would instruct *them* on how to wear make-up, sometimes putting the heavy eye shadow and eyeliner on them himself. Then they'd sit yoga-style on his big bed, with Elvis in the middle, and he would tease them, saying Frances was jealous because he kissed Gloria, or Gloria was jealous because he hugged Heidi, going on to change the order of the names. Then he would turn out the light, and they would lay there, Elvis putting one arm around a girl on each side, with the third laying atop his feet.

No one would speak a word until Elvis decided that it was late. Then he'd sit up, kiss each girl good-bye, and say, "I love you. See you tomorrow." Then Lamar would carry them home, hoping none of the parents would be waiting to tear him apart.

None ever were. And, after all, their activity had been perfectly chaste, however psychologically satisfying it had been for all parties.

Obviously, then, Elvis needed someone to baby more than he needed a sex partner. He craved the attention of someone who adored him without the threat of sexual pressure, much as a mother would. And now in his room, cuddling Priscilla in his arms on the bed, it was not so much love and romance or even sex that he spoke of. It was Gladys.

"I just wish Mama could have been here to meet you," he said. "She would have liked you as much as I do." Lamar says that Elvis always looked for girls who would baby *him,* even if they were just babies themselves. Considering the pictures of Priscilla taken at the time, with her short, dark hair, it's not hard to believe that when Elvis looked at her, he saw her with the eyes of a little boy, a child who missed his mother.

Soon, Priscilla would visit Elvis in his room four nights a week, and from her own recollections, nothing more ever went on there than it had in Elvis's bedroom at home with Gloria, Frances, and Heidi. Do I believe it? I don't want to get into Elvis's intimate sex life. But he told me on a couple of occasions that if a nice girl turned out *not* to be so nice, he wanted nothing to do with her. I know he cared quite a bit for Priscilla, and so I find it easy to believe he never touched her until he thought the time was right for them to marry. He said he didn't want to ruin her life. That sounds melodramatic in the social climate of the nineties, but that's exactly what it amounted to with the psychological and social delineations of the fifties.

That Christmas, the Presleys threw a holiday party at 14 Goethestrasse. Vernon invited Davada "Dee" Stanley and her husband Bill, an American Master Sergeant. Elvis invited Priscilla, and his two new friends Joe Esposito and Charlie Hodge, who came often to the Presley home. When Elvis and Priscilla managed to be alone, he presented her with a brightly wrapped box, which contained a gold watch with a large diamond set in the lid, and a pearl-and-diamond ring. Priscilla was aghast at such extravagant gifts, but she gladly put them on.

"Thank you, Fire Eyes," she said softly, using her new pet name for Elvis. Exactly what he responded is unknown. Elvis, with his history of baby talk, already had four hard-to-take nicknames for Priscilla--"Nungen," which was an affectionate twist on "young one," " 'Cilla," "Little One," and the one he began using with increased frequency, now that its former owner didn't need it anymore: "Sattnin."

Chapter 7

Drugstores, Hollyweird,
And Wild Times

Early in February 1960, Grandma Minnie Mae, Red, and Cliff Gleaves came home to Memphis in anticipation of Elvis's discharge on March 2. For two years, Elvis had counted the days until he could return to the security and sanctity of Graceland, and now that the day was almost here, he was torn. Priscilla would be remaining in West Germany with her family.

Colonel wanted Elvis to return to the States the same way he'd left--by troop train and ship. But the army had had enough of mobbing teenagers, and insisted that Elvis return by Military Air Transport Service C-118, departing from Frankfort's Rhein-Main Airport with seventy-nine other G.I.s aboard. That plane would be followed by another. This one carried Lamar, Elisabeth Stefaniak--the young woman Elvis had dated before he met Priscilla and who'd later signed on as his secretary--and about two thousand phonograph records. Also aboard was Vernon, who'd recently grown a gangsterish, Boston Blackie moustache at the request of his friend, Dee Stanley, who had begun divorce proceedings against her husband.

Elvis asked Priscilla to ride to the airport with him, giving her his combat jacket and his new sergeant's stripes. He promised to call her as soon as he got home, and Priscilla said she'd write him on pink stationery and address the letters in care of Joe, so Elvis would be sure to know they were from her. They huddled in the back of the car for one last moment, squeezing hands, and then he hopped from the car and returned to the throngs of fans. Priscilla yelled his name, her voice swallowed up in the scratch of sound.

When the plane set down at McGuire Air Force Base at eight in the morning, a snowstorm made the airfield look like a miniature scene in a shake-'em-up snow globe. Elvis, still terrified of flying, was glassy-eyed himself, having popped a handful of sleeping pills in the air. At nearby Fort Dix, New Jersey, he sprinted for a waiting limousine, and a half-dozen teenage girls made a dash for him. Elvis's soldier pals took it all in, laughing and shaking their heads. One of them yelled after him: "Go get 'em, Elvis!"

But Elvis had more on his mind than girls. In a moment, he would face a two-hour press conference, attended by dozens of reporters and photographers. The press also had celebrity welcomers in their midst. Actress Tina Louise was there, representing a New York radio station, as was Nancy Sinatra, who had two lace-front shirts for Elvis, which she explained were presents from her father.

For the first few minutes, the bulk of the attention fell on Colonel Parker, who had been Elvis's shadow while he was still in the States, but who surprisingly never visited Elvis in Germany--either because he had too much to do in this country positioning Elvis for his comeback, or because as an illegal alien he didn't have a passport. Colonel did his usual showman bit, warning the press to behave, instructing photo-graphers on how close they would be allowed to his "prize," making sure the television lights were just right. Then he stepped aside, raised his left hand in a signal, and Sergeant Elvis, looking every inch the patriotic soldier boy, strode into view with his right hand posed in a confident wave.

As usual, Elvis didn't, or wouldn't, say anything to explain himself that his interviewers could grab onto. ("The army sure changed me, but I can't tell offhand how.") His performance was mostly to smile his famous crooked grin which, in the old days, broke into a full sneer. Elvis was about to put the sneer into retirement, though, since it had outlived its usefulness in shaping his early persona as a mix of tough guy and teddy bear, threatening and alluring at the same time.

In the early days of his career, Elvis had mastered his press conferences with charm, boyish good humor, ardency, and a kidding sense of self-mockery. Now it was more important for Elvis to act earnest--less sex-crazed and raunchy, and more concerned with old-fashioned values. When someone inquired about the young American girl he'd been seeing in Germany, Elvis gave no sign that he was nursing a significant flame. "She is very mature, very intelligent, and the most beautiful girl I've ever seen," he said. "But there's no romance. It's nothing serious."

Nobody dared ask what an army veteran was doing with an underage girl--hell, I guess they knew--and the questions were mostly trivial, on the order of whether Elvis would grow his sideburns again. Colonel stepped in whenever the questioning got too close to the bone, such as when a reporter asked how much Elvis's army pay had been.

"I don't know," Colonel charged. "I don't get a commission on that." And then he asked the reporters to "please state that the government gets 91 percent of [Elvis's earnings] in tax." So, even though his Boy's gross earnings in 1959 had been $1.9 million, Colonel swore, "Elvis is not a millionaire," an entirely believable statement once you pondered the fact that Graceland was mortgaged for $134,000, and Colonel was taking 25 percent for himself.

Suddenly, it was over. "Been real nice," Elvis said. "Good to be home."

Two days later, as Elvis rode a private train back to Memphis, Senator Estes Kefauver stood in Washington and babbled a tribute to Elvis into the *Congressional Record*. There was more hype, as well, since Colonel provided Elvis with a dress uniform that inadvertently promoted him with four stripes on the sleeve. Whenever the train stopped en route to Memphis, Elvis looked out to wave to hundreds of fans eager to welcome him home, while thousands waited patiently in Memphis.

But Elvis's happy homecoming was shadowed by anxiety. His mother was gone. His father was keeping fast company with Dee Stanley, a woman Elvis detested as too blond and too silly, and who would visit Vernon at Graceland while waiting for her divorce. And Elvis himself had fallen in love with a fourteen-year-old girl, a situation even he recognized as being

A provocative photo of Elvis out back of Graceland. I at first remembered it as a pre-army birthday party shot, but it's apparently immediately post-army (or so I'm told). Yes, Sergeant Presley's hair was *that long* when he returned in March 1960, and the top of the cake does read "Welcome Back, Elvis"--but it still has an earlier feel to it as far as I'm concerned.

too gothic and weird for normal public consumption, even in the South.

Then there was the matter of his career. Colonel had decided that Elvis's real money would come from motion pictures, since he could easily make three or four a year. His next movie was scheduled to be "G.I. Blues," a military salute guaranteed to cash in on his army career. Quite rightly, Elvis joked to the press that, "It's not about my actual experiences in the army--they couldn't film that!"

But as much as Elvis disliked the idea, he understood its commercial appeal. After that, he wanted to go back to making films in the dramatic vein of "King Creole," or at least involve himself with roles in which he didn't sing, strum a guitar, or kick his legs in a chorus line.

He told Colonel about it in language as straight as he could muster, but he wasn't sure Colonel understood, or cared. Colonel said, "You can do the greatest movie in the world, and the greatest acting job, maybe even win a hundred Oscars. But if the movie doesn't make money, then you're a flop."

Elvis saw the logic of that, but he didn't see why he couldn't have it both ways. Above all, he didn't want to look like a cartoon character up on the screen, playing a good-natured, but essentially dim-witted drifter who changed his name and his clothes, but otherwise looked the same in every film. It was no longer enough to just entertain people--he wanted to *reach* them, as he hoped he had in "King Creole."

And what would happen to his music? The majority of Elvis's fans had moved out of adolescence now, just as he himself had. They no longer demanded music that reflected teenage rebellion or raw sexuality, but romance. Young people --especially young women--falling in love and marrying and having children, craved a certain amount of tenderness. Now they asked Elvis to conduct his life according to conventional standards. They may have been attracted to him *because* he seemed rough and rowdy, and challenged every rule, but now they wanted him to fit into, if not *polite* society, prevailing society.

In short, they hoped he'd be safe, and even a little predictable--which, of course, was anathema to a truly creative artist. On August 16, 1977, a reporter asked John Lennon what he thought about the fact that Elvis had just died. "Elvis died," he said, "the day he went into the army."

And yet Elvis had years ago learned to give the boss what he wanted. His perversities were no longer on the surface, and he was no longer the defiant kid who massaged his artistic integrity into a framework that, by good fortune, the public had also loved. In the process, he had gotten too accustomed to a comfortable life to risk losing it, for himself or his family-- again because, "We Presleys have been poor as far back as I can remember." And so he would try to be content within those musical and cultural limitations, even if he winced at hearing Colonel tell one movie director, "All we want is songs for an album."

On his second post-army recording session, he would cut "It's Now or Never," a Caribbean re-working of the Neapolitan classic "O Solo Mio," and the recitation ballad "Are You Lonesome Tonight?" Both songs showed off the new maturity of his voice, but it was not coincidental that they were also acceptable to even the most conservative of grandmas.

And when Frank Sinatra, the very symbol of American mainstream popularity, invited him to make a guest appearance on his ABC television special in May of 1960--Elvis's first TV show since his return to the States--both Elvis and Colonel gladly accepted. Elvis would appear for six minutes, sing two songs on his own and two with Sinatra (in a turnabout, Frank would croon "Love Me Tender," and Elvis "Witchcraft"), and collect a fee of $125,000. Sinatra would call the special, "Welcome Home, Elvis," and broadcast it from the Fontainbleau Hotel in Miami Beach. No wonder Sinatra's daughter had brought Elvis two lace-front shirts!

And yet, only a few years before, Sinatra had called Elvis's music "deplorable, a rancid-smelling aphrodisiac," and rock music in general "the most brutal, ugly, degenerate, vicious form of expression it has been my displeasure to hear." Was Elvis now positioning himself for inclusion in the Rat Pack?

The first time I saw Elvis when he got back from Germany,

I could see almost instantly that he was a changed man. Part of it was simply physical. To me, he looked the best he had ever looked in his life. His hair, in the days before he started dying it panther black for the movies, was dark blond or brownish, highlighted by the sun. And while it was nothing for him to wolf down five bacon sandwiches slathered with mustard at one sitting, his physique was muscular and trim.

For as long as I knew him, Elvis never talked at length about the effect his mother's death had on him, or even how much he missed her. But he really didn't have to, because he carried it with him, in the look on his face, in his actions. When he first came back, he couldn't bear to go to the cemetery to visit her grave--he could hardly stand to drive past it--and while he kept up a front around the rest of us, his Aunt Lillian would catch him sitting around looking sad with his head down, or staring out at nothing in particular, just missing Gladys and wondering what he could have done to help her. For Elvis, losing his mother was like becoming an infant again and finding he had no mother. It was the loneliest emptiness imaginable.

I sometimes envisioned him walking around Graceland in the thin hours of the morning, talking to her, looking for her, trying to feel her presence, the same way he and his mother had visited Jessie Garon's grave and talked to him about ongoing family matters when they still lived in Mississippi. But then the Presleys had a penchant for talking to the dead in the present tense. Lamar, after all, said that when Gladys died at the hospital, Elvis took him in to see the corpse, patted it on the stomach and said, "Look here, Sattnin, here's Lamar." At times, I don't think Elvis fully realized that she was gone.

One thing I did know for sure: Elvis wasn't sleeping. He started looking awful in the face, his eyes droopy and strange. I asked Lamar and Red what was going on, and at first they didn't say much. Then it came out that Elvis had started taking "speed" in the army--Dexedrine--so he wouldn't nod off on guard duty. A sergeant had handed out the pills to Elvis and several others, and Elvis, who despised getting up at dawn, began taking them regularly just to get through the day. The problem was, he'd also started taking sleeping pills just before his induction, partly to try to curb his sleepwalking, and because his anxiety about his career was so overwhelming. Now it was getting so that he needed pills to get to sleep, and pills to stay awake.

After awhile, I asked Elvis about it, and he said it wasn't anything serious--the only real problem was getting the stuff, even though it didn't constitute hard narcotics. He said that in Germany he bought them by the quart jar from the pharmacist at the post. Then he came up with the kicker, his idea of a perfect solution:

"Let's buy a drugstore!"

I thought he was kidding. "Elvis, what would you do with a drugstore?"

"Well, if we had a drugstore, we could do what we wanted."

"Elvis, you'd have to go back to Germany and get that pharmacist to run it. You can't just go in there and start dispensing pills."

A look of surprise crossed his face, and then he broke into a sheepish grin. "Oh, yeah," he said.

I was still working in construction when Elvis came home from the army--still getting up early in the morning and going to bed at a reasonable hour--and so I wasn't spending that much time at Graceland. But whenever I did go out there, I was amazed to see how much things had changed since Gladys's death. First of all, he began having Graceland completely redecorated, choosing bizarre color schemes and, as someone once said, "all the furniture you *wouldn't* buy."

That didn't mean much in itself, but Elvis's behavior did. When his mother was alive, we slipped around with girls, and we did other things, but at two or three o'clock in the morning, that house was vacated. Now there was no one at Graceland to answer to, since Vernon, who was frolicking there with Dee Stanley under Gladys's very roof, was hardly Elvis's moral governor. Besides, he almost never bucked Elvis, except to complain about money. And, of course, this was legally Elvis's house.

With Gladys dead, Graceland was no longer a home. In

fact, it was more like a whorehouse. Now Elvis could do anything at all, and that included shacking up all night, throwing nude swimming parties, everything. We'd go down to the gates every evening about six or seven o'clock, and all these girls would come up to the house. We'd weed them out, and keep some of them there later and later, and then they'd start spending the night.

Elvis had his dates, of course, but the guys were doing the same thing. Some of the girls we knew, and some we'd just met the first time. But they wouldn't leave until ten or eleven o'clock the next morning. If Gladys had lived, Elvis's whole life would have been different. I don't think any girl would have spent the night, and certainly there would never have been a girl living there full time. When Priscilla came to visit, I guarantee you she would have stayed in a guest room, just as Natalie Wood did.

When Elvis first told me about Priscilla--that she was fourteen years old and that he was trying to figure out a way to get her over to the United States--I just shook my head. "I can't believe it, Elvis," I said. "Well," he declared, "I'm just crazy about her." Then I knew he was serious, and I didn't find it hard to believe at all. He liked younger people because he felt older women had been around more, and done more. If he was going to have a woman around who really meant something to him, he didn't want her to be trashy. He also wasn't interested in a woman who had been married, divorced, or had children--a particular turn-off for Elvis, who was repulsed by the idea of childbirth. A psychiatrist might say he had a madonna-whore complex. All I know is that he simply felt more comfortable with young, fresh people.

He also said, "You know, Alan, a fourteen-year-old girl is far more advanced than a fourteen-year-old boy, in almost every way--physically, emotionally, intellectually." I didn't believe that for a long time, although now I know it's true. But I did know that if he really wanted this particular fourteen-year-old, he'd get her.

In April of 1960, Elvis and the entourage--which now included his army buddies Charlie Hodge and Joe Esposito, as

Elvis serenading a bunch of "frauleins" on the "G.I. Blues" set, which started production in May 1960. (Photo: Maria Columbus)

well as Red West's cousin, Sonny--rented a $2,500 railroad car and headed out to Los Angeles to make "G.I. Blues" with Juliet Prowse for Paramount and Hal Wallis. Of all the people Elvis hired through the years, Red and Sonny were the toughest, except for the karate experts he hired later on. Of course, I always say--and to a great extent I mean it--that out of all of us, Elvis was the toughest. But Red and Sonny were also into karate, which Elvis had discovered in the army, taking private lessons from a martial-arts instructor named Hank Slemansky, and later Ed Parker. He was so keen on it that he insisted on doing his own karate stunt in "G.I. Blues." He was still basically learning, though, and he broke a small bone in his hand.

When the guys got to California--I stayed in Memphis working construction for the next two movies--they met up with Colonel Parker, who installed them in the Beverly Wilshire Hotel. This is where we'd stayed during "King Creole," and Colonel planned on making it Elvis's permanent headquarters on the West Coast.

The movie went off without a hitch, except for the fact that Elvis complained constantly about the quality of the songs, and about the fact that he "felt like an idiot breaking into song while I'm talking to some chick on a train." Colonel sympathized with him, told him he'd take care of it, and the movie came out exactly as it was filmed.

Most of the critics took note of a new, toned-down Elvis on the screen. Bosley Crowther, of the *New York Times,* wrote, "Gone is the wiggle, the lecherous leer, the swagger, the unruly hair, the droopy eyelids, and the hillbilly manner of speech."

"G.I. Blues" was made in fewer than sixty days, and then Elvis came home to relax before heading back out to do "Flaming Star." Elvis had just had a brief off-camera affair with Juliet Prowse, saying, "She has a body that would make a bishop stamp his foot through a stained-glass window." But he saw a good bit of Anita Wood back in Memphis, and he gave her a diamond necklace.

I wasn't sure what that meant. I knew that Anita was crazy about Elvis--she'd written him faithfully while he was in

Germany--but I also knew that she wasn't exactly thrilled about the stagnant nature of their relationship, since Colonel, thinking it was bad publicity, didn't want Elvis telling anybody she was his steady girl. Elvis had placed her in the "good girl" category, so their relationship was chaste, and therefore, any physical involvement was on hold until marriage. Anita was probably in flux about Elvis, not knowing whether to wait for him or find someone who was serious about matrimony. Maybe the diamond necklace was a reward for sticking around.

Then there was the matter of Priscilla. Elvis continued to talk about her as if she were the girl for him, and *Life* magazine had even photographed her as "the girl he left behind" in Germany. Anita says Elvis told her when he was still in Germany, "Now, Little, don't you believe anything you read, 'cause I'm not datin' anybody over here." Anita laughs about it today. She says, "I knew he was lying!" But then Elvis had a tendency to do that, especially in matters of romance. He told me that he'd written Anita from Germany and told her he loved her--that she was the *only* girl he'd ever loved in his life --and that it scared her so bad he didn't hear from her for six months. Anita says he lied about that deal, too. It was probably just a convenient way of explaining why he was keeping company with someone else.

Then again, Elvis had other domestic problems to worry about. On July 3, his father married the dreaded Dee in Huntsville, Alabama, at the home of her brother. Elvis, who instantly acquired three brothers, Billy, 7, Ricky, 6, and David, 5, stayed home. The official line was that Elvis was elated that his father had found someone to share his life. In truth, it was years before he forgave Vernon for what he saw as a betrayal of his mother. After all, Gladys had been dead less than two years. No matter what the press reported, or whatever Dee herself says today, Elvis never afforded her the slightest measure of affection. When she and Vernon returned to Memphis and moved into a house of their own near Graceland, Elvis in a way put them into a sealed-off compartment of his mind, seldom to be disturbed.

In August, Elvis went back out to California to begin work

on "Flaming Star," a 20th Century-Fox picture with a forty-two-day shooting schedule. The script was written in part by Nunally Johnson, whose diverse work included an adaptation of John Steinbeck's "The Grapes of Wrath," and "How to Marry a Millionaire." Elvis's role, that of a half-breed caught in a race war in small-town Texas, had been written for Marlon Brando, who turned it down. Elvis would do more than a credible job with it--he knew something about being an outcast, even if he weren't a Kiowa Indian. And Don Siegel, who would later make his mark with Clint Eastwood pictures, brought a surprising sensitivity and intelligence to the direction.

Siegel understood what Elvis wanted to accomplish as an actor, and he later told a Los Angeles newspaper that, "When Elvis gets ready to do a serious scene, he closes himself in and is absolutely unapproachable to anyone but me...Elvis has a very complex, but a very interesting personality." But "Flaming Star" would be a comparative flop in Elvis's movie catalogue--it contained only one musical number, and the mix of action and brooding emotion wasn't quite right. Colonel would take particular notice.

The entourage had been out in Los Angeles for about a month when they suffered an embarrassing eviction from the Beverly Wilshire Hotel. Elvis and his friends had been asked to vacate hotels in Europe when they got especially rowdy, but back in the States, Elvis wanted the guys to keep it down. One night, the guys forgot they weren't at Graceland, where water fights--usually involving squirt guns--or fireworks extravaganzas were common occurrences.

At home, it was okay to take things to the limit, which sometimes meant that somebody got banged up a little. But not in a public place. This particular night, it started when somebody slipped on the kitchen floor and accidentally cut himself with a broken bottle. When Elvis stooped over to render aid, Red, Sonny and Joe grabbed him from behind, and pinned him to the floor. Then Sonny held his legs, and Joe held his torso, while Red rubbed his hand repeatedly over Elvis's nose, sending him into an frenzy.

Elvis was just about ready to explode, when Red yelled,

"Let him go!" At that point, Sonny and Red high-tailed it out the door, but when Joe tried to do the same, he slipped, and Elvis tackled him. Joe managed to scramble free, but when he tried to get up, Elvis knocked him down and began rolling and kicking him across the floor. Still infuriated, Elvis picked up a guitar and whacked him hard on the elbow, and Joe screamed bloody murder.

Red and Sonny heard Joe yell, and turned around to see what was happening. Elvis, madder than anyone had ever seen him, took off after them, chasing them through the fire-escape door, and down the steps to another floor of the hotel. But Red and Sonny had too much of a head start, and when Elvis saw he couldn't catch up, he yelled at the top of his lungs and threw the guitar with all his might.

That probably would have been it, except for the fact that one of the hotel's live-in guests, a little old lady no less, chose to investigate the disturbance, opening her door at the precise moment the guitar whizzed down the hall. Elvis stopped and apologized--the guitar had missed her by inches, shades of Dodger--but the old lady knew him only as a racket-causing hooligan, and jumped back in her room and called the front desk. The next day, Elvis and his party were asked to check-out. Permanently.

Elvis was rightfully embarrassed over this, and he took some kidding about it for years. But the "inner circle," now dubbed "El's Angels" for such displays of rowdiness, was getting too big to stay in a hotel for an extended period of time. These were mostly young men in their twenties, guys who'd never been exposed to the things that hanging out with Elvis brought them, and it was natural that a group of young bachelors would get a little wild sometimes.

The solution, Colonel said, was to rent a house big enough for all, a house with plenty of bedrooms and sound-proofing, in a private and secluded section of town. And so in September, they moved into an Oriental-style house at 525 Perugia Way in the Los Angeles suburb of Bel Air, with a view of the Bel Air Country Club.

The home, which had previously been owned by both the

These were taken in the back yard of the house on Perugia Way in Bel Air in May 1961, when we were filming indoor scenes for "Blue Hawaii." Notice the little cigar in his hand--you hardly ever see a picture of Elvis with a cigar, because he thought cigars looked too much like the *real* Mafia! He smoked them, but mainly, he just held them to keep from biting his nails. When Elvis sat down like this, his leg was always twitching, his foot was going all the time--he was a very nervous person.

Shah of Iran and by the Ali Khan and his wife, actress Rita Hayworth, was said to have been designed by famed architect Frank Lloyd Wright. It was shaped sort of like a bagel, the structure winding around a fifty-foot patio and lush greenery. Inside, Elvis found it installed with a black cook and houseboy, and furnished with contemporary California pieces, offset by plush white shag carpet. For the next two years, he would stay there whenever he was on the West Coast, the house becoming a sort of Graceland West, headquarters for some great times and, from what the guys told me on their trips home, some wild parties.

When Elvis came back to Memphis that fall, he was still in a party mood. In October, I went over to Graceland for a little game of touch football, where things got rougher than I expected. Somehow, Elvis fractured his finger, and Joe took him to Baptist Hospital. Everybody made a big deal out of it. He stayed overnight, which I thought was a bit excessive, but I guess they needed to check him out. The next day, we had our picture in the newspaper, a smiling Elvis looking right at me and holding up his good arm, and the five of us bending over him in bemused pose. In Hollywood, the informal football games would grow to real matches, and everybody would suit up in jerseys that said "E.P. Entp.," for "Elvis Presley Enterprisers," and play other stars' teams. You'd never know who'd show up to play on Elvis's side, from Ricky Nelson, to Max Baer, Jr., to Gary Lockwood. Even Pat Boone came out once or twice.

In the months after Elvis's discharge, it was obvious that Colonel intended to make good on his promise to put Elvis in back-to-back movies. Right before he went out to Los Angeles that November to start work on "Wild in the Country" for 20th Century-Fox, he pulled me aside one night.

"C'mon back to work, Alan," he said.

"I don't know, Elvis."

"Tuesday Weld is in this movie, man."

"Really!"

I had a thing for Tuesday Weld, and Elvis had preyed upon my weakness.

Walking with Tuesday Weld during filming "Wild In The Country."

I was back on the bus.

"Wild in the Country" also co-starred Hope Lange and Millie Perkins, who would break her wrist slapping Elvis in one scene, and who would ironically go on to play Gladys Presley in the 1990 ABC-TV network series, "Elvis." Gary Lockwood, who would become a good friend, was also in this picture, as was Christina Crawford, who years later would write a best-selling book about life with her actress-mother, Joan.

The plot of "Wild in the Country" revolved around a punk named Glenn Tyler, another of Elvis's characters struggling against the dominance of an older woman. This time it was psychiatric social worker Lange, who hoped to turn him around from a certain life of crime and desperation when she discovered his writing talent.

The original script, which high-brow writer Clifford Odets ("Golden Boy") adapted from a novel by J.R. Salamanca, called for Elvis's character to sink into deep depression and commit suicide by inhaling carbon monoxide in a closed garage. That's the way they shot it, too, until Colonel issued a veto.

"The fans would never go for a weak Elvis!" Colonel said, waving his ever-present stogie, and shifting his considerable weight from one foot to another. He'd already sabotaged the drama by talking studio head Spiros Skouras into sticking six production numbers in the picture, two of which were mercifully cut.

And so, after coming back to Memphis in December, we all trekked back to California in early January 1961, to reshoot the ending so that Elvis's character could overcome his disadvantaged background and--in true Hollyweird style--triumph over adversity.

"Wild in the Country" would be Elvis's last opportunity to stretch into a dramatic actor of consequence, or to tackle a literate, credible script. For virtually the rest of his movie career, he would be thrust into one insufferable musical comedy after another, none of which would be more than a predictable star vehicle, and none of which would vaguely approach reality.

(Center photo)
Signing autographs at
the motel, January
1961. That's me on the
left, with Joe Esposito
and Gene Smith on
the right.

Elvis liked "Wild in the Country." But director Philip Dunne would later say that it fell between the cracks, that "audiences who might have liked Clifford Odets's drama wouldn't buy Elvis and his songs, and Elvis fans were disappointed in a Presley picture which departed so radically from his usual song-and-sex comedy formula."

That January, when we went back to reshoot the ending, the studio threw Elvis a twenty-sixth birthday party, and photographed a bunch of us standing around eyeing the cake. Afterwards, Elvis sat at a small table at the motel and signed pictures for all the local kids who had hounded him for autographs while he was making the film. One day, Colonel told them, "If you'll just let us work and do the movie, I promise you he will sign every autograph, and pose for every picture." And he did. He must have signed for four or five hours.

Elvis never snubbed any fans in those days. Other than the time he was making movies, Elvis was never too busy to sign an autograph if somebody came up to him.

Pictures that came to Graceland, however, were another story. We wouldn't worry Elvis if he were studying a script, and we wouldn't ask, "Elvis, could you sign these forty-three pictures and twenty-five albums?" So, the guys and I would forge those signatures all day long. Sonny really practiced a lot, and he was the one who could forge it the best, although Joe was pretty fair. Elvis never dotted his "i," so when we forged his signature, we never did either. Elvis would look at them, and say, "Hey, that's pretty good!" Hell, no telling how many people in the world think they have an authentic Elvis signature, when they really have a Sonny West.

I kept my crush on Tuesday Weld all the way through "Wild in the Country." It wasn't hard to do, because she was unbelievably sweet to us, sending cases of local vintage wine over to our motel. If I don't remember anything else about this movie, I'll remember it as the picture where Elvis finally let us have liquor behind the bar at the house in Bel Air and at the location hotel. He would drink a little bit himself, but he never drank around the house. It was Hope Lange, who was a terrific person, who finally changed his mind about that. She even

A shot of me with Hope Lange.

(Center photo)
The cast party at the end of "Wild In The Country." That's Joe Esposito (to Hope's left) and me (second to her right) lending encouragement as she cuts the cake.

Hope Lange with Elvis, and yours truly behind Hope.

had him drinking vodka.

One night she came over to the house, and she asked if we had any liquor. Elvis got kind of nervous. He turned to us and said, "Uh, is there anything here to drink?" He knew there wasn't anything behind the bar, but he suspected we had some in our rooms. We said, "Yeah, Elvis, we've got some vodka," and brought it out. After that, he said, "We'd better stock the bar." Before, though, we'd go out to someplace like the Moulin Rouge for some special event, and Elvis would order orange juice for us. Then one of us would excuse himself, pull the waiter over in the corner and whisper, "Put a little vodka in that stuff!"

By now, Elvis was finally paying us a salary. I think we started off at $100 or $125 a week. That wasn't a lot of money, even then, but it didn't cost us anything to travel with Elvis. Because we lived with him on Perugia Way, we ate there, and if we went out, he picked up the whole tab. If we were on location for a movie, the studio took care of everything. So being paid a salary was a lot like getting an allowance. Later, we'd get raises, and sometimes Colonel would give us a bonus. Plus, whenever Elvis signed a big deal with a studio, he'd come back to the car and pass out hundred-dollar bills. Vernon would have keeled over if he'd known that.

The only time we had to pay our own lodging was if we took little side trips on our off days. Location shooting for "Wild in the Country" was done in Napa and Calistoga, California, and we'd go to San Francisco on Saturday nights, after the shoot finished that day. The general plan called for staying at the Mark Hopkins Hotel and watching the football game on Sunday, and then driving back Sunday night.

Elvis was in a bit of discomfort during this movie. The newspapers reported that a local physician treated him for a "minor infection," which was fancy talk for the fact that Elvis had a huge boil on his rear end. The studio doctor lanced it one Saturday, but it was still killing him. It hurt so much he couldn't sit down--he had to just kind of lean on his hip, or lay in a chair. Even riding in the limousine sent him howling.

This particular Saturday, we decided to go to San Francisco

as usual, but the only way Elvis could handle the ride was if he got stoked up on pain pills. I don't know how many he took, but it altered his sense of propriety. About fifteen or twenty miles out of San Francisco, we were stopped for some reason when a car pulled up and the occupants started smarting off at us. Of course, they didn't know it was Elvis. They just saw it was a Cadillac limousine with a bunch of people in it.

With that, Elvis, overly sensitive from his posterior problems and his hopped-up head, pulled out a little Derringer he'd recently started carrying. He liked the "polite gangster" effect the gun made with the tiny cigars--either Have-a-Tampa Jewels or Rum Crooks--he'd smoked on and off for the last few years, and now here he was sticking the damn thing out the window! Those guys weren't prepared for that. The looks on their faces! They sped off like the lead car in a posse chase.

When we got to the Mark Hopkins, Elvis immediately went to bed. But about one or two in the morning, the rest of us got antsy.

"Y'all want to go out?"

"Yeah!"

Two or three of the gang stayed behind with Elvis--we always had to make sure someone was with him in case he needed anything--and the rest of us went downstairs and hailed a taxi.

"Cabbie, take us someplace where something's going on."

"Sorry, sir, everything's closed in San Francisco. It's too late."

"You mean there's *no place* to go?"

A funny expression meandered across his face. "I know a couple of little after-hours places, but they're...."

We cut him off. "Great! Take us there."

"Well-l-l-l," he stuttered, "they're kind of private."

"Don't worry, we'll take care of you."

The cabbie saw dollar signs.

Thirty minutes later, we drove under a bridge to an odd-looking building with a funny door. The sign read, "The Broken Drum." We went up, knocked, and a porthole popped opened. A pair of dark eyes looked us over. Then, the door opened with a musty creak.

We were just little guys from Memphis, Tennessee, and even though we'd been to Hollywood, and Charlie and Joe had been to Germany, we really hadn't seen all that much. I, personally, was about as green as a new billiard table and twice as square, so I thought I'd died and gone to heaven when a handful of beautiful girls came up and started talking to us, sitting down and getting friendly.

We'd been there about five minutes, sipping drinks out of coffee mugs and thinking, "Godalmighty, this is a dream come *true*," when next thing we knew all the girls were up on their feet dancing. Except they were dancing with each other, and kissing on each other, too.

I looked at Sonny, he looked at me, and together we said, "Let's get the hell out of here. I think we're in the wrong place!" We hustled out of there and crawled back to the hotel, and by the time we got there, we were practically convulsing, we thought it was so funny. That was our introduction to San Francisco, and a hell of an introduction it was.

"Wild in the Country" marked another new experience for me--my first time to get on camera, as an extra in the courtroom scene. Some of the other guys worked, too: The movie opened with a fist fight between Elvis's character and some little troublemaker, which Red West played to brief, but total, perfection. We weren't in the union yet, but since we were on location, we could work, even though it was just for the experience and the glamour. You had to be a member of the Screen Extras Guild to get paid.

Naturally, we started putting a bug in Elvis's ear about letting us join the extras guild, and later on--I forget which picture, exactly--he finally got us in. An extra who appeared in a crowd scene was paid $27.50 per day, plus overtime. If you had a line, you got more. Mostly, whenever you saw people in the background in his movies, we'd be among them. If Elvis were singing in a nightclub, for example, I might be sitting at a table. I can usually spot myself in Elvis's movies, if I look real close and I'm not eating popcorn when the scene comes up.

Actually, all of the guys are in the movies. Once we joined the union, we divided the money up. I would work, say five

A posed "screen test" photo of me for my role in "Wild In The Country." I was supposed to play a court bailiff in the trial scene, but even though I got all dressed up in uniform, they never did use any footage with me in it!

Tuesday Weld and Brenda Lee with Elvis during "Wild In The Country." Tom Diskin, Colonel's assistant, invited Brenda to the set. Wolf, Tuesday's white German Shepherd, also squeezed into the shot (at lower right).

(Below) Elvis and I talk with a few "Wild In The Country" cast and crew.

days, and Joe might work only two, and Red three. But we'd take all the money and put it in a pot and split it up. That way, there wasn't any dissension. It was a good deal for all of us. We didn't argue over who would work, either. When the director said, "I need three guys in this movie," there wasn't any backstabbing. At least, not at this stage of the game.

On "Wild in the Country," Elvis dated Nancy Sharp, a wardrobe girl he'd met on "Flaming Star." In a way, Elvis was like the song "Love the One You're With." There was no doubt in my mind that he cared about Anita Wood, and that he was in love with Priscilla. But that didn't stop him from appreciating beautiful women, especially if they were petite brunettes. Elvis thought he had to be, well, Elvis. He had an image to maintain. Just how that image differed with each person's perception came to full light that Christmas, the December he came back to Memphis before he got his release on "Wild in the Country." That was the Christmas Elvis worked a miracle. Using Dee and Vernon as a shield, Elvis persuaded Priscilla's step-father, Captain Joseph Beaulieu, to let Priscilla come to Graceland for Christmas. She would fly from Frankfort, West Germany, to New York, where Vernon and Dee would meet her, and escort her back to Memphis. They, of course, would also serve as chaperones during her visit.

Priscilla stayed at Graceland about two weeks, returning to Germany early in January, just before Elvis went back to finish "Wild in the Country." We eventually ended up going to Las Vegas, where she bought sexy, grown-up clothes and had her hair done. I was the one who took her shopping.

It's funny the memories we have of that trip. I'll never forget going to shows in Las Vegas with a fourteen-year-old, and Priscilla says she'll never forget the amphetamines Elvis gave her to let her stay up long enough to enjoy them. Likewise, her parents have probably never gotten over the shock of Priscilla arriving back in Germany looking like a Vegas hooker. But when she first arrived in Memphis, we didn't see Elvis *or* Priscilla for about five days. They just went into his room and disappeared.

So much for chaperones.

Elvis, always copying my best on-camera techniques, adopted my hand-on-hips pose.

Colonel Tom Parker dressed as Santa on the set of "Wild In The Country."

CHAPTER 8

White Cotton Panties
The Orgy Years

Of all the things I remember best about living in the house on Perugia Way, the two-way mirror takes the cake. Sonny is the one who instigated the thing. He'd read about two-way mirrors in a book, and one day he came in with one and announced he'd found a new way to have fun. He couldn't afford anything better than an el-cheapo model, because the good ones were really expensive. This one was small, maybe three-by-two feet.

The idea was to install it in the den, so we could watch the fireworks when a guy and a girl got amorous. The guy would know what was going on, but the girl didn't have a clue, and they'd put on a little show for us. Everybody just stood back and watched and snickered. The amazing thing was that none of the girls ever caught on.

At first, we weren't sure how Elvis would react to the idea of his friends standing around watching unsuspecting young women get it on with his buddies. He took one look through the mirror, though, and that was it. He thought it was a gas. In fact, when it started getting cloudy and fading, Elvis bought the next one himself.

Granted, not everybody thought it was great. One time one of the guys was performing what I'll call a love act with a young lady, and Elvis and Tuesday Weld and I stood in the closet watching. Tuesday had had a little bit too much to drink--which is why I think she consented to watching anyway--and after a little while she said, "I don't want to sit in here and watch people screw! Let me out of here!"

Tuesday was probably one of the nicest people we ever worked with. I'd put her at the top, right along with Ann-Margret and Ursula Andress. In a lot of ways, Tuesday was

Me and my pal Wolf (Tuesday Weld's dog) in the yard of the house on Perugia Way, May 1961.

like Elvis. She'd led a special life. She'd never had a little-girl life, because she'd been an actress from almost the day she was born. We got pretty close to Tuesday, and in fact, she was one of the few people in Hollywood who could come over to Elvis's house anytime she wanted. Even after she and Elvis stopped dating.

Their romance never was a particularly big one. They met while making "Wild in the Country," and dated only occasionally. Mostly they were just good friends.

During the movie, Tuesday used to bring her big white German Shepherd, Wolf, over to the house. When she stayed overnight, she slept in Elvis's room, and Wolf slept in mine. I was pretty crazy about the dog, and because of that, Tuesday and I had a kind of bond. Of course, I'd had that big crush on her, but now I valued her in a different way. Sometimes she'd come over and not even see Elvis. We'd just sit in my room and talk.

One day, Tuesday announced she was going to get rid of Wolf because she did so much traveling, and because she couldn't really spend much time with him, even when she was at home. He'd fallen off a cliff by her house one time when she wasn't watching him as closely as she should.

I told her I really hated to see her give him away, so finally she said she would just give him to me. Well, that got me as excited as a kid at a carnival, because Wolf was a great dog. Back then, you didn't see many white German Shepherds. But as time wore on and she never quite got around to bringing him to me, Elvis gave her a hard time about it. He said, "Look, Tuesday, you don't have to give Alan the dog, but if you're not going to give it to him, tell him. Don't keep leading him on."

Not long after that, we were getting ready to go to Las Vegas, when Tuesday came over. "Okay, Alan," she said. "I can't give you my dog. But I do have a present for you." I got all primed for something great, and then I saw that she had two hamsters in a little cage. My face fell. "Hell, Tuesday," I said. "I don't want any goddamn rats!"

We went on to Vegas, and that was that. But when we got back to California, Tuesday again came by the house. She said, "Alan, I've got another present for you." I didn't know what to expect, but this time Tuesday didn't disappoint me. She'd gone out and bought me a white German Shepherd puppy. It was about the prettiest puppy I'd ever seen, and she'd paid an astronomical amount for him, about $500. I named him Wolf, like her dog.

Eventually Wolf got too much for me, just as his predecessor had gotten to be a handful for Tuesday. It seemed like I was traveling more and more, so Wolf stayed with my parents back in Memphis. Finally, when they moved out of their house, they gave him to another family, who agreed to take care of him until I had a place of my own. But when I eventually came home to Memphis, I couldn't get in touch with them. I was really sorry. Wolf was a good dog. I had him for six or eight years.

It was just like Tuesday to give me such a great gift, because she had a generous nature. Guys like Sonny always talked about what a body she had, and, of course, it was true. But she was also an incredible person. Eventually, she married Gary Lockwood, who co-starred in "It Happened at the World's Fair." After that, she and I and Gary used to go around together, or I'd go over to their house. A couple of years ago, she was in an Elvis-themed movie, "Heartbreak Hotel," playing the mother of a kid who kidnaps Elvis and brings him home as a surprise. The world premiere was held in Nashville, and when I heard Tuesday was supposed to be there, I drove the two hundred miles to see her. I hadn't talked to her in years, although I'd gotten a message from her once or twice, and I was really looking forward to seeing her. Somehow, I couldn't believe that she would actually be there, and I was right: She didn't show. I'd give almost anything to see her again.

The social interaction at the house on Perugia Way was a real mix of ordinary and extraordinary, weird and normal-- kind of like Elvis himself. You never knew for sure what was going to happen next. But we had some great times, and some fun times, and not just by peeping at naked people in the next room.

Elvis loved playing practical jokes, so I couldn't resist playing one on him occasionally. Like the time we got onto the subject of my middle name.

I was named for my aunt Nellie. Jewish people like to name their kids after dead relatives, and somehow they managed to get Alan out of Nellie. Alan Elliott Fortas. Don't ask me where the Elliott came from.

Anyway, Elvis knew my name was Alan E. Fortas, because that's the way I signed everything. I never actually used Elliott, just E., even on official documents. One time in California, we were sitting around the house when Elvis asked, "Hog Ears, what does that 'E' stand for?"

I knew I had him, and I settled back in my chair.

"You know, Elvis, I never wanted to tell you because I knew you wouldn't believe me, but it stands for Elvis."

He looked at me like I'd just told him he had a brother living in Omaha. Then he thought it over.

"Aw, c'mon. I don't know but two people named Elvis, and that's me and my father, and he just uses it for a middle name."

I could tell he didn't really know what to think.

I stared down at my lap, real serious like.

"I just never brought it up, Elvis, because I knew you would never believe me, and I knew you'd think I was kidding. But I figured the right time would come along, so I never pushed it."

Elvis chewed on his bottom lip. Finally, he bounded out of the chair and came over to me.

"Let me see your driver's license," he demanded.

I dutifully took out my license, but Elvis got no help there.

"See, Elvis, I never use it. Just the E."

By this time, I had trouble keeping a straight face. But I could see that Elvis was beginning to buy into it.

"Now, really, Alan, you swear?"

George Klein happened to be there that day, and Elvis told him to get on the phone to Baptist Hospital to see if they had my birth certificate on file. Of course, birth certificates are on file in Nashville, but when the hospital came up short, nobody thought about calling the state capital. I'm not sure they would have told them, anyway. But I had a good laugh out of it. To the day he died, Elvis wasn't sure *what* my middle name was. I really had him going. "I don't believe it," he finally said. But then, because he couldn't stand not to know for sure, he added, "Just never bring it up again!"

Elvis's personality was so quicksilvery, though, that you knew you could tease him, but not too much. In other words, the guys' relationship with him was based on companionship, fleeting pleasures, an air of magic, and an ability to joke around--as long as we didn't lean on it too heavily. Things got worse as the years--and his drug use--wore on. Then, too, Elvis was beginning to drink a little bit, usually Screwdrivers, and he knew only one way to do it--chug-a-lug--because he hated the taste of liquor. And he particularly despised beer. He used to say that all he could remember from the time he was a kid was empty beer cans strewn around his relatives' houses. As a result, we could drink anything we wanted to around the house *except* beer.

In his especially explosive periods, Elvis would just haul off and fire one of us whenever we got on the bad side of his temper. I remember the time that Sonny got fired, for example. Tuesday called me and said she was coming over that night, and that she was bringing along a girl named Kay whom she wanted Elvis to meet. I checked with Elvis, and he said, "Fine, tell 'em to come up."

When they got there, Sonny had the idea that Elvis was with Tuesday, mostly because they were deep in conversation. Sonny went to fix a drink at the bar, all the while smiling and coming on to Kay. Sonny thought he was making progress when Elvis popped up between them, proceeding to give Kay that matinee idol swagger and telling her how pretty she was. Then, just as suddenly, he went back to Tuesday. Sonny moved in again.

Sonny was just getting his lines down when Elvis reappeared, this time giving Kay a small kiss on the cheek. When she smiled, Elvis kissed her hard on the mouth. Kay obviously liked what she got, and kissed him back.

Sonny was justifiably ticked. Shaking his head, he came across the room to where Gene Smith and I were sitting on the couch. "He's smooth as silk, Sonny," I said. "No shit. He shot me right out of the saddle," Sonny pouted, wearing a long face.

Elvis never missed anything that went on in a room, and in a minute or two he came over to see why we had our heads together. Ever since the army, when he started taking "uppers" with some regularity, Elvis's temper had been quicker than usual. He was doing just light drugs--stay-awakes and sleeping pills--but he could get downright mean at times, mostly from the paranoia that comes from popping junk like that. Naturally, then, he assumed we were talking about him. His voice was tense and hard.

"Sonny, what's the matter with you?"

Sonny was ready. "I can't believe it, man. You have *changed!*"

Elvis recoiled. "What are you talkin' about? What can't you believe?"

"I can't believe that Tuesday Weld is up here, and you've gotta fool with the girl I want to be with," Sonny said, the steam building up.

"Hey, wait, man, you've got it all· wrong," Elvis barked. "First of all, I'm not with Tuesday. Tuesday brought Kay to meet *me*. Besides, it's my house, and you're trying to tell me who I can talk to and who I can't!" With that, Elvis picked up a Coke bottle and held it high like a weapon.

Sonny, who'd been drinking a little bit himself, jumped up and squared off like he was going to throw a punch. Elvis dropped the bottle. "Man, I can't take this," Sonny blurted. "I'm quittin'."

Sonny started to stride out of the room, when Elvis blocked his path. "You're not quittin' man, you're fired!" Elvis yelled. Sonny no sooner got the first words of his next sentence out, when to everybody's astonishment, Elvis pulled back and hit Sonny flat on the jaw. It was the first time any of us ever saw Elvis hit one of his employees.

Sonny was dazed, but it was more from amazement than from the blow.

"I can't believe you did that!" he said. "I can't believe it!" He just kept repeating it, stunned. There were tears in his eyes.

"Tell you what you better do, Sonny," Elvis said, cooling down. "Just pack your clothes and leave."

The rest of us stood still, silent as graves. Then Sonny went into his bedroom and started to pack.

In a little while, Elvis stuck his head in Sonny's room, and saw him stuffing things into paper bags and boxes. Elvis disappeared for a second, and, repentant, came back with a suitcase. He held it out to Sonny, along with some money. Later, I drove Sonny to a motel. Elvis's fits of temper never lasted very long, and Sonny eventually came back to work. But after that, things were kind of touchy between them.

That wasn't the most bizarre behavior Elvis would indulge in by far, but it's a fair example of the reason you can't make Elvis into a boy-next-door. That was the problem with the ABC-TV series they tried in 1990. They wanted him to look like a simple guy, and he wasn't. He could be extraordinarily complex, especially when his chemistry was altered by drinking or drugs. He wasn't a hoodlum, and he wasn't a bum. But he also wasn't the guy-next-door.

On the other hand, Elvis wasn't a patsy. If somebody tried to chase him down an alley, he wouldn't run--he'd turned around and fight him. Just like he sang in "Trouble," from the "King Creole" soundtrack, "I never looked for trouble/But I never ran." Still, none of us were prepared for his drawing back and hitting Sonny.

Except for the time he was actually making a movie, Elvis kept the same kind of schedule in California that he kept in Memphis. In other words, he turned night into day, and day into night, rarely crawling out of bed before two o'clock in the afternoon. We pretty much stayed to ourselves, though. We didn't go to Hollywood premieres or parties. We had some friends there, usually people we'd worked with, and we invited a couple of them to the house and entertained them, although not in the normal fashion that Hollywood entertains. We didn't have big, elaborate catered dinners, for example. When we were working and not partying, a night for us was watching TV, shooting pool, going for a swim, or just sitting around talking.

Part of the reason for that was because Elvis was a little insecure with big stars, and because he always had to be in control of the situation. Even when somebody like Tuesday Weld, or Joan Blackman, or Connie Stevens came over, a lot of times he wouldn't get up to welcome her. He'd just stay glued to the television--which he usually watched with the sound off --or keep on doing whatever he was doing. Eventually he'd come around, but at first he'd tell one of us to take her coat, and see what she wanted to drink. As the boss, he couldn't be bothered.

Rude? Of course. But again, he had to be in charge. That was one of the reasons he had the Memphis Mafia, for control and insulation. He couldn't stand to be alone. But I think one reason he didn't play the Hollywood game of going to pre-mieres and showy events was because he'd told his audience he wouldn't get above his raising, and he meant it. In public, at least, he lived by the limits that he thought his fans had set. He allowed *other* people around him to make changes for him, like Colonel, of course, but he was afraid to alter the essence of who he was because he was afraid of losing it all.

The idea that Colonel kept him away from people--kept him a prisoner--is absurd. Colonel had no input like that whatso-ever. That was Elvis's doing. He could have gone a few places --people in Los Angeles are pretty blase about stars in their midst, even Elvis Presley. And in fact, when we were working late at the studio, and it was overtime and they wouldn't prepare dinner for us, Elvis would buy dinner for the whole cast and crew at the Formosa Cafe. Otherwise, though, he didn't patronize it, and he distanced himself from much of the superficiality of the Hollywood way of living and doing busi-ness because he didn't want to be swayed by it. At the same time, he cut himself off from people who could open him up to new experiences and ideas.

Singer Jim Ed Brown tells a story about Elvis's early "Loui-siana Hayride" days, when Elvis never ordered anything other than a bacon, lettuce and tomato sandwich on the road, for breakfast, lunch and dinner. His explanation was that he was just used to his mother's food--she was a wonderful Southern cook, he said--and he was saving himself for one of her big meals. Too unimaginative to try something new? Closer to the truth would be the explanation that he was uncertain which of the silverware went with certain dishes, or that he didn't completely understand the menu. Rather than expose his ignorance, he stayed with what he knew. In a lot of ways, he never got beyond that.

The few people who could come and go at the house whenever they wanted to, then, were people who posed no threat to Elvis. Usually, they were people who catered to him. Tuesday was one, although she was certainly less subservient to him than the others. And a guy named Wes, who'd won a number of James Dean look-a-like contests. It was incredible how much this guy looked like Dean. He got some acting gigs out of it, but then he went into music, and he could sing fairly well. The house was open to him all the time, not because he was a James Dean look-a-like--although that didn't hurt--but because he was a nice guy. Nick Adams could come by, and John Ashley, the actor. And for quite a while, Johnny Rivers, when he was still an unknown.

These particular years of Elvis's life are usually called the Hollywood years, or the movie years. But they could probably also be called the orgy years. When I first went out to California, it wasn't all that wild. I can remember being in the Perugia Way house one night, when Elvis was there with a date, and the rest of us sat there with our thumbs in our mouths. Elvis looked around and said, "You know, I don't understand this. I have a date, but nobody else up here has a date. What's the problem?"

One thing led to another, and I finally said, "Well, I can get a date, Elvis, but I don't really feel like it tonight." And Joe said, "Well, I can, too." Elvis looked at both of us and said, "I bet neither one of you can get a date." Esposito and I started arguing back and forth, each of us accusing the other of being too ugly to get a girl, when we ended up betting fifty bucks as to who could get a date the quickest.

"I'll beat you back here, and when you come back to this house, I'll have a cute little girl sitting here beside me," I bragged. Then I got on the phone and started calling. But heck, this girl was mad, this one was out of town, this one was asleep, this one had a date. I was going from A to Z in the phone directory, calling everybody I knew. I was getting downright panicky.

Next thing I knew, Joe left the house and came back with a woman. Of course, he'd just picked somebody up off the street. He must have told her he'd split the money with her, because as soon as he got there and took the fifty, he took her back to wherever he got her. But we used to do stuff like that all the time, especially when I first got out there.

But when Elvis was in a partying mood, things could move on the Bacchanal side pretty quickly. And when we weren't working, that would be just about every night. If we were making a movie, we received just a few guests every evening, but things would be over early. Of course, on the weekends, we partied nonstop. Things would start popping after dinner, about ten o'clock. In the early days at Perugia Way, when we'd go out looking for our own dates, we knew to look for girls for Elvis, too. The perfect ones for Elvis were on the order of Priscilla. They had to be small--no taller than five-feet-two-inches--and they couldn't weigh more than about 110. And he definitely preferred brunettes, like his mother. More important, they had to be young. If they'd celebrated their eighteenth birthday, Elvis's eye began to wander.

A lot of people assume the worst, and the most lascivious reasons for this, and maybe they're true. But in some ways, I think Elvis saw *himself* as belonging to that age group. Certainly in many ways, his emotional growth had stopped about the time his career took off: Once Elvis saw what the audience wanted, he went to extremes to insure the inherent formula didn't change too much. In other words, Elvis was afraid to grow up--and positively mortified of growing old.

A lot of these girls were movie extras and starlets, most of whom converged on the studios where Elvis worked. Almost every Elvis picture had a party scene with dozens of pretty girls, and when the casting call went out, the guys and I got up early in the morning and went over to the studio to check out the applicants, casually dropping the information that Elvis was having a party in Bel Air. We didn't do that too much, because the casting directors didn't exactly approve. And we could get most of the girls we wanted, anyway. They were easy to find in Hollywood--we'd talk to them in clothing stores, or really just anywhere.

After a time, these parties got to be as orgiastic as Elvis's Paris romps. When the news got out, one girl telling another, women swarmed all over the lawn, waiting to get in, their cars parked all up and down Elvis's quiet street. They came in a steady stream, showing up in all kinds of outfits--some wearing pants, some with halters and bikinis barely covering their dignity, some decked out in fur-trimmed jackets or nicely filling a little black chemise. Whoever was on the door would pick them out like the judge of a beauty contest, and when they passed muster, the big brown portal would open for admittance. Some of them, honest to God, would stand out there until two in the morning, even though one of us on the door would try to give them a polite brush-off, like, "Try again." Sometimes there would be fifty girls to us eight guys.

Elvis's parties were supposed to be casual affairs, but in truth they were carefully orchestrated ceremonies during which Elvis held court. A girl was allowed entry to the elegant foyer, shown through the proper living room--where a painted photograph of Elvis, Gladys and Vernon posed in front of Graceland hung over the fireplace--and guided into the den, the scene of the parties. There, Pepsis, chips and other adolescent refreshments, as well as alcohol from the wet bar, were waiting. Elvis usually sat in front of the television, making rude remarks about whomever was on the screen.

Some of the girls would sit at his feet, and they almost always laughed at what he said. A couple of the guys would, too. Elvis knew it was forced laughter, and that most of the guys who did it had a reason--they wanted to get closer to him, to assume a position of some responsibility, and hope to avoid the routine firings that popped up from time to time. Some of us tried our damnedest not to fall into that trap, and I think Elvis respected us for it.

Basically, Elvis just wanted everybody to have a good time and be themselves. But when he was in a sarcastic mood or ticked off at somebody, there was no telling what he would say, either to the television or to his guests. He'd pull out one of his little stogies or sometimes a pipe, and occasionally if one of the guys didn't rush right over and light it, we'd get a humiliating dressing down: "Do I have to sit here all night, or are one of you jerkheads gonna give me a light?" Some of the girls thought it was big stuff, and others saw it for what it was-- Elvis liked to look big in front of the women. Episodes such as this were rare, though, and woefully sensationalized in Albert Goldman's biography, *Elvis*, which made Elvis out to be some kind of monster, which he wasn't. But one thing was certainly true: We were no longer traveling companions, but "yes" men.

Women, especially, who didn't agree with Elvis put themselves into a kind of frightening jeopardy at times. I'll never forget the night that Christina Crawford, who'd had a bit part in "Wild in the Country," and who was Joan Crawford's adopted daughter, challenged him about something, the particulars of which I've long since forgotten.

Elvis wasn't used to anybody crossing or even disagreeing with him, let alone a woman, who, in Elvis's skewed sense of Southern etiquette, never talked back or challenged the opinion of a man, especially not the King of Rock 'n' Roll and a big Hollywood star. At that juncture, Elvis no longer felt he had to be chivalrous.

Christina, who was very intelligent and opinionated, wanted to set an example, to show Elvis that he might be famous, but that she knew somebody just as famous. Furthermore, she wanted him to know that being well-known didn't give him a license to be an insensitive bore. She pushed her point a little too hard when an almost palpable streak of rage flew across his face. The next thing I knew, he had Christina by the hair, dragging her across a marble coffee table, and into another room.

Some of the guys remember that he kicked her in the rear

and had somebody throw her out of the house. I don't remember that, but I do remember that he cursed her out pretty good. It really shocked her, but, of course, she was wrong to smart off like that in Elvis's own house. The next day, she sent over an apology and five cases of Pepsi. It was hardly a sacrifice--her step-father was a Pepsi bigwig--but still a nice gesture, since she knew that Pepsi was Elvis's favorite drink.

Everything was cool after that, and if I'm not mistaken, she later came back to the house. But that incident would set up a fearsome pattern. Two years later, Elvis was playing pool with the guys and their dates, when he took umbrage at a remark one young woman made, and threw his pool cue at her, injuring her shoulder. And many years later, when he was far more shrouded by drugs than he was at this time of his life, he hurled a dinner knife at Joanie Esposito, Joe's wife. The thing was headed straight toward her eye when Sonny West instinctively threw his hand up and blocked it. During the time I was with Elvis, he apologized for such deplorable acts. In later years, though, I hear he just figured the woman had it coming.

Even though the girls outnumbered us six to one at these parties, we waited to put the moves on anybody until Elvis made his pick. To do otherwise might invite the kind of horrible confrontation Elvis had with Sonny over Tuesday's friend, Kay, or maybe even worse. It wasn't that we all just sat like dummies until the end of the night when Elvis invited a woman to retire. Deep down, Elvis wanted us to be successful with the girls, and we could usually narrow it down to two or three starlets that he liked and had his eye on. All the same, we pretty much just socialized until after the motorcycle rides or the late movie, which wound up sometime after half past one.

By the stroke of two, however, Elvis began inviting guests to accompany him to his bedroom. "Guests," the plural form, is the right word, for Elvis sometimes picked not one, but two or three young girls to spend the night--shades of his bizarre hijinks with the teenage Heidi, Frances and Gloria back in Memphis.

Exactly what Elvis did with these girls, I don't know. He

152

always told us he never completed the sex act, though. He said, "I've got to be careful. I can't afford to get someone pregnant and ruin my career." Which is why none of the guys believe these stories about Elvis's illegitimate love child--or children, I guess it is now, with the emergence of a guy who calls himself "Elvis Presley, Jr." We never heard Elvis mention the mothers of these children, or helped him arrange visits with them, as at least one of them asserts in a book.

It was about this time that Elvis asked me to go down to a little studio in Hollywood and have some tapes made for him. Elvis would have a lifelong interest in soft-core pornography, but now he wanted his blue movies custom-made to conform to his ultimate erotic turn-on: the sight of young girls wrestling. He didn't really like to see them do other things--he just wanted wrestling. And he didn't like to see them naked, because a completely nude woman turned him off. Girls who shared his bed said he complimented their bodies, but that he preferred it if they covered up a few essential parts. I remember Elvis saying that a hundred times: "It's much sexier seeing a girl in panties than seeing her walk across the floor naked, because it always leaves a little bit to the imagination."

The girls in the tapes, then, could wear only one thing: white cotton panties. A lot of people think that's pretty weird, but I never really thought so. I lot of men are into two girls. Elvis told one of the guys that the fixation came from an incident in his childhood, when he accidently saw two little girls fall together on the ground, their dresses flying up to expose their crotches. In Elvis's mind, he also saw the telltale signs of puberty protruding around the edges of the panties. From that moment on, the image of pubic hair and white cotton panties became his most potent erotic fantasy, the payload to transport Elvis to the height of sexual arousal.

Sometimes, while either watching the girls in his bedroom or perusing the tapes I had made for him, he would get a most defiant erection, which he would relieve either by masturbating, or, if the girls were actually there, dry humping one of his lucky guests through his slacks or pajama bottoms. Elvis, for as long as I was with him, didn't wear underwear--he hated the only styles available for men at the time, the baggy boxer shorts and the Jockeys--and he was embarrassed to let the girls view his penis.

Whether that spoke volumes about Elvis's self-image, and his fear of mature, adult sexual relationships, it is only fair to include the information that Elvis was, like so many country boys of the time, uncircumcised, a situation that would fill the adult Elvis with shame. He was even shy about it with the guys. He always used the stalls, and not the urinals, in public rest rooms, for example. And when he'd get dressed, he'd put on his shirt first, and let it hang down to cover himself, and then he'd put on his pants. Every so often, he would complain that it "hurt a lot" when he engaged in intercourse, since the foreskin tore and frayed with the friction in the vulva. When he withdrew, his penis was sometimes bloody.

A couple of us suggested that a minor operation would alleviate that condition, but Elvis would always say that when a man put if off until his age, the pain was unimaginable, even in the healing process. And so Elvis went to his grave with his penis intact.

The interesting thing about the sex tapes was that by the late sixties, Elvis staged his own bedroom antics with one of the first Sony home video cameras and tape recorders. We originally got the camera to see what was going on at the front gate, but in no time it disappeared into Elvis's room. By now, he was no longer content with just seeing the girls wrestle, but asked them to perform lesbian sex. At the end of one of these sessions, Elvis sprang in front of the camera with an angry hard-on, and proceeded to jack off with the ultimate precision.

Eventually, Elvis's taste turned to what is commonly referred to as "cat films," or tapes of women fighting, usually over a man. They started out rather mildly, with the women sitting together talking, when suddenly the action shifted to argument. At that point, the women would punch and claw and smack each other, all the while sending out a terrific howl --which is how the genre got its name.

For Elvis, though, the exciting part was yet to come--when the women tumbled to the floor and their legs went up, giving

the viewer a clear shot of their panties! In most cat films, one of the partners was invariably an older, heavier woman, rather coarse in her looks. Elvis's favorite film of this type had just such a woman, and the psychological implications of why he loved these films so--the beating up of women, and his obvious identification with either the tough, aggressive woman, or the weaker "girl" (a term used in medieval days to mean the passive sex partner of either sex) who allowed it to happen--don't require a Ph.D. to understand. And it's not difficult to connect them with the underlying feelings of identification--and of latent anger--that must have surfaced during his slumber parties with the teenage Gloria, Heidi and Frances.

One day Elvis up and destroyed a lot of his tapes, and Joe and Vernon trashed a lot of the others, particularly the ones that put Elvis in a compromising position. Still, a couple of them supposedly escaped the purge, and I later heard that they surfaced on the black market in Los Angeles. I tend to doubt it. Maybe so, but I never knew anybody who had one.

Whenever Elvis made his pick of women at the party, it was now safe for the rest of us to get cozy with whoever was left, providing she'd have us, of course. A lot of the girls were happy to go bed with anyone even vaguely connected with Elvis, both because of his glamour, and because they thought the contacts might lead to being cast in one of his movies.

Not too many of us slept alone at the end of one of these bashes. Whoever did, though, was assigned "Night Duty." That meant he'd lay down fully clothed in the living room to catch a few winks before dawn, when he'd dutifully rise to drive home Elvis's nubile young prey.

Yours truly posed in front of two of Elvis's limousines--one of my jobs was to keep them cleaned and gassed up.

Chapter 9

Pineapples And Passion Fruit
"Blue Hawaii"

In January of 1961, Elvis signed a five-year contract with Hal Wallis, one which called for Elvis to make a movie a year. To celebrate, he went out and bought a Rolls-Royce Phantom V from a Beverly Hills dealer, only to bring it home and have Gladys's chickens and peacocks peck away at their reflections in the elegant finish. I would have wrung their puny necks, but Elvis hung on to them because they'd been his mother's. Instead, he chose just to have the car repainted four or five times.

I ended up driving the Rolls almost exclusively, and while it wasn't the most dependable car in a lot of ways, we had a lot of fun with it. For instance, I remember driving it home from California one time, and stopping to buy gas in Forrest City, Arkansas, a small country town about sixty miles from Memphis. Elvis always liked to have the Rolls gassed up and washed, in case he wanted to show it off or take somebody for a ride.

The gauge said the car was almost empty when I pulled into the station. It had a big tank for its time--held about twenty-five gallons--and it took a while to fill it up. Apparently, Forrest City, Arkansas, had never had a Rolls-Royce grace its little streets, and word traveled like wildfire. The attendant was still pumping away when I looked around and discovered the whole town standing there gawking. There were lots of "oohs" and "aahs," and talk about the car maybe belonging to some celebrity.

Elvis didn't want the general public to know whose car it was, so he always told me to say that I was just delivering it for an automobile service. I was ready, then, when the first predictable question rang out of the crowd.

"Whose car is that, mister?"

"I don't know," I said. "I work for a service in California. I was just paid a hundred dollars to deliver it to Memphis."

A hush fell over the crowd. People reached out a tentative finger to touch it, or moved closer, like Gladys's chickens, to see their reflections in the paint.

Finally, a scrawny guy elbowed his way to the front.

"I know whose car it is," he said in a confident drawl.

"Tell me," I said. "I wish I knew."

He pointed a bony finger to the "RR" on the grill. "Roy Rogers!" he announced, a big grin crawling across his face. "That's whose car it is!"

The crowd erupted in admiration. "You're probably right," I answered. "I never thought of that. Yeah, it's Roy Rogers' car!"

Then I handed the attendant Elvis's credit card, which read "E.A. Presley." The gas jockey either never stopped to look at it, or he was too stupid to figure out that "E.A" was Elvis. I drove off laughing so hard I wondered how they kept from hearing me all over Forrest City.

A few days after he first bought the Rolls, Elvis packed up for Hollywood, where he began recording the soundtrack for "Blue Hawaii." On March 25, we touched down at Honolulu's International Airport. Here, Elvis would film his biggest box-office success, and give a live performance--at a benefit for the USS Arizona--that would rival his more famous concerts.

Four months earlier, Colonel had read an editorial in the L.A. *Herald-Examiner* asking people to donate money for a memorial to the big ship, sunk nineteen years earlier at Pearl Harbor. With that, the idea for the benefit was born. Colonel planned to use the event, just as he had Elvis's appearance on the Sinatra television special, to make him a respectable middle-class commodity.

Country comedienne Minnie Pearl was on the bill for that concert, and she was amazed to find three thousand screaming fans on hand when the plane touched down, many of them trying to push the fence over to get to the plane. With police and security guards holding the fans at bay, Colonel went over to Minnie and told her he wanted her to stay near Elvis when they got inside: He wanted them to be photographed together. By this time, Minnie's amazement had turned to fear. The young women had very nearly knocked the fence to the ground, and she was afraid she might be trampled if she stood too close to their idol.

From Minnie's viewpoint, everything eventually came off without incident. For Elvis, it was a different matter. Before we got on the plane, Elvis told one of the guys that he wanted to change clothes to meet the fans and photographers, and ordered a fresh outfit packed in a carry-on bag. But when the plane landed, we discovered that the bag had somehow been stowed with the rest of the luggage. One of the reasons the fans started breaking down the fence was because the plane sat on the tarmac for half an hour while somebody located Elvis's bag. Things got crazier when Elvis started walking to the car. Hands began grabbing him from every direction, trying to put leis around his neck, trying to touch his arm. Elvis loved that intense display of affection from fans, but it also made him hyper as a high-wire artist.

That night, Elvis, Minnie and the others put on their show, raising $52,000 for the memorial, quite a sum in those days. All of the guys got dressed up for this event--put on tuxes or white dinner jackets--and Elvis wore his famous gold lame jacket. He balked at wearing the pants, though. He'd always hated them, even though Colonel Parker thought the suit, designed by Nudie the tailor, was terrific. Aside from the fact that he didn't think the suit fit right--Elvis was fastidious about how his clothes hung on him, and this gold job was almost impossible to alter--he complained that one time he got down on the floor to sing a song and $500-worth of gold came off the pants. They were incredibly hot and heavy, so this time he opted for regular tuxedo trousers.

Elvis was visibly scared--it had been a long time since he put on a real show--but he tapped into a kind of tremulous sensuality he hadn't expressed on stage since before the army. At one especially dramatic point, he fell on his knees and slid some twenty feet to the front of the stage without missing a note. Nobody knew it at the time, but this would be his last live performance until the so-called "Comeback Special" of 1968--seven seemingly interminable years.

Minnie Pearl recalled later that on the day after the benefit, she and a number of the other musicians on the show went down to Waikiki beach to lay in the sun. They were cavorting and kidding and having a big time, when they turned and looked up at Elvis's penthouse in the Hawaiian Village Hotel. Elvis was standing alone on the balcony. They hollered and waved at him, and he waved back, looking, as Minnie put it, like a "solitary figure, lonely-looking." Minnie interpreted that to mean that Elvis was a prisoner, unable to leave his room for the fans. A lot of people believe that, or they think, again, that Colonel orchestrated his isolation.

In truth, Colonel didn't keep him anywhere, because Elvis could do what he wanted, and did. The only input Colonel had was with contracts, making sure Elvis showed up to do his movies, and advising him not to do interviews, something Elvis didn't enjoy anyway. He never said, "Elvis, don't go to this theater," or, "Don't go out on the beach," or anything like that. He never mingled in Elvis's private life. That's why they had a good relationship, at least when I was around. They may have had their disagreements, particularly in the latter years, and Colonel may have had to whip Elvis into shape a few times. But Colonel made sure Elvis had the money. What Elvis did with it was his business. If Elvis didn't go out on the beach to join Minnie and her friends, it was because he didn't want to go.

Just why Elvis went to Hawaii to make movies--and to do the benefit--is another question. Of course, it was a great, exotic location, perfect for fanciful romance movies like Elvis's. But not many entertainers went over there at the time. I know that Colonel loved it there, but I've always thought he had something else going there that we didn't know about.

For example, it was wholly out of character for Colonel to want Elvis to do a benefit of *any* kind, especially if it meant flying a band in for one day, and then flying them right back out the next. As an example, in years to come, when Richard Nixon's White House invited Elvis to sing--a performance com-

Two nice shots of Colonel taken on the set of "Blue Hawaii": standing on the beach with Patti Page (top), and a rare picture in which he looks like he's planning some kind of strategy. Knowing the Colonel, he probably was.

pensated only by the honor of having been invited, Colonel replied that they couldn't make exceptions for anyone: Elvis didn't sing unless he got paid, $25,000 plus traveling expenses and lodging for his band. "Nobody asks Elvis Presley to play for nothing," Colonel huffed.

On top of it, Colonel, who almost always insisted that Elvis not do interviews--his rationale was if you did it for one station, you'd have to do it for all--loved to have Elvis interviewed for the top Hawaiian rock station, KPOI. The biggest stations on the mainland wanted Elvis on their radio, but Colonel said no. And here, for KPOI, Elvis not only did interviews for the station, but *commercials*. Go figure.

Did Colonel own at least a part of the station? By making Elvis available on numerous occasions, did Colonel somehow erase the enormous gambling debts he'd been piling up for years? I don't know, but you'd have thought he did, the way he catered to the management and staff. We went back to Hawaii a lot through the years, and every time we did, Colonel arranged for Elvis to cut a spot for KPOI. I remember asking Colonel about it, and his explanation was that none of it would be heard back on the mainland, so it was all right, and it promoted good will while we were on the islands.

In contrast to his periods of ill-temper on many of the movie sets, Colonel was especially playful while we were in Hawaii. He was always clowning around with the crew. One day he took a pineapple, stuck a cord in it, and put it in his briefcase, and then went around interviewing people on the set, telling them he was reporting for KPOI, or Radio Pineapple. Colonel was perfectly serious when he did it, and while I saw a lot of people staring at that briefcase, wondering what the hell was in it, nobody questioned the Colonel. Most of them gave a detailed, straight-laced interview about the making of "Blue Hawaii"--to a prickly, yellow fruit. It was absolutely nothing, of course. But it just shows how the Colonel loved making things happen. If things got too boring on the set, he would liven them up.

Two days after the USS Arizona benefit, Elvis began filming "Blue Hawaii" on the island of Oahu. With Joan Blackman as his love interest, and Angela Lansbury as his mother, Elvis was cast in the role of Chad Gates, the heir to a pineapple fortune. The premise of the film argued that Chad wanted to make something of himself apart from his wealthy family, but the logic fell apart when the script had him become a tourist guide--hardly a lofty ambition for a boy trying to show he can make it on his own.

No matter how implausible, the plot turned on the happy ending of Elvis/Chad coming to terms with his family after handing all the travel arrangements for a convention for his father's pineapple company. Hal Wallis told the press, "Once again we tried to parallel Elvis's own life with his screen personality." Right.

Actually, it didn't matter. The soundtrack for "Blue Hawaii" eventually sold more than five million copies, an astonishing feat for such a lame collection of songs, distinguished only by "Can't Help Falling in Love."

"Blue Hawaii" was one picture where we didn't need to liven things up too much, because it was probably as much fun as any movie we ever did. A lot of sweet little girls--ingenues --worked on it, including Pam Austin, who everybody liked a lot. And, of course, Joan Blackman, the co-star, had been Elvis's first date when he went to Hollywood. She was living at the Hollywood Girls Club then, and Elvis had gone and picked her up like a regular fellow. Eventually, something went bad between them--it had to do with their differing attitudes toward interracial dating--and Elvis would say he didn't like her much anymore. But for awhile, we saw quite a bit of Joan at the house.

Joan wasn't an ingenue, by any means, and at this stage of the game, only the young ones turned Elvis's head. The movie was full of such young women, and Elvis had a habit of keeping them out all night, which rankled Hal Wallis no end. Wallis would take the girls to dinner each night, and as soon as the meal was over, they'd say, "Mr. Wallis, thank you for a lovely evening, but we have to go to sleep now." And then they'd come up to Elvis's suite and sit and play records and talk until three in the morning.

Elvis and "Blue Hawaii" co-star Pam Austin, one of the many ingenues that he dated off the set (April 1961).

Finally their close-ups told on them. It got back to Wallis that they reported for work looking baggy under the eyes, and practically yawned in the middle of a scene. Wallis got so mad that he moved all the girls from that wing of the hotel and put a ten o'clock curfew on them. That meant that they had about three hours to play after we wrapped at the end of the day.

Elvis went steaming off to Colonel, who understood the validity of Wallis's complaint. But Colonel delighted in an opportunity to needle Wallis about anything under the sun, from money matters to better working conditions. And so Colonel puffed his way over to Wallis to talk about orgies between his star and the nymphets who filled up the crowd scenes.

One thing led to another, and Colonel told Wallis he understood that dealing with such matters put him under a lot of pressure. Colonel said he didn't like to see Wallis so burdened.

"Tell you what, Hal," said Colonel, pulling a pair of dice from his pants pocket. "I'll shoot you double or nothing for the movie. If I win, you pay double, and you can go back to California. If I lose, we'll do the picture free. One roll of the dice."

Wallis looked him square in the face.

"You're crazy, Parker."

Whether Wallis had already heard of Colonel's long-standing gambling habit, I don't know. Later, I asked Colonel, "Would you really have rolled the dice, double or nothing?"

Colonel slid the cigar across his yellowed teeth.

"Well, if I told him I would, I'd'a had to."

But Colonel knew he was safe. A guy like Wallis wouldn't have gambled that big on one roll of the dice for anything in the world.

Half the time, I think Colonel did stuff like that because he knew it would make a good story. I was a sucker for Colonel's stories, and all of his antics, really.

One of the tricks Colonel liked to play on the movie sets was seeing if he could hypnotize us. I never knew whether he really thought he was hypnotizing us--probably not--or whether he just wanted to see how far we'd go along. You never knew

"Blue Hawaii" press conference at the Hilton Hawaiian Village Hotel. I'm standing on the right behind Red West (in the Hawaiian shirt). Joe Esposito stands over on the far left.

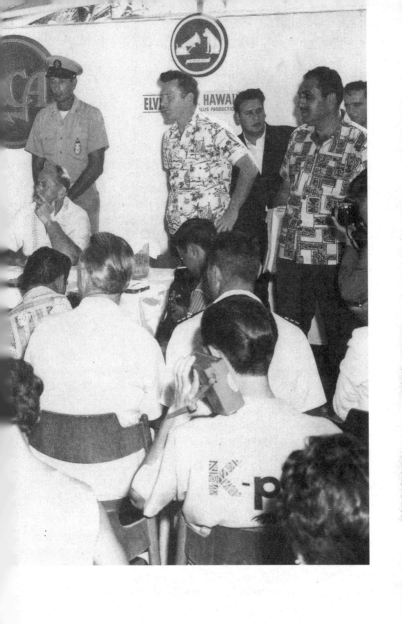

what Colonel was thinking, and he was always four steps ahead of anybody. Anyway, we'd all play our roles. Colonel would get out a pocket watch and swing it in front of our faces, and we'd act sleepy and pretend he had us deep in his power.

Some of us were better subjects than others. I usually started laughing before it was over. But Sonny West was a great subject for Colonel, and Colonel loved using him, because Sonny would act like he was really in a trance. I remember one time in Hawaii he got us going on that, and when he thought he had us "under," he'd say, "Go over and pick up that microphone and sing like you're Elvis Presley." Or, "Go up to Mr. Presley [meaning Vernon] and tell him you want a raise." Some of us would actually do it. And the rest of us would laugh our tail-ends off.

Of course, a lot of people thought Colonel had Elvis in a permanent trance, including, perhaps, Hal Kantor, who wrote the screenplay for "Loving You," in which Elvis's character was manipulated by a cunning manager. I'll say this, though. Colonel may have made bad judgments about Elvis's movie career, and he may have taken more than his fair share of Elvis's money. But this was hardly a Faustian pact. And nobody complained until Elvis died. What people tend to forget is that Colonel kept Elvis on top for twenty years. Without Colonel, he probably would have been a Jimi Hendrix, a blaze of talent quickly doused by drugs and self-destruction.

Wallis, who I think respected Colonel, never seemed to care for any of the Memphis Mafia. When we went back to Hollywood to film the indoor scenes for "Blue Hawaii" in April, it was obvious that he regarded us as hangers-on who distracted his star. To some degree, he was right. I felt his disdain in a personal way one day at the studio, when I went to the set and casually flopped down in a chair. Hell, I didn't know there were names on the back of them. He came over and glared a hole in my face, and went into a slow burn. "There are two hundred chairs on this sound stage, and you have to sit in mine!"

"Blue Hawaii" was the first movie I worked in as an extra where I was actually recognizable on the screen. The irony

Shooting scenes for "Blue Hawaii." That's Jennie Maxwell on the left, and a Paramount script man on the right.

Elvis between takes on the "Blue Hawaii" set.

was that my favorite moment on the screen is one in which I'm not identifiable--when I'm out paddling in a canoe with Patti Page.

Patti didn't have billing in the movie, but her husband was Charlie O'Curran, the movie's musical director, so she was just there every day on the set. Patti was a wonderful person, very sweet and fun-loving. And so when the director needed an anonymous couple in an outrigger to be seen way off in the distance of Kauai, well, Patti and I just volunteered. Back on the mainland, I'd go to her house a few times, and she'd sing for me, especially "The Tennessee Waltz," her big hit, which I loved. And she signed a copy of her book for me, "From your canoe partner on 'Blue Hawaii,' the singing rage, Patti Page."

Mostly, though, I appeared in crowd scenes. It wasn't much, but it was enough to make my family and the folks back home in Memphis proud.

One of the old Memphis crowd came to see us toward the end of "Blue Hawaii." As far as Elvis was concerned, Anita Wood was still in his life, although Elvis was having his pick of starlets almost every night. Whether Anita thought Elvis might still marry her, I don't know. She was probably out in California trying to establish a movie career, since Elvis had at one point gotten her a bit part in a film. Or maybe she was there to see about a recording career, since 1961 was the same year she cut two Elvis novelty records.

One night, Elvis, Anita, Lamar and I were in the car coming home from the studio, when Elvis pulled a Hank Williams routine in the back seat. This was a limousine, big and roomy, and Elvis was half-way laying down in the back, with his head in Anita's lap. When we pulled up at the house, Anita yelled out.

"Alan, Elvis isn't breathing! He isn't breathing!"

"You gotta be kidding."

Lamar jumped out of the car and ran into the house, screaming for somebody to call an ambulance.

About that time, Elvis started laughing. Turns out, he and Anita had cooked up the whole thing. "I just wanted to see what you guys would do," he said, flashing a grin.

Of course, there was no predicting when Elvis would spin into one of his moods, or get on a kick of some kind. It was about this time, in fact, that he got on his suit kick.

One of my jobs was to buy Elvis's clothes for him. I remember the time we were in Memphis, when Elvis called me and said, "Alan, what's the name of that real nice mens' store here?"

"Julius Lewis's, Elvis. I used to work down there in high school." Elvis had never been in there.

"What's that real nice suit they carry?"

"Oxxford." At the time, an Oxxford suit was about three hundred dollars, but I didn't tell him, because he didn't give a damn how much they were.

He said, "Go down there and tell the guy to send me twenty suits, altered and everything."

I said, "Oxxford doesn't make a suit with the western pocket, Elvis, remember?" I wanted him to know that, because Elvis hated it if the pocket bulged or stood open. That didn't happen with western pockets, but it often did with traditional cuts.

"No problem. Tell them to cut the pocket out and sew the pocket up. You know what colors I like--black, blue, no brown, and no green."

So I went down there and saw my friend, Bill, the manager, and told him Elvis wore size 32/32 pants--32 waist, and 32 length--and he wanted all his pockets cut out and sewn up, and he took about a 38 or 40 suit coat.

"Elvis wants twenty of 'em, Bill. Alter 'em and bring 'em out."

Bill looked at me like I had just escaped from the local looney bin.

"You're serious," he said.

"Yep, I'm serious."

"We've never had an order like this. That's $6,000. Suppose they don't fit or he doesn't like them?"

"It doesn't matter, Bill. He'll probably just throw 'em in his closet and forget about 'em.

"We'll have them out in two days."

Then again, sometime later, he did basically the same thing. "Buy me twenty-five pairs of pants--blues, greys--and a bunch of shirts." Or, "I don't have any socks. Go buy me some socks." So I came back with a hundred pair. He never told me to take them back. He just said, "Fine." But two things I never bought for him: Underwear and blue jeans.

I didn't buy underwear for him because, as I said before, he didn't wear any, except when he had to in the army. With the tight, tapered pants of the day, you couldn't wear boxer shorts, and why he didn't wear jockey shorts, I don't know. Maybe he didn't think they were sexy, or maybe he simply grew up without wearing them and didn't see the necessity later on.

As for jeans, I never bought those because he didn't like them and refused to wear them. I suppose it reminded him of having to go to grade school in overalls, a sure mark of a country boy. It even bugged him when a couple of the guys would wear jeans. He'd say, "Man, here we are in Hollywood, California, doing a million dollar movie and driving around in a $35,000 Rolls Royce, and you guys come out in blue jeans."

One day Elvis decided to put a stop to it. He called us all together and said, "Boys, I've decided everybody's going to wear suits and ties." A couple of the guys grumbled. I said, "Elvis, we don't have any suits." He said, "Don't worry, boys, we're gonna buy suits and ties, and I'm payin' for 'em."

And so, like some ragamuffin army, we all marched into a high-priced mens' store in Beverly Hills. Elvis bought himself twenty-five or thirty narrow-lapeled suits and skinny ties, and the rest of us four or five suits, ties, and dress shirts. At one point in the dressing room, the guys let out one long, collective sigh. But Elvis looked as gleeful as an I.R.S. agent on an audit. "We're gonna dress accordingly," he beamed.

For a couple of days there, we all sat around like funeral home attendants, dressed in somber dark suits and shoes. Nobody complained, because we knew it wouldn't do any good. Then one day, Elvis took off his tie. The next day, he didn't wear one at all.

I said, "Elvis, wait a minute. We're all wearing ties and suits, but you're not." He thought a second and wrinkled his brow. "Okay," he said, "we're going to change it. If I come down in a suit and tie, y'all be in one. If I come down in casual clothes, y'all do the same." It sounded complicated, but we all agreed.

Pretty soon, it got to where we were changing wardrobes twenty times a day. After awhile, Colonel saw us and nearly dropped his stogie. "Forget them suits, boys," he said, walking off and chuckling way back in his fatty throat. "Make y'all look like you're ninety years old."

Chapter 10

Better Living Through Chemistry
"Follow That Dream"

The spring and early summer of 1961 found us back home in Memphis. The idea was to unwind a little bit before returning to California to begin Elvis's next picture, "Follow That Dream." Elvis owed RCA some records, so he'd go to Nashville in June and cut some tracks for an album called "Pot Luck with Elvis," and a back-to-back single of "Little Sister" and "(Marie's the Name of) His Latest Flame," a song that just happened to include the name of Colonel's wife.

Colonel didn't want Elvis cutting many songs that his publishing company, Hill and Range, didn't publish or administer. And even though the writers there didn't have to worry about living up to a certain standard as far as Colonel was concerned, it was in the interest of Doc Pomus and Mort Shuman--some of the best writers Elvis ever had--to make Colonel happy when they could. Why not flatter the big man by putting his wife's name in a song? That virtually guaranteed that Elvis would record it.

Elvis would try to relax and do some normal things back in Memphis, like buying a bigger boat to use on McKellar Lake, and selling his sixteen-foot Glasspar ski boat to George Klein and me. It didn't last too long--with a Johnson 75 outboard motor on it, the bottom busted out when we hit a wave one day. But what the hell, we were trying to be regular guys again. Red West took normalcy one better by marrying Pat Boyd, one of Elvis's secretaries.

It was obvious to me on that trip home that I was a different guy than I'd been before we left. Courtesy of Elvis, I'd been introduced to the wonderful world of narcotics, hypnotics and stimulants. We were living on Dexamil, Dexedrine, Placidyl, Valium, Percodan, Seconal, Tuinal, Nembutal, and sometimes

Demerol, mainly to be able to continue Elvis's day-for-night schedule, and still be alert and on the movie set by seven in the morning. I didn't know what the hell I was doing.

Elvis had started taking Dexedrine and Dexamil in the army, and when he got back to the States he was still popping them pretty regularly. Which meant, of course, that he couldn't sleep. When he got to Hollywood, he found he had a lot of company in the jet set.

"Here's how you get to sleep," somebody finally told him. "You take a Seconal." One thing led to another, and with different doctors only too happy to supply a wealthy celebrity, Elvis discovered Hollywood was a junkie's haven.

There were a number of private doctors such as this, but we found it was almost as easy to get pills from the studio doctors. Each studio had its own physician, and they'd give you just about anything you wanted--the old Judy Garland Syndrome. And we'd make trips to Vegas, where drug store pharmacists would practically hand them over. We used to spend hours in the drugstore across the street from the Sahara Hotel, getting a crash course in pharmacology. Before I went back on the road with the guys, they found a friendly supplier in a druggist at the Chrysler Pharmacy, conveniently located in the Beverly Wilshire Hotel. That guy absolutely loved Elvis, and he'd give him anything he wanted for a dollar a pill. Most of the time I was with Elvis, though, we all had doctors' prescriptions to get what we wanted. It was easy as pie.

I had begun my nightmare affair with drugs in a seemingly harmless manner, which I suppose is what all drug addicts say. Mine started with diet pills right after Elvis got home from Germany. I took them, along with the other guys, both to lose weight and to stay up all night. A couple of us were working regular day jobs, and then partying all night long. I'd complain about not getting enough sleep, and Elvis would say, "Here, Alan, take this, and you'll be fine."

Pretty soon, Elvis was keeping the *Physician's Desk Reference* by his bedside. That way, when he talked to the doctor, he already knew what to ask for. If Elvis called and said he was in a lot of pain and a doctor said, "How about if I give you codeine?" Elvis knew the drug's effects. Then he'd say, "Oh, no, that doesn't set too well with me," and he'd rattle off the adverse reactions often associated with the drug. "I need something else, maybe something stronger," he'd moan. He knew almost as much about drugs as the doctor.

In July of 1961, Elvis trekked back to Nashville to cut the soundtrack of "Follow That Dream," and a week or so later, we went back out to Hollywood to start production on the picture for United Artists, with co-stars Joanna Moore (later the wife of actor Ryan O'Neal and the mother of actors Tatum and Griffin), Arthur O'Connell, and Simon Oakland.

"Follow That Dream" was the first of the long line of crappy pictures Elvis would make that would seal his fate as a wasted presence on the screen, just as the soundtrack would take a dip in quality even from the mediocre "Blue Hawaii" songs. If the title song was nothing more than a pleasant little rhythm number, reflecting the optimism of youth, such tripe as "I'm Not the Marrying Kind," "Sound Advice," and "What a Wonderful Life," set a kind of new low standard for him. Now it was clear that the hard-core clutch of fans could be happy hearing his voice wrapped around any collection of empty filler. But it would be seven years before Elvis would place a song on the country charts, and after "(You're the) Devil in Disguise," in 1963, he would never again appear on the R & B chart.

The screenplay of "Follow That Dream" was based on the 1957 novel, *Pioneer, Go Home* by Richard Powell. The plot centered around a chance occurrence--Elvis's beat-up wreck of an automobile runs out of gas--and the fact that Elvis's character, with the unlikely name of Toby Kwimper, decides to homestead in Florida with his off-beat hillbilly family. Before the picture's end, Elvis manages to break up a craps game, demonstrate his judo, and take on the state welfare system. He also falls in love with a pretty young girl played by actress Anne Helm, who winds up moving in with his family and growing up in his home--a twist that foreshadowed Elvis's relationship with Priscilla.

We filmed "Follow That Dream" on location, mostly around

(L. to r.) Colonel (in the straw hat), Elvis, Anne Helm, me, and Gene Smith on the set of "Follow That Dream." (Photo: Maria Columbus)

Tampa--Colonel's old stomping ground--Ocala, Yankeetown, and Crystal River, Florida. Elvis went down there on a rented bus, while Lamar pulled Elvis's new boat, a twenty-one-foot Coronado, from the back of the white Chrysler station wagon. I drove his Cadillac limousine.

The limousine ended up costing poor Lamar a lot of grief. He was sitting in the damn thing one day when they were ready to use it for filming. Since he was already in it, one of the crew asked him to drive it for the shot. It was parked right near the water. One guy told him to move it back, and another guy told him to bring it forward, and Lamar got mixed up and the limousine somehow went back and sank in the sand--all the way down to the axle. It botched the whole shot.

Elvis was really mad at Lamar. But when everybody at the studio started yelling at him, saying, "You ruined it! You cost us all this money!" Elvis took Lamar's side. "Listen, y'all," Elvis snarled. "That's my limousine, and y'all better be quiet about why it ruined the shot. We'll just re-do it." Elvis could get down on us when he felt like it, but he didn't want anybody else to jump on his employees.

We stayed at the Port Paradise Hotel, situated on a little lagoon out in Crystal Bay, which opened out into the Gulf of Mexico. It was a beautiful place, and the rooms were great, with little kitchens. Joe and I cooked breakfast for Elvis when he got up in the morning, and in fact, the only way we *could* get him up was to start loud arguments. We'd go into Elvis's room and start frying bacon and eggs, and I'd yell, "Dammit, Joe, you're cooking the bacon wrong!" and we'd carry on like crazy.

You'd think that would make Elvis mad as a hatter, but he'd always stumble in in a good mood. He'd say, "You guys are like two old women arguing in the kitchen." He must have liked it, because he always ended up laughing.

Crystal River was an odd place for a lot of reasons, not the least of which was the fact that the studio had gone down there and built a beach. They even hauled the palm trees from California and put them in the ground. One night a huge storm came up and washed the entire beach away, palm trees

Elvis visiting on the set of "Follow That Dream." (Above) With his father Vernon, stepmother Dee Stanley Presley, and step brothers Ricky and Billy Stanley.
(Photo: Maria Columbus)

(Right) Elvis with Vera Presley, who married Grandpa Jessie after his divorce from Minnie Mae. That's me behind the two kids, who unfortinately I cannot place.
(Photo: Maria Columbus)

(Left) Another "Follow That Dream" shot. (L. to r.): Bitsy Mott, Colonel's brother-in-law; Joe Esposito; Red West; Tom Diskin, Colonel's assistant; Sonny West; me, and Frank Esposito, Joe's brother. Gene Smith sits on Colonel's lap.
(Photo: Maria Columbus)

and all, and they had to come around and stick them back in. Now, you might ask why they just didn't go someplace in Florida that already had beaches? Who knows? Maybe Colonel *owned* Crystal River. It was mighty close to Tampa, the winter home of all those carnival shows Colonel used to shill for. All I know is that we had a good time down there.

We finished filming in August, but some of us stayed on a little while to soak up some sun. In October, Elvis went to Nashville to record a session that included "Good Luck Charm," and a couple of the guys went with him. The rest of us drove back to Memphis, where we dropped off the boat, and then headed out to Los Angeles. Elvis would start "Kid Galahad" in a couple of weeks.

Before we left Crystal River, I gave George Klein a call. George mentioned his vacation was coming due, so I said, "We'll just pick you up when we drop the boat off, and you can ride to Los Angeles with us." But when we got to Memphis, there was no room for both George and his luggage, so we put his bag on top of the station wagon and covered it with a tarpaulin. The only trouble was, toward the end of the trip we hit the kind of storms that Noah wrote home about. When we got to L.A., we peeled George's suitcase off the top of the car, and everything he owned was drenched. We had to just take it and put it in the bathtub.

When things like that happened, life as Elvis Presley's traveling companion didn't seem so glamorous. It didn't seem too cool, either, when second-string stars tried to snub us. That didn't happen too often, but when it did, it hurt.

George and I were on that same trip from Memphis to L.A. when we went through Gallup, New Mexico, and heard on the radio that Freddie Cannon was playing there that night. Freddie had had a couple of good records, "Tallahassee Lassie" and "Way Down Yonder in New Orleans," and we were nuts about his voice, a high, hopped-up kind of instrument.

We would loved to have stayed over to see Freddie's show, but we needed to get on to L.A., and we'd planned on driving straight through. I told George, "There aren't very many motels in Gallup, so if he's here yet, I know where he's staying.

A couple of odd-looking shots from a "Follow That Dream" pow-wow, both showing Elvis--and almost everybody else--smoking a cigar. Seated around the table (l. to r.): Joe Esposito, Billy Smith, Lamar Fike, director Gordon Douglas (in the hat), Elvis, Colonel, me, Gene Smith, and Tom Diskin. (Photo: Maria Columbus)

I also know the people who run the motel, because we usually stay there when we drive through to California. Let's just go by and say hello."

We pulled into to the motel, and sure enough, the lady remembered me. Freddie was there, all right, and she told us which room. I knocked on the door, and a guy answered.

"Yeah, can I help you?"

"Hi. My name's Alan Fortas, and this is George Klein. We're with Elvis Presley. I know Freddie Cannon's staying here, and we just wanted to stop and meet him and tell him how much we like his records. We're on our way out to California."

By the time I got the last sentence out, I realized that the guy *was* Freddie Cannon. He kind of looked at us, and then he said, "Is Elvis with you?"

"No, he's recording in Nashville."

He stammered a little bit and said, "Well, uh, Freddie's asleep."

I wanted to say, "Hey, man, I know who you are now! Don't pull that on us!" Instead, I calmed myself down and decided to play the game. "Okay," I said. "Just tell him we stopped by and that we really like his records."

We got back in the car, and the more I thought about it, the angrier I got. That guy was full of it, and I was mad as hell.

Two days later, we were in L.A. Elvis was in California by then, and there was a knock at the door. I got up to answer it, and there stood Johnny Rivers and Freddie Cannon. We originally met Johnny in Memphis. His real name was John Ramistella, and although he was born in New York City, he grew up in Baton Rouge. About the time we caught on to him, he was living in Nashville with Audrey Williams, Hank's widow. This was before his big hits, of course. Johnny was real nice looking, young, a kind of semi-country rock 'n' roll singer. And even though Audrey had seen a lot of miles roll by on her odometer, she looked pretty good, too.

The problem was, Audrey dug into that boy like a tick on a flop-eared hound. Johnny was only seven years older than Audrey's own Hank, Jr., but she had to have him. And she wouldn't let him leave! It took the Nashville Mafia to get him out of town, mainly a fella named Skull, who used to sit in the Rainbow Room in Printer's Alley. It was heavy.

When Johnny got to California, he was still young and struggling, and everybody just seemed to like him. He started playing the Whiskey-a-Go-Go, doing a kind of live disco act, and the guys went down to see him quite a bit, even though Elvis wouldn't go to the Whiskey because it was so crowded. Pretty soon, though, Johnny was added to the list of Hollywooders who could come and go at the house whenever he liked.

Anyway, here were Johnny and Freddie Cannon, standing at the door at about three o'clock in the afternoon. Johnny said, "Alan, I've got Freddie Cannon with me, and he wants to meet Elvis." I got red-faced all over again. "Elvis is asleep," I said, and I slammed the damn door in his face.

I walked back down the hall, and Elvis yelled, "Hey, Fortas, who was that?" I said, "Johnny Rivers and Freddie Cannon. Freddie wanted to meet you, but I told them you were asleep."

"Wait a minute," Elvis growled. "I want to meet him." I mumbled something under my breath, and walked outside and called them back. But I was still angry. I said, "Look, Freddie, we stopped in Gallup, and you wouldn't see us. Don't ever pull that crap on us again, okay?" He apologized, and later, he and George got fairly tight. To this day, whenever George sees him, he says, "Freddie, you woke up!"

In November, we started production on Elvis's tenth movie, "Kid Galahad," a boxing film based on an old *Saturday Evening Post* story of the 1930s. It had already been filmed twice, most notably in the thirties with Edward G. Robinson, Bette Davis, Humphrey Bogart, and Wayne Morris, who played Walter Gulick, Elvis's role.

Gulick was called upon to beat boxing at its own game, to emerge untouched from a corrupt and often violent underworld, winning not only the matches but the girl. As if that weren't enough, in this updated version, Gulick was also required to have a fabulous singing voice, although the songs were hardly worthy contenders--only the winsome love ballad, "Home is Where the Heart Is," packed a punch.

(Right) On the chilly set of "Kid Galahad." (L. to r.): Billy Smith, Ray Sitton, Marty Lacker, Joe Esposito, Elvis, Lamar Fike, Red West (behind Lamar), and Sonny West. (Photo: Maria Columbus)

(Below) Joe, paper in hand, has moved to the left, Lamar is now behind Billy, Ray is on Elvis's left, Red and Sonny have moved off, and I've come in at the right. (Photo: Maria Columbus)

Elvis's co-stars were Gig Young, Lola Albright, and our friend Joan Blackman, who once again played his love interest. Their off-screen romance was long over by this time, however, and now Elvis was seeing Connie Stevens, who would quickly break up with him. Elvis had Joe pick her up in the Rolls -Royce one night and bring her back to the house, where all the guys sat around with their dates. Connie thought Elvis should have picked her up himself, and that he should have arranged for a romantic dinner alone. When it was obvious that their ideas on dating were just too different, Connie demanded to be taken home.

Elvis talks with Joan Blackman and director Phil Karlson (probably) on the set of "Kid Galahad." (The tall studio chair on the right of this photograph is discussed further in the photo caption, pages 188-89.)

We shot most of "Kid Galahad" in Idyllwild, California, about a hundred miles east of Los Angeles, in the San Jacinto Mountains. Elvis rented a house for the four-week shoot, and everything seemed to run as smooth as clockwork. But "Kid Galahad" was set in the summer, and, quite naturally, it snows sometimes in the mountains in November, even in California. We ended up finishing the picture at the United Artists studios in Hollywood, which meant that Elvis couldn't go home for Christmas. That Christmas on Perugia Way was the first and only time he wouldn't spend the holidays at his beloved Graceland.

Sonny West had a bit part in the movie, and I thought once again that the most I'd be able to get on camera was in yet another crowd scene. But this was a Mirisch Company production, and I'd gotten to know an assistant director, Dave Salvin, fairly well. One day, Dave said, "I've got a little part for you, Alan."

Even though Dave was a buddy, I didn't want to fall victim to the kind of humiliating trick I'd suffered during "King Creole." So I said, "All I want to be is an extra, Dave. I don't care about the part." Of course, I would have traded a small, but significant portion of my anatomy for a real role, but I stayed cool.

Sure enough, there was a little part for me, a scene in which I would make my speaking debut. A line! I would play a laundry man. In the film, Elvis, who's supposedly won his fight, is standing around the town square when I pull up in a laundry truck. I get out and shadow box with him and say, "Nice goin', kid." Before the shot, I told Elvis, "I'll probably mess it up so they'll have to do it ten times." But it went fine. And I was rewarded with a check for $125, which went into the Memphis Mafia "extras" pool.

By the time "Kid Galahad" was filmed, the Mafia had taken on a new member, Marty Lacker. Marty was born in New York City, but he'd moved to Memphis in 1952, where he went to Humes High School his last year with Elvis, Red West, and George Klein. He and George were great friends--Marty had been a radio program director and disc jockey--and everybody liked Marty pretty well. After he got out of the army, he started coming out to Graceland, and now Elvis had invited him to come to California. Marty had played on the Humes football team with Red, and I think that appealed to Elvis.

(Left) The studio gave Elvis that chair to use during location shooting for "Kid Galahad" (the star and the director got tall chairs), but see how high it is? Elvis very seldom sat in it, because he liked to sit with the rest of the cast and didn't want to be "above" them when they talked.

All the people on the set seemed to be ex-boxers and fighters and semi-fighters. Elvis once asked Mushy Callahan, the stunt guy, "Who's that over there?" Mushy said, "Just call him 'Champ'." Elvis called out, "Hey, Champ!" and about twenty people turned around.

(Detail for above photo, l. to r.): Lamar Fike and Ray Sitton on Elvis's right, Marty Lacker, me, and Joe Esposito to his left.

At first, Marty didn't stay all that long. After a little while, he went back into radio, but when Elvis asked him to come back to the group two years later, he joined for good. Soon he was handling some of the important bookkeeping and secretarial work, and he and his wife, Patsy, and their family lived in one of the Graceland apartments, over what had once been the garage. We called him "Moon" because of his bald head.

When "Blue Hawaii" came out in November of 1961, it got a number of favorable reviews. The *Hollywood Reporter* said it offered "a new setting to exploit the singer's appeal." And *Variety*, which ranked it number two on its "National Box Office Survey," said it "restores Elvis Presley to his natural screen element--[the] romantic, non-cerebral film musical."

That wasn't exactly putting Elvis in the same league with Laurence Olivier, but it was far more positive than the reviews of "Wild in the Country." Colonel took careful notice, especially when "Blue Hawaii" became Elvis's top-grossing film, and the soundtrack stayed in the number one spot for twenty weeks. As far as Colonel was concerned, the formula was perfected. If Elvis had serious aspirations as a film actor, he'd have been better off a dead man than endure the mindless parade of dreadful pictures Colonel had in store.

In many ways, of course, he became exactly that, and it showed. Film critic Pauline Kael would later take one look at him and succinctly sum up that Elvis Presley had become "a bloated druggie with dead eyes." At the end of 1961, though, not one of the people closest to Elvis really saw it coming.

CHAPTER 11

"The Original Rock 'N' Roll Lolita"

By the time we made "Kid Galahad," Elvis had rented a Mediterranean-style house at 1059 Bellagio Road in Bel Air. Exactly when we moved in, I don't know. But it was sooner than most of the Elvis books say--January of '62--because Marty Lacker remembers we were already in the Bellagio Road house by the time he came on "Galahad."

We originally moved because Elvis thought we'd outgrown the Perugia Way house, especially since the neighbors didn't care too much for legions of girls parked along the street and standing out in front of the door. It looked like a male bordello to them. In a way, they were right.

The Bellagio Road house was an elegant place, all done up with marble. In some ways, I think it was a little too fancy for Elvis's taste. Whatever the reason, Elvis didn't like the Bellagio Road house very much, and we weren't there all that long--a matter of months or maybe a year--before we moved back to Perugia Way. The owner ended up enlarging the Perugia Way house for us, and offered to redecorate anyway we wanted. That was a great offer, because it wasn't everyone who wanted to rent to eight guys, even though Elvis paid a premium price, and took care of repairs when the house and furnishings got damaged. We stayed there until 1965.

We hadn't been at the Bellagio Road house but a few days when Elvis mourned the fact that we hadn't brought the source of a lot of our fun on Perugia Way--the two-way mirror. "Heck," he finally said. "I'll just spring for a new one." This one was the size of a picture window--five-by-five feet--a huge mama.

There was a cabana at Bellagio Road, where our female guests changed from their street clothes to their bathing suits. Sonny, who'd bought the first two-way mirror, thought the cabana was a great place to put the new mirror. Except for one thing. It would work only at the back of the cabana. And to get to the spot where we could look into the mirror, we had to crawl under the house. The first time we had girls changing in the cabana, I looked up, and Elvis had crawled under the foundation.

"Good, Godalmighty, Elvis, what the hell are you doing under here?"

Elvis, with dirt on his cheeks and a big smear across his forehead, got a sheepish grin on his face. He didn't say a word.

"I can't believe you crawled under there gettin' all dirty. Hell, they'll *let* you look, Elvis! All you got to do is go up to them and ask."

Elvis thought about it a second, and then he said, "Yeah, but it's a lot more fun this way."

Fun for him maybe, but for the rest of us, it was just too much of a hassle. And so the mirror didn't get used that much. The weird thing was that as our leases expired on these different houses and we went to look at new ones, all of the guys would walk around checking not so much if the house would accommodate Elvis and his twisted band of friends, but if there were a place for the mirror.

We ended up carrying that thing all over Hollywood. Finally, we just had it put in a crate, and ended up bringing it back to Graceland. I'll bet it's still in the attic there today.

Life at Bellagio Road was pretty much the same as it was at Perugia Way. Girls came and went, and a handful of Hollywood guys also knew they were welcome.

At the end of March 1962, Elvis was set to begin work on "Girls, Girls, Girls," a typical babes-in-bikinis musical, masquerading behind the thin plot of Elvis-the-fisherman saving his charter boat from a rich dilettante who cared nothing about the sea. Elvis's co-stars were Stella Stevens, Laurel Goodwin, and Jeremy Slate, with oriental actor Benson Fong on hand as a modern-day Confucius.

The director was Norman Taurog, who'd done "Blue Hawaii," and who would make more Elvis pictures than anyone else. Taurog, who was sixty-three years old at the time we went into production, was a former child actor. As an adult, he'd continued to treat his young stars like kids, keeping a supply of candy bars in his pockets as rewards for good performances. He'd done a lot of the Dean Martin and Jerry Lewis comedies, which pleased Elvis way down deep, since Martin had been one of his idols.

Taurog was one of the few directors who'd ever tell Elvis what to do. Elvis loved it, because he was still eager to learn, and he bought Taurog a Cadillac to show his appreciation. "I was always proud of Elvis's work," Taurog said before his death in 1981, "even if I wasn't too proud of the scripts. I always felt that he never reached his peak."

In Elvis's eyes, "Girls, Girls, Girls" was the beginning of the end of his career as a serious actor. He hated the frivolous production numbers, and he spared no emotion in telling Colonel how humiliating it was to have to sing to a crustacean ("Song of the Shrimp"). The soundtrack was filled with junk songs, like "We're Coming in Loaded," but it also contained the jaunty "Return to Sender." A huge hit single--it got to number two and stayed on the charts fourteen weeks--"Return to Sender" came on the heels of two other big records, "Can't Help Falling in Love" and "Good Luck Charm," which made it to number one.

Elvis wouldn't have another number one record until "Suspicious Minds" in 1969. But Colonel turned a deaf ear to his complaints. The "Girls, Girls, Girls" soundtrack reached number three on the charts and "went gold" (sales in excess of a million dollars), and in May of 1962, the movie industry voted Elvis the top box-office draw. Tests such as these were the only true measurements Colonel respected. The *Los Angeles Times* deemed the picture "no better or worse than other previous Elvis epics. It's just a matter of whether you can take it."

We went on location to Hawaii for "Girls, Girls, Girls," and just as the last time we flew into the Honolulu airport, five thousand fans showed up to say hello. Somehow in the crowd, Elvis lost his watch and his tie clasp. One of the girls inadvertently pulled his favorite diamond ring off, and Elvis was furious when he found out it was gone. The next day, the unthinkable happened: A girl's voice was on the phone, saying, "Elvis's ring came off in my hand and I want to bring it back." She did, too, and left it at the desk at the Hawaiian Village Hotel.

"Girls, Girls, Girls" may have been one of the low points in Elvis's movie career, but it was the high point of mine. I didn't have a line in the picture, but I ended up being on camera more, in the scenes in which Elvis takes his fishing crew out on the boat.

It happened almost by accident. The boat was fairly small, so Taurog said, "I'll take three people out a day. We'll alternate, and the rest of you can stay on the beach."

We'd leave early in the morning, and we'd stay out until six or seven o'clock at night. When we came back in, we smelled like tuna. One day they used me as one of the deck hands, so I had to go back out almost every day after that, because now I was established as a crew member. In one scene where we're unloading the boat, Elvis throws me a fish and I catch it. Hardly high drama. But of all of Elvis's movies, that's the one in which I'm most recognizable.

After shooting wrapped on "Girls, Girls, Girls," we came home to Memphis for a rest. Elvis wanted to revisit his old haunts, and just like old times, he got his friends together for a trip to the fairgrounds and the all-night shows at the Memphian Theatre.

It was about this time that Lamar decided to go off the payroll and quit the road. He'd never really be disconnected from the group, and in fact, he went back with Elvis full time in 1970. But in 1962 he moved to Nashville to become the road manager for singer Brenda Lee, while simultaneously acting as Elvis's liaison with Hill and Range, the publishing company that handled Elvis's music.

Nobody could replace Lamar--he was his own three-ring circus and tent show--but now Elvis asked Richard Davis to come to work for him. Like several of the other guys, Richard had a football connection--he first met Elvis in a pick-up game in Memphis. Richard would work as a kind of valet to Elvis for the next seven years.

Another member of the entourage came aboard on this trip home, too. He weighed forty pounds, stood three feet tall, and

he gave us more fun and more headaches than any other member in the history of the Mafia. His name was Scatter. Never has there been a chimpanzee like him.

Scatter had been a Memphis TV star. He belonged to Captain Bill Killebrew, who appeared on a local television station, usually with Scatter. Killebrew worked in public relations for a bread company, but he was also an artist--he drew sketches on television, too. It was the early days of TV, when viewers weren't the sophisticated lot they are today, and the flickering tube threw out a lot of different kinds of oddball shows.

We were home in Memphis in the spring of 1962, then, when Killebrew brought Scatter over to Graceland. He was looking to sell him, and I guess he figured Graceland was the kind of untamed place where a monkey would feel right at home.

If Graceland wasn't savage enough, Hollywood certainly was. But Scatter was a little wilder than any of us imagined. There was no telling what he would get into, and, of course, some of us helped him find his way. We dressed him in little boys' clothes, and at least one of us helped him acquire a taste for straight scotch and bourbon, which he would drink sitting on a bar stool next to the rest of us.

Scatter was a real party animal, all right. We had a friend named Brandy who was a former stripper, and who was a regular at our parties. As a guest, not a stripper. She used to get down on the floor and wrestle with the chimp and some-times simulate sex with him. People nearly choked, they were laughing so hard.

Some of the girls at our parties were afraid of him, though, and others thought he was downright adorable. Until he'd masturbate in front of them, that is, or lay on the couch and raise their skirts as they walked by. I honestly don't know where he learned to do that. Chimps often play with them-selves, but we didn't put him up to it, and we didn't teach him how to look up a girl's skirt. He figured that out on his own. Sonny and I stuck him in a bedroom one time with a couple who were making love, and Scatter ran in chattering like

Forty pounds of trouble. Scatter was responsible for more fun and created more pandemonium than any other member of the Memphis Mafia.

crazy--just excited, you know--and jumped on their backs. It may not sound funny now, but the chimp was the life of the party.

I was the one who usually took care of Scatter, and since I normally looked after the cars, Scatter and I often went for a drive in either the limo or the Rolls-Royce. One of my favorite pranks was to tool around Hollywood with Scatter sitting on my lap. I'd put a chauffeur's cap on him, and when a car came along, I'd duck down so it looked like Scatter was actually driving. More than one car went off the road taking it all in, and Elvis thought it was so funny that he looked everywhere for one of those trick circus cars, but he never found one.

Scatter gave us a good scare one day when we were at the studio watching the dailies. One of the guards came into the screening room and said, "By any chance do any of you own a chimpanzee?" I said, "Yeah, he's locked up in Mr. Presley's dressing room." The guard said, "No, he's not, buddy. He's sitting at Mr. Sam Goldwyn's desk right now."

That about gave me heart failure. I could see all of Mr. Goldwyn's mementoes and important papers strewn all over the floor. But when I got in there, Scatter was just sitting calmly in the chair, looking as if he were contemplating a big Hollywood takeover or the casting of his next picture.

The long and the short of it is that Scatter got to where we couldn't handle him, mainly because there were so many people fooling with him. We were going out of town one time, and we were about to board him, when I got the brainstorm to take him to Gene Detroy, who had the famous Marquis Chimps. They were a big act in Vegas and on TV, like the orangutans they use now. Elvis said, "Good idea."

I called Gene and told him who I was, and said that we had this chimp we couldn't control. Could we bring him over?

"Certainly," Gene said. "I'd love to see him." Elvis got excited. "I want to go, too," he said. So the three of us padded over to Gene's house.

"We can't discipline the chimp anymore, Mr. Detroy," I said. "He won't even wear his clothes anymore."

Detroy looked surprised. "He used to wear clothes?" He

Me and the wild chimp of Bel Air in the back yard. Scatter, who was mostly my responsibility, could be a real gentleman when he wasn't overstimulated by too much human attention.

For a short time, until we had to send him back to Memphis, Scatter got to mingle with the stars. Here he is with actor Gig Young.

turned to his trainer: "Take Scatter back and dress him."

A few minutes later, preceded by an unbelievable racket and commotion, Scatter came out, fully dressed, and sat down. He behaved like a perfect gentleman. We couldn't get over it.

We told Gene that we were going out of town, and that we thought we'd board Scatter while we were gone. "Why don't you leave him with me?" he offered. "I'll put him through a refresher course. And I might take him with me on some of these fairs and carnivals."

Detroy kept him for about a month, and when we came back, Scatter was a changed chimp. He'd performed at some of the fairs, and he was disciplined and orderly. But as soon as we brought Scatter home and people started fooling with him again, he went right back to his old ways.

The worst part was that with so many people going in and out of the house, he started just walking out on his own. Our next-door neighbors were having a big cocktail party one time, when Scatter sauntered over and stood in the door screeching "Ooh! Ooh! Ooh!" at the top of his lungs, the way chimps are wont to do. People froze in their tracks, with their mouths hung open, and half-eaten canapes in the hands. A woman screamed and slumped to the floor. "There's a wild ape in the house!" someone yelled, and then all hell broke loose--total pandemonium. Scatter no doubt thought it was hilarious, but it scared those people half to death.

The neighbors had put up with a lot, having eight guys living next to them. But this was the last straw. They came over and said, "Look, you can't have a chimp in Bel Air. He's got to go, and that's final." And so we sent him back to Memphis.

Chimpanzees who've been around people all their lives can't really be confined by themselves, because then they get lonesome, and their personalities change. That's what happened to Scatter, who got violent and unpopular once he was put in a cage at Graceland. One day he bit the maid, and then mysteriously died two days later. We think the maid poisoned him, of course, but another theory is that all that drinking gave him cirrhosis of the liver. I think he died of a broken heart.

When it was time to return to California after our Memphis hiatus in the summer of '62, Elvis bought a Dodge motorhome rather than suffer his fear of flying. The motorhome was convenient, but it was also the scene of one of the scariest moments we ever had.

Elvis had been reading the *Physician's Desk Reference* for some time now, and lately he'd graduated to medical books. He let it slip to an interviewer from *Parade* magazine at one point, saying he read them because he'd thought about becoming a doctor in high school, and that his interest in medicine was still keen. The truth, of course, was that he read them so he could tell how many pills he could take, and in what quantity, to get high and still stay alive. Even so, he made some near-fatal errors.

The October after Elvis bought the motorhome, for example, he and Gene Smith drove it back to Memphis from Hollywood. Gene was wired from all the dope he was taking, plus all the extra that Elvis had given him. In fact, he'd been so wired for three days and two nights on speed that he couldn't sleep.

We were in Arizona, and it was freezing outside. Elvis was driving the bus, and he gave Gene 500 milligrams of Demerol, which is a synthetic opiate. Gene took the little white pill and waited to fall asleep. But forty-five minutes later, when he was still stoked to the skies, Elvis gave him another hit. An hour went by, and Gene was still bouncing off the clouds-- trying to fix stuff on the bus, working on things under Elvis's feet--trying to do everything, he was so out of it.

Finally Elvis told him, "Look, Gene, go back in my bedroom, man, and get some sleep. Those pills will kick in before long." So Gene went back in the bedroom, and after a while, Elvis told Billy to go check on him. In the meantime, Gene had opened the window back there, and a terrific draft had blown in on him. So when Billy tried to wake Gene up and couldn't-- the stuff had finally hit him--he felt Gene's face, and it was just ice cold. Gene's heartbeat had probably slowed down, and his breathing, too. But mostly he was cold from all that cold air coming in on him. Well, Billy just freaked out. It hadn't been that long since he'd found Junior Smith dead in his bed, maybe from an overdose, and he thought it'd happened again.

Billy came running back up to the front of the bus, yelling, "Elvis! Elvis! I think Gene's dead! I shouted in his ear and he didn't move a muscle, and he's cold to the touch!" Elvis pulled over to the side of the road real quick, and he had his seat belt on, and he jumped up so fast the seat belt almost cut his damn legs off.

Of course, we all ran back there, but Gene wasn't dead. He was just cold from the window being open. He wasn't coming around, though--that was true--so we got him out and dragged him along the side of the highway. He was okay. He'd just been up for three days, and he had two big hits of Demerol in him. It scared the shit out of Elvis, though. He said, "Goddamn, I ought to kill your ass!"

By the summer of '62, Elvis was so fed up with the movies he didn't know what to do. It was all girls and sunny climes, the same story line with different characters and different clothes. When Elvis got frustrated, he took more pills. None of us wanted to see that happen, although a couple of us, like Gene and I, were taking them ourselves, just not at the levels Elvis was. We were glad, then, when we started filming "It Happened at the World's Fair," since it looked to be a little bit different, if only on the surface. Location filming was done at the real World's Fair in Seattle, where Elvis was protected by forty off-duty policemen.

Colonel had traveled to Seattle months ahead of time to arrange for everything, including our stay at the New Washington Hotel. As usual, Colonel insisted on a hotel with quarters that could be sealed off from the rest of the building, so he could keep us relatively isolated, with one or two policemen guarding the entrance ways.

I guess that was necessary for security reasons, but with our traffic slowed down, it made for some mighty long nights. When we got bored, we were likely to indulge in one of Elvis's favorite pranks. It started when one of us would call room service. By the time the bell boy got up to the suite with the

The day that pro-football star turned actor Jim Brown came to the set of "It Happened At The World's Fair" to meet Elvis.

(L. to r.): Billy Smith, me, Richard Davis, Jim Brown next to Elvis, Joe Esposito, Marty Lacker, and Jimmy Kingsley.

food, we'd have everything out of the room. There wouldn't be a stick of furniture anywhere. We'd be sitting on the floor.

The bell boy, of course, couldn't believe there wasn't any furniture in the room, and he'd run straight down to the desk. By the time the manager came up, the furniture would all be back in place, and the manager would just sort of back out the door, mumbling some excuse about why he came up. When he left, we'd laugh like hell.

At other times, Elvis would turn that around on us, and the guys would be the object of his fun. Somebody would come to the house and want to see him, and Elvis would say, "Tell him I'm not here. Just make excuses." So we'd go down and say, "Elvis is asleep." Or, "Elvis is gone." Then we'd look around and Elvis would be standing in back of us, and the guy would look at us like we were morons. Not so funny then.

The plot for "It Happened at the World's Fair" was about as silly as the rest of the recent movies--Elvis was a pilot without a plane, hanging out at the World's Fair. There, he fell in love with a nurse (Joan O'Brien) at the first-aid station. He also semi-adopted a little orphaned Chinese girl (Vicky Tiu), to whom he fed an endless stream of junky fair food--if it wasn't on a stick, they didn't eat it.

Gary Lockwood played Elvis's buddy, but the real co-star of this picture was Elvis's outfits, which cost more than $9,000. Sy Devore, the wardrobe man, reported that the clothing broke down to ten suits at $285 each, thirty shirts at $10 a piece, four sports coats at $200 each, two cashmere coats at $225 a piece, fifteen pairs of slacks at $85 each, and fifty-five ties at $7 a throw. Pretty pricey for the times.

Only one decent song came out of this film, "One Broken Heart for Sale," and it was noteworthy only by comparison. Mostly Elvis had to sing fluff such as "Cotton Candy Land" and "Take Me to the Fair." What I remember most about this movie was taking pictures on the set when the guys weren't serving as extras in the crowd scenes. Joe did a little better than the rest of us. He had a bit part as a carnival worker in a scene where a lady wins a doll.

Elvis trivia fans remember that Kurt Russell, the actor

Exterior and inside snapshots of Elvis and co-star Joan O'Brien during filming of "It Happened At The World's Fair."

Three memories from "It Happened At The World's Fair": Horseplay with actor Gary Lockwood (above); Colonel in a bow-tie (left); Gene Smith and me taking it all in (below). Red West, who played a character called "Fred" in the movie, sits behind me.

who later played Elvis in a 1978 television movie, made his film debut here. He's the little kid who kicks Elvis on the shin. But in the end, "It Happened at the World's Fair" was just another movie in what was becoming a numbing series of months before the camera. The reviews said about the same thing.

Far more intriguing things were happening in Elvis's life at the end of 1962, not the least of which was the Stateside arrival of young Priscilla Beaulieu. For more than a year, Elvis had worked on Priscilla's step-father, Captain Joseph Beaulieu, to allow her to come to Memphis for another visit.

Once she arrived, however, Elvis decided he wanted her to stay for good. She went back to Germany as planned, but then Elvis told her father he hoped she'd return to Memphis to live. I doubt if Elvis came right out and said he wanted to marry her when she got a little older, but I imagine that idea was implicit from Captain Beaulieu's point of view.

Elvis argued that she would live with Vernon and Dee in their own home--not at Graceland--and that she would finish her studies at Immaculate Conception High School, a proper Catholic girls' academy. He and Captain Beaulieu got together in person to talk about it when Elvis was making "Fun in Acapulco" in Hollywood, and Captain Beaulieu took a leave of absence, bringing Priscilla with him. After some understandably tense moments, it was agreed that she would probably attract less attention cloistered away at Immaculate Conception than she would at a public school.

Just why Priscilla's father agreed to let his daughter become the concubine of the world's most famous rock 'n' roll singer, I don't know. Maybe Priscilla just lived in a state of perpetual swoon while she was away from Elvis, and her father thought a week or two with him in the States would put an end to her schoolgirl crush. Then again, maybe he was hoping the two would marry, and Priscilla would be financially set for life. The official reason the Beaulieus gave was that they wanted their daughter to attend school in the United States, not Germany, and Elvis was only too kind in helping them realize their dream.

Whatever the real reason, I was fairly dumbfounded by the bizarre aspects of this arrangement (*Vanity Fair* magazine would eventually call Priscilla "the original rock 'n' roll Lolita"), and I was also a little concerned about Elvis's growing fascination with young women just passed puberty.

I also wondered if Elvis intended to be faithful to Priscilla, since he'd never once been monogamous in the years I'd been with the entourage. He always had several women on the string at any one time, and that included Anita Wood, who tended to fade in and out of the picture.

Back in 1955, Elvis had left his sweetheart, Dixie Locke, in Memphis while he went on the road playing dates and getting friendly with the young girls who had begun to follow him throughout the South. He expected Dixie to wait patiently for him--no matter what kind of behavior he might have engaged in--and so he was flattened when he came home and learned that she was engaged to someone else. Elvis had never learned his lesson. Then again, maybe it was in the genes. Elvis's paternal great-grandmother, the never-married Rosella Presley, had ten children and never bothered to tell them who their father, or fathers, were. She herself was the daughter of Dunnan Presley, who kept four wives simultaneously.

Captain Beaulieu would find reason to fly to San Diego frequently through the years, doubtless to keep an eye on his step-daughter and her unlikely squire. That first Christmas, Elvis held a party at Graceland and introduced Priscilla to about thirty of his friends and business associates. Earlier, he'd given her a toy poodle named Honey. Captain Beaulieu was probably both relieved and chagrined to hear that Elvis also slipped a diamond ring on Priscilla's finger. But Priscilla also slipped a little something of her own to Elvis that Christmas: The demand that Anita Wood be cut out of his life forever.

Chapter 12

Wheeling And Dealing
"Viva Las Vegas" And The $5 Million Ashtray

As the years went by, Priscilla and I developed what I felt was a fairly close relationship. I did a lot of driving for her, particularly when we were in California, and I was only too glad to do it. Elvis liked for only one or two of the guys to drive, because he didn't trust just anybody. So I was the one who drove Priscilla to San Diego to see her father. I'd usually drop her off, and either stay there in town or go across the Mexican border to Tijuana and fool around. Then, when Priscilla was ready to go back to L.A., she'd call me, and I'd pick her up and off we'd go.

We talked a lot. I eventually came to know her whole family--her father and mother, her sister and brothers. We spent a lot of time together. Some of the guys thought she was cold and calculating, especially as the years went by and she began to resent the time Elvis spent with the guys. I thought she was an extremely nice person. A beautiful person. A little *young,* maybe, but a sweetheart.

When I think back on it, Priscilla must have lived hard that first year. She had to wear those little Catholic school uniforms, for instance. Here we all were, living in Hollywood, doing movies, going to Vegas, and she was getting up every day going to high school in her uniform! She'd come home from school in the afternoon, and when she'd get to the Graceland gate, she'd call the house to find out where we were. If we were in the backyard, she'd come in the front door. If we were in the front of the house, she'd come in the back door. She never wanted us to see her in her uniform.

Elvis tried to teach her how to dress when she was out of the Catholic garb, and how to use make-up. Some people think he tried to make her look as much like Gladys as possible. I don't know. I think that's just what he knew, so it was natural for him to do that. I think he had her dye her brown hair black so it would make her look more like *him*. He dyed his own hair because he thought people looked sexier with dark hair than light. He used to say, "Valentino had black hair, and the women loved him."

I thought Priscilla was pretty smart for her age. There were certain things she didn't know, of course, but she was only fourteen or fifteen years old, and heck, she'd been living in a foreign country. She'd go to the hairdresser, for example, and leave a fifty cent tip. Now, fifty cents was worth a lot more then than it is today, and it might sound like a pretty nice tip for a fifteen-year-old schoolgirl. But it was still an inadequate tip for Elvis's girlfriend, and somebody had to tell her that. Priscilla didn't take it too well--she was close with a dollar, having grown up in a service atmosphere with a strict step-father.

Of course, Priscilla never did stay at Vernon and Dee's house. She took up residency at Graceland that very first day, one of the best-kept secrets of Elvis's career at the time. But Elvis's grandmother Minnie Mae was there, and they'd gotten close in Germany.

Minnie Mae was a trip. When she wasn't cooking Elvis's favorite foods, she was playing rollicking gospel music on an organ Elvis gave her. Tall as a beanstalk and just as thin, she was angular and hard as the frozen ground of winter. But she was also cool. She wore sunglasses day and night, and decorated her room with the presents that Elvis's fans mailed in by the truckload. Like Gladys, she dipped snuff with a vengeance.

In January 1963, Elvis and the group--he'd now started referring to us as the Memphis Mafia to the press, jokingly calling us his "disciples," or "The Twelve" in private--loaded up the motorhome and headed back to Hollywood to begin work on "Fun in Acapulco." Although the film was set in Mexico, all of Elvis's scenes were filmed at Hal Wallis's Paramount Studios. A second camera crew traveled to Acapulco for background and "color" shots. That spiffed up the look of the movie, and a good thing it was. Even Elvis's hard-core fans were getting tired of the manufactured, low-budget look of his films.

"Fun in Acapulco" teamed Elvis with Swiss born sex-queen Ursula Andress, who played a hotel social director to Elvis's singing trapeze artist--a trapeze artist who just happened to have a fear of heights. The plots of the movies were getting more and more absurd--Elvis also had a romantic interest in a lady bullfighter! And the songs were equally moronic: "There's No Room to Rhumba in a Sports Car," for example.

One irony with the plot, however, is that Elvis's manager is a nine-year-old Mexican boy who gets him a job singing at the hotel, for which he demands 50 percent of his income. A couple of years later, Colonel Parker would do exactly the same thing.

"Fun in Acapulco" was Ursula's second picture released in America--she'd done the James Bond movie "Dr. No" the year before--although she'd been in movies since 1954, mainly in Italy. There was a lot of speculation that she and Elvis were having an affair, but Ursula was married to John Derek, the actor-turned-producer-director, and Elvis didn't fool around with married women. He was intrigued with her, though, because she had been romantically linked with James Dean for a time.

One of Elvis's secretaries, Becky Yancy, said that Ursula used to call him at Graceland, but I think that she and Elvis were truly just good friends. For one thing, she wasn't his type--neither dark-haired nor petite. When we came back from Hollywood and somebody brought up her name, Elvis blushed a little and said something about how big her shoulders were. "I was embarrassed to take my damn shirt off next to her," he said, laughing. And it sounded like the truth.

On the other hand, I fell madly in love with Ursula the minute I met her. I'd heard a lot about her, and I'd seen "Dr. No," and so we got along well. We sat and talked a lot on the set, and one day she gave me a big bunch of her publicity pictures. They were pretty revealing. I said, "Ursula, who takes these pictures?" She said, "My husband, John, does." Turns out that he'd photographed her for *Playboy*.

I just couldn't get over them, and I asked her, half-kiddingly, "Does he need people to help him take 'em? Hold reflectors or anything?" And she said, "Yes, all the time." I said, "Well, next time he needs any help, be sure to call me."

I thought that was it, and then one morning about eight o'clock the phone rang. I'd stayed up shooting pool until six, and I was pretty groggy when the maid came in. "It's Ursula Andress on the telephone," she said. Ursula was sunny and energetic. "Get over here!" she purred. "We take pictures at eight-thirty!" Well, there was hardly even time to get dressed. But with breakneck speed, I was over at Ursula's house, a big beautiful home with waterfalls back in the hills. John began telling me what was going to happen, what equipment he was going to use and how I could help. But, of course, all the time I was thinking, "I wonder if she's going to be in the nude or in a bikini?" I was revved.

About thirty seconds later, Ursula walked out in a pair of blue jeans and a football jersey, eating an ice cream cone. That was the picture. I said, "Ursula, don't ever call me again to take pictures." She sent up a raucous howl. Ursula was super, though. I was crazy about her.

When we got back to Memphis, Elvis spent a lot of time riding his motorcycle with Priscilla and getting back into his old habits, renting the fairgrounds and the movie theater. We watched "Lawrence of Arabia" and "To Kill a Mockingbird" until we knew every line of dialogue. Usually his taste fell to things like the campy "Village of the Damned"--one of his all-time favorites--but since he was stymied doing all these formula pictures, he also liked to watch good acting and films with meaty stories.

I felt sorry for the guy. He seemed increasingly tense--pent-up--and he often complained of needing a place to go to be alone with his thoughts. That's when Marty Lacker arranged for his brother-in-law, Bernie Granadier, and Marty's sister, Anne, to design the Meditation Garden there at Graceland. It would end up being one of the true pleasures of his life.

But as bad as I felt for Elvis, my heart also went out to Priscilla. Elvis continued with his usual nightly drug ritual--three or four Placidyls, Seconals or Tuinals. And he gave

Priscilla uppers and downers, too, when he thought she needed "medication" to be able to keep up with both his schedule and her school work. She had a rough time of it, going to school, being Elvis's companion, and learning to grow up all at the same time. When she graduated, he threw a big party for her, and gave her a new red Corvair--her first car. Soon after, Priscilla enrolled in the Patricia Stevens Finishing School in Memphis, where she learned to model.

As memory serves me, Priscilla modeled dresses at lunch-time at a local restaurant a time or two, using a fictitious name. And she studied ballet at the Jo Haynes School of Dancing, again using a fake name at the recitals. Elvis was proud of her. But I think he patronized her to some degree, and found her appearances a little amusing, as if it were quaint that she would have the chutzpah to perform when she "belonged" to the world's greatest entertainer. I thought she was right to seek out other interests and to assert herself as somebody other than Elvis Presley's girlfriend.

But as it turned out, Elvis had another girlfriend waiting in the wings, although nobody knew it yet.

In 1963, Colonel Parker struck a deal with Metro-Goldwyn-Mayer that made his client the highest-paid actor in Hollywood. Colonel told the *New York Times* that Elvis received a million dollars for each film, plus 50 percent of the profits. The contract demanded a picture a year for five years. But alas, the MGM bosses shared Colonel's view that quality was hardly of utmost importance in the Presley vehicles. And so Elvis was doomed to at least five more hokey, low-budget formula pictures in which he essentially recited the same dialogue in different locales. An MGM employee was quoted as saying, "They could be numbered [instead of titled] and still sell."

Elvis didn't talk much about business to us. That was private. But sometimes he'd let us know something was about to go down, and the MGM deal was one of those events.

We were all still asleep at ten o'clock one morning when Colonel called Elvis and said, "Meet me at MGM Studios in thirty minutes. It's important that you be there. I wouldn't call you if it weren't."

A mid-sixties birthday party for Colonel. The cake reads "Happy Birthday To The Colonel From His Pals At MGM." (L. to r.): Jimmy Kingsley, Richard Davis, actor Nick Adams (sporting a beard), Colonel's wife, Marie, Billy Smith in front of Colonel, Joe Esposito to Elvis's left, and me to Marty Lacker's right.

So we all trotted over to MGM, were Colonel was waiting. Elvis went in with him, and about an hour later, he came out carrying a glass ashtray, laughing his head off. We were sitting in the car, stone-faced with boredom. Somebody asked, "What's goin' on, man?"

Elvis said, "Man, you wouldn't believe this. Colonel just finalized the biggest deal we've ever signed in California. But he saw this ashtray on the table, and he said he wouldn't sign the contract unless the ashtray went in with the deal."

That was Colonel. Why did he do such things? Because he was a con artist to a certain degree, yes. But you have to be to get ahead in California. I think he pulled the ashtray caper because he liked to fool with people's heads. It was a psychological advantage, a way to put them slightly off kilter. In other words, Colonel snookered MGM on some point or another, and he used the ashtray to divert their attention and help him work his wily ways.

Colonel called such ploys "snowing" his opponent. He was so proud of being a "Snowman," in fact, that he had a huge cardboard snowman propped up next to the wall in his office. But he took it a step farther when he founded the "Snowmen's League of America," inspired perhaps by Hal Wallis's calling Colonel "America's Number One Snow Man." Colonel had phony membership cards printed up that said admission to the league was limited to those "skilled in evasiveness and ineptitude." And a code which bound the members stressed "the snowman's willingness to see the other man's problems and show the greatest understanding without financial involvement." If he took a shine to you, he made you an official member.

He also had certificates printed on authentic green stock paper. I still have mine. It reads: "Snowmen's League of America" across the top, and then there are lines to type in someone's name over either "Temporary Member" or "Lifetime Member--Maybe?" Down below, in big letters, it reads: "Chief Potentate Col. Tom Parker," with, "This membership can be cancelled at any time by any potentate snower," in smaller letters. The final line says, "Special Chief Executive Snower

Colonel Tom Parker, Chief Potentate of the Snowmen's League of America, and my membership certificate (about a third of its actual size).

Bob Hope Citation." The whole thing is set off by a drawing of a snowman waving his arm and smoking a big cigar--a snowman who looks a lot like Colonel Parker.

Colonel loved it. In retrospect, I understand his hidden glee: The illegal alien not only makes millions in his adopted country, but rubs its nose in it at the same time.

The first picture in the MGM deal was "Viva Las Vegas," which co-starred Ann-Margret, often talked about as "a female Elvis Presley." Born in Sweden and reared in suburban Chicago, Ann-Margret Olson had made only two pictures, "State Fair" and "Bye, Bye, Birdie." Elvis himself had been asked to sing two songs in "Bye, Bye, Birdie," a request Colonel had refused. However that would have affected Elvis's career, "Bye, Bye, Birdie" made Ann-Margret a star, and now she was hot as a firecracker. Talented as both a singer and dancer, she had worked as part of comic George Burns' act in Vegas, and she'd appeared on television, mixing a spread-to-the-cheek-bones sensuality with the reserve of a Midwest Homecoming Queen. She was also sultry and flirtatious on the screen--a perfect Hollywood sex kitten. Men would have died for her.

"Viva Las Vegas" was one of Elvis's best post-army pictures, in large part because of the real chemistry--and passion --between its stars. On screen, Elvis always knew how to look at a woman with a sweet promise of adventure, but "Viva Las Vegas" was something else again. In it, he plays a character named Lucky Jackson, a race car driver who falls in love with a hotel swimming instructor, Rusty Martin (Ann-Margret). The plot takes an improbable turn, of course--Lucky's money for a motor for an all-important race gets sucked down the drain of the swimming pool, leaving Lucky no other choice but to go to work as a waiter and vie against Rusty in the employees' talent contest. In the end, he wins the contest, the race *and* Ann-Margret, who, unlike most of the leading ladies in Elvis's other pictures, seems like a real flesh-and-blood woman instead of a cardboard cut-out.

That July, we arrived in Las Vegas to start filming locations for the movie. Colonel arranged for Elvis to occupy the Presidential suite at the Sahara Hotel for two weeks, which meant we took the entire top floor.

A lot of people in Vegas were into drugs, and since we were dating girls from the different shows who also did drugs, we indulged ourselves more than we'd planned to while we were there. Vegas is a pretty loose town, and one thing just led to another. One day we walked across the street from the Sahara to a pharmacy in a little shopping center. The guys started looking around, buying tooth paste and other usual toiletries, when the next thing we knew, Elvis was behind the prescription counter. He'd charmed the pants off the pharmacist, who gave him all kinds of stuff. It was almost as if the pharmacist said, "Look at this. Do you know about these?" showing him all kinds of new pills.

Las Vegas was the town where Elvis bombed in 1956, and he'd never forgotten it. He had an ambivalent attitude toward it. One minute he was soured on it, and the other he wanted to live it up and enjoy it for all it was worth.

One day we were downstairs at the dice table in the Sahara, when we noticed a fellow standing next to us. He was a polished guy, no bum. Elvis started talking to him, and eventually he said to Elvis, "That's a beautiful watch you're wearing." Elvis said, "Thanks. Yours is sharp, too." The man thanked him, and then Elvis said, "Would you like to trade?" The guy said, "Are you serious?" Elvis said, "Yeah," and they both unstrapped their timepiece and handed it over.

We went out for the rest of the night and didn't think anymore about it. The next morning, the man tried to get Elvis on the phone. Well, nobody could get through to Elvis-- not even his father--so the call came to me.

"Listen, I'm the man who traded watches with Mr. Presley last night."

"Yeah, I remember you."

"Well, I don't think Mr. Presley realized that the watch he traded me was an award from RCA Victor. It says so on the back." I told him I'd tell Elvis when he woke up, and I'd call him back.

About four or five o'clock, Elvis woke up and I told him what the guy had said.

"Tell him to forget it," Elvis said. "A trade is a trade. Find out what it said on the back of the watch, and then tomorrow take my other watch out and have the same thing engraved on it."

He knew that the watch meant a lot more to that guy than it did to him. But then Elvis just naturally enjoyed doing things for people, because he was always more of a giver than a taker. He felt that he'd been poor all his life, and now that he was a superstar, he could afford to make somebody happy, especially if all it took was trading watches.

And yet Elvis could be incredibly thoughtless, too. For example, as much as nobody really wanted to admit it, since Priscilla was sitting home in Memphis reading movie magazines, it was clear that Elvis was about to begin an affair with Ann-Margret. At first, before we even got to Las Vegas, we kind of ignored it. George Klein had come out to see us in California, and we were sitting around in the Perugia Way house when Elvis told us he was getting ready to start "Viva Las Vegas" with Ann-Margret as his co-star. Then he said, "I've got a date with her tomorrow night. I'm going to pick her up at eight o'clock."

We sort of looked at each other. "Wonderful," we said. "Who do you want to go with you?" He said, "Nobody. And when I get back to the house, I don't want eight guys hanging around, either."

And so it began. Once we got over to Nevada, they went motorcycle riding all the time. Hondas were big then, and Ann-Margret was an accomplished rider. They rode in the film, too.

Elvis was really smitten with her, and he wanted to treat her to the best of everything. One night we went to the New Frontier to hear one of Elvis's favorite rhythm-and-blues and gospel singers, Clara Ward. The guy who ran the New Frontier was from Memphis. His name, as I recall, was Smith, and he kept telling Elvis, "Please come stay at my hotel. Not only will you get free rooms, but free laundry, free food--just name it." So we went there that one night, and the waitress asked

Ann-Margret, who was twenty-three years old, for some identification.

That embarrassed Elvis, and as we walked out, Mr. Smith came up to Elvis and said, "Elvis! How you doin'?" Elvis said, "Let me tell you something, Mr. Smith. If I ever come back in this goddamn hotel again, you tell the waitress never to ask anybody I'm with for any fucking I.D.!" He never stopped walking while he said it, and the poor guy had to practically run to keep up with him, trying to make things right again. We knew Elvis was mad enough to burst into flame to use language like that.

Elvis got steamed again a short-time later when he discovered that one of the assistant directors was equally infatuated with Ann-Margret, and virtually lived for seeing her face on screen. So much so that he directed the cameramen to shoot an inordinate number of close-ups of her over Elvis's shoulders, virtually cutting Elvis out of a lot of the action. Elvis fumed about it and finally went to Colonel, who turned things around in a hurry.

In late July, we went to Hollywood to shoot the interiors at the MGM Studios in Culver City. Elvis, Ann-Margret, Billy Smith and I rode together in Elvis's Rolls-Royce. I was behind the wheel, but after awhile, Elvis said, "Here, let me drive." Billy and I moved to the back. It was cold as a hooker's heart that night on the desert, and I asked Elvis to turn on the heat.

The Rolls, which had broken down once or twice at the most inconvenient times--such as when Elvis was waiting with someone he wanted to impress--didn't have the best heating and air-conditioning system. When it was moderately warm in the back, it was burning up in the front. Elvis was hot-natured anyway, so he just couldn't stand that much heat. Meanwhile, I was shivering away back there, and again I asked, "Hey, man, can't you do something about this? We've got frost on the windowpanes here!"

"Naw, Alan, it's too damn hot up here!"

Well, Ann-Margret had this beautiful white fur coat. Suddenly she said, "Here, Alan, you take my coat and cover up and get warm." Billy and I crawled under it, and man, it was

Elvis with actor Cesare Danova in a scene from "Viva Las Vegas." I also
made it into the scene--that's me at the far right in the western shirt.

heaven. It had perfume on it like I'd never smelled in my life. Just unbelievably good. Better than Georgio. Of course, Billy and I were from Memphis, Tennessee, and we didn't know anything about perfume--only if it smelled good or not.

By the time we arrived in Los Angeles, we were positively reeking with it. The next day, I went up to Ann-Margret and said, "You've gotta tell me the name of that perfume. I might want to buy some for some little girl sometime."

Ann-Margret probably knew I really just wanted some of that perfume to remind me of her, and I thought she was playing me along. She said, "No way I can tell you the name of that perfume. Uh-uh. Nope."

This went on for months. I'd ask her every time I saw her, which was frequently, because she spent a lot of nights at the house. Still, she refused. Finally, she admitted that the reason she didn't tell me was that she really didn't know--that it was probably a combination of several perfumes that lingered in the coat. But she was always great to me, and I loved her. I called her "Rusty Ammo," a take-off on the name of her character in "Viva Las Vegas."

By now, Elvis and Ann-Margret's relationship was seriously entangled. For a while, he managed to keep it from Priscilla. But then in early August, one of the Memphis papers ran a story with the headline, "It looks like Romance for Elvis and Ann-Margret." And in a few weeks, Ann-Margret herself was telling reporters that they were engaged.

Just what Elvis told Priscilla, I don't know. He probably said it was just publicity for the movie, and nothing else. In truth, he'd bought Ann-Margret a round bed to enhance their lovemaking, and he talked about her all the time. In November, the paper ran a follow-up story, "Elvis Wins Love of Ann-Margret."

Such stories are often fabricated tales to spark the sale of movie tickets, but I believe Ann-Margret really did care a lot for Elvis. And I think she truly wanted to marry him, even though she knew full well about Priscilla, and used the code names "Scoobie" and "Bunny" when she telephoned him at Graceland. (The guys joked that "Thumper" would be more appropriate.) I don't know exactly how he managed to do it, but Elvis enjoyed the company of a gorgeous redhead in California and a smoldering brunette in Memphis. How many of us are as lucky as that?

Chapter 13

"What A Friend We Have In Elvis"

Despite the fun he'd had on "Viva Las Vegas," Elvis still moaned that his film career was racing to hell on rollerskates. He was right: His second picture under the MGM contract was "Kissin' Cousins," an eighteen-day shoot with a budget of only $800,000, produced by Sam Katzman, "King of the Quickies," who'd also done "Rock Around the Clock" in 1956.

The novelty of the picture--which went into release before "Viva Las Vegas"--was that Elvis would play dual roles, one a blond mountaineer from a moonshining family (Jodie Tatum), and the other a black-haired air force officer (Josh Morgan). Elvis the airman had to talk his country cousin--the blond Elvis--into allowing a nuclear missile silo to be constructed near the Tatums' moonshine still. Pamela Austin and Yvonne Craig got the top female billing, but among the group of mountain girls who try to capture the soldiers was Maureen Reagan, Ronald Reagan's eldest daughter. On its release, *Variety* would report that "Kissin' Cousins" was "a pretty dreary effort...Elvis needs and merits more substantial material than this."

In October of '63, Elvis went to Nashville to record the movie's soundtrack, since the producer thought the songs, with such titles as "Barefoot Ballad," "Smokey Mountain Boy," and "There's Gold in the Mountains," would sound more authentic coming out of the country music capital instead of California.

Elvis was offended by phony material such as this, but he enjoyed the change of pace of recording in Nashville and, in January 1964, he went back to cut a couple of tunes apart from the soundtrack. One was "Memphis," the Chuck Berry tune which had also been an instrumental hit for Lonnie Mack. Elvis loved the song, and felt it was well-suited to his voice. More to the point, he was desperate to record something decent that would put him at the top of the charts again.

Just how difficult that would be became apparent when a new British group named the Beatles soared to the number one position in late January with "I Want to Hold Your Hand," repeating the triumph a week later with "She Loves You."

Beatlemania was in full bloom, and Elvis was scared. Stuck in a contract of making one dreadful movie after another, he hadn't set foot on a live stage in so long he could barely remember the last time. His records occasionally broke into the Top 10--"Bossa Nova Baby," the latest, climbed to number eight--but he knew he was really just hanging on. When the Fab Four appeared on the "Ed Sullivan Show" in February, Colonel Parker sent a congratulatory telegram in Elvis's name, which Sullivan read aloud on the show. The Memphis Mafia, however, knew better than to mention the Beatles in Elvis's presence.

For now, there was no real time for Elvis to work on improving his music. In March, he began production on his sixteenth film, "Roustabout" for Paramount. This time, he played a down-on-his-luck singer who brings in the customers at a fortune-teller's teahouse. Tired of such unscrupulous ploys, Elvis leaves to become a carney, his singing talents working wonders to keep Barbara Stanwyck's midway alive in the midst of a takeover by a larger outfit. "Roustabout" wasn't a terrible film, but it was far from distinguished. There were really only two memorable things about it--Elvis's performance of "Little Egypt," which, like "Girls, Girls, Girls," was originally recorded by the Coasters, and Raquel Welch's walk-on, her first appearance in a movie.

I'm not sure if "Roustabout" was the movie we were working on, but it was around this time that Ed Hookstratten came into our lives. One of the most powerful attorneys in Los Angeles, Hookstratten represented half of everybody who was anybody, and knew the other half personally.

Elvis didn't have a lawyer in California, and didn't think he needed one until the day Richard Davis rounded a corner in Bel Air and steered Elvis's station wagon smack into tragedy. Richard had been on the movie set when Elvis decided he needed a couple of pieces of wardrobe from home. Richard went to get them, and on the way back to the studio, he turned the corner at the exact moment a Japanese gardener, oblivious to traffic, backed out into the street. Richard ran right over him. The gardener was dead.

Colonel knew that Elvis needed somebody sharp to represent him, since it would be a fine line whether Richard acted on his own going back to the house and fetching the wardrobe, or whether he was acting on Elvis's command. Nobody wanted to cheat the gardener's family out of a rightful settlement, but Colonel knew that whether Richard was running an errand or simply doing a favor would be an important distinction in court.

Enter E. Gregory Hookstratten, otherwise known as Ed. Colonel put him on retainer, beginning an association that would last virtually until Elvis's death, since it would be Hookstratten who would handle Elvis's divorce, and Hookstratten whose name was bandied about whenever the notion came up to replace Colonel as Elvis's manager.

I don't recall how the lawsuit turned out, but my recollection is that the two parties settled out of court. Mainly I remember what a number the accident did on Richard, and how he wouldn't drive for a long time. I remember, too, that Elvis insisted we sell the car.

After that, Ed started coming by the house occasionally. I liked him. He was a flamboyant character, a guy given to country clubs and fraternizing with the jet set--I especially recall seeing him in golf get-ups, for example, rather than a suit and tie. If you looked through a book of pictures of lawyers, you'd stop at his photo and say, "This is a typical Los Angeles attorney." But he was also a hell of a nice guy who fit in really well with everybody because he was cool. And once he found out my uncle was Abe Fortas, we really hit it off. Often when he came by the house, he'd come back into my room to talk. I looked forward to his visits.

Our old pal Johnny Rivers was still coming over to the house, too. Elvis had really taken a shine to Johnny, and one particular night, he played him a test pressing of "Memphis," which he'd cut in Nashville a couple of months before. Elvis was particularly proud of his rendition, and he thought it might open some doors to letting him cut the kind of muscular material that made him famous.

It was always a period of months between the recording sessions and the release of the records, but Elvis never dreamed somebody would steal his song before the darn thing ever came out. Johnny told him he loved it--thought it was a great groove. And then, the next thing you knew, Johnny cut it himself, with the same arrangement. "Memphis" was Johnny's first hit, going all the way to number two, and it made him a star. Elvis wouldn't release his own version for a long time, then, because he didn't want to look as if he were copying Johnny. After that, Johnny was on Elvis's shit list, forever barred from coming to any of Elvis's homes.

Johnny's record was released just as were starting to film "Girl Happy" for MGM, and Elvis, who was still a little reticent in the company of show business folks, got especially leery of them around this time. Frankly, I think he was just afraid of being upstaged.

We were over at MGM one day when the guys and I saw Steve McQueen working out. Elvis loved Steve McQueen. He'd seen "The Great Escape" something like twenty times. He knew all the dialogue, everything. Elvis's dressing room was on one side of the street, and the gymnasium was right above it on the other side of the street, so that if you came out of Elvis's dressing room, you could see the windows of the gym. McQueen would work out every morning when Elvis was in make-up, and the guys and I would talk to him through the window.

One day McQueen said, "You know, I'd love to meet Elvis." And I said, "Well, he'll be coming out in about fifteen minutes. I'll introduce you." So a few minutes later, McQueen was hanging out of the window, waiting to meet Elvis. I went into the dressing room, where Elvis was reading his script.

"Guess what, Elvis," I said. "I've been talking to Steve McQueen, and God, he really wants to meet you! He's waiting at the window."

"Oh, yeah?" Elvis said, nonchalantly. "Yeah," I said. "When

we walk out, I'll say, 'Steve McQueen, meet Elvis Presley,' and you can say hello to him."

Elvis just sat there reading his script, acting as if I were talking about the weather. When the time came to leave, Elvis walked out of the dressing room and calmly got into the Rolls-Royce, never once taking his eyes off his script. "Elvis!" I yelled. "Elvis!" He never looked up.

Of course, you couldn't tell Elvis anything, and he especially wouldn't do something just because you told him he should. It was like, "Hey, I'm the boss, and nobody's gonna tell me I've got to do it." You had to use psychology on him. Like the time all the guys wanted to go see James Brown at a club in Los Angeles. Elvis had always been a fan of James Brown, and we'd heard that he was leaving to go to Europe, and they were giving him a going-away party at this little place in Hollywood.

Well, one of the guys got excited, and made the mistake of saying to Elvis, "Hey, let's go to this James Brown party! Everybody's going!" Elvis said, "Nope. To hell with James Brown. I'm not going."

Elvis didn't have anything against James Brown--he respected him. We'd been to a bunch of his shows in Memphis and other places. But we should have said, "James Brown is playing tonight, Elvis, but hell, you wouldn't want to see him." Then he would have said, "Yeah, I would, too! I'd love to go down and see him. Let's go." That's the way you had to do him.

Well, I sure as heck wanted to see James Brown, and I wasn't going to let Elvis ruin it for me. I got a couple of the guys together--I think it was Sonny, and Richard, and Jimmy Kingsley, who was a movie stunt man who'd started hanging out with us--and we went. The place was really packed with stars. Even the Rolling Stones were there.

After the show, we went back to James's dressing room. I had on a watch that Elvis had given me, a watch that he gave away to basically everybody. It had a Jewish star on it, and as it turned, it would become a cross, and then turn back again. It wasn't expensive--the kind of thing you order a hundred at a time and get 'em for about fifty bucks a piece--but it was made

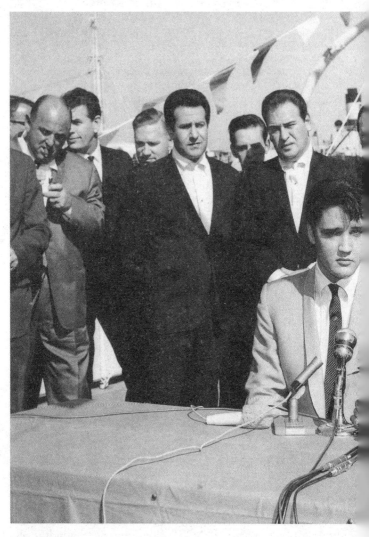

February 13, 1964. Elvis finally managed to donate FDR's presidential yacht, the "Potomac," which he'd paid $55,000 for a couple of weeks before. He first offered it to the March of Dimes--he'd wanted to donate it as a national shrine (FDR suffered from polio)--but the charity felt it couldn't afford to maintain it. Finally, Danny Thomas accepted it on behalf of St. Jude's Hospital of Memphis in a ceremony aboard the yacht.

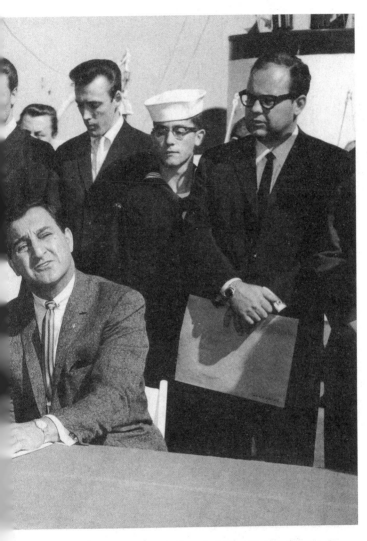

At the left, Colonel lights a cigar. Directly behind Elvis and Danny Thomas are Joe Esposito, Billy Smith, me, Marty Lacker, Jimmy Kingsley, and Richard Davis.

by a jeweler and it looked sharp.

James took one look at it and said, "Godalmighty, that watch is really sharp!" I said, "Elvis had them made up. I'm sure he'd want you to have one." And I took my watch off my wrist and gave it to him. One thing led to another, and we ended up staying up all night and talking to James. It got to be five, and then six o'clock, and finally, I said, "Man, I've gotta leave. I've gotta pick Elvis up at seven-thirty and take him to the studio."

I was driving home when it hit me: "What am I going to tell Elvis when he asks where my watch is?" It would be just like him to say, "What time is it, Alan?" Then I'd say, "I don't know. I don't have my watch." And he'd demand to know where it was, and the stuff would hit the fan. Then again, maybe he'd remember trading his RCA watch with the stranger in Vegas, and he'd understand how these things happened.

Maybe not.

I took Elvis to the studio, and then I went up to Joe and told him what happened. I said, "Give me another watch, man." Because it wasn't like we had only ten of them--we had boxes of them. Joe said, "Oh, I don't know, Alan," just to see me squirm a little. Finally, he gave me one, but I ended up telling Elvis, anyway. I was sweating bullets when I told him, but he just said, "No problem, Alan." That was the thing with Elvis. You never knew what his reaction would be.

About a month later, Jackie Wilson played the same club. Elvis told me, "We're goin' to see Jackie Wilson. Make sure you're at the house at 7:00 p.m." I said, "Uh-uh. You wouldn't go to see James Brown, so I'm not goin' to see Jackie Wilson." And I didn't. He and Priscilla and a whole bunch of them went without me.

Such behavior on my part was grounds for dismissal, and I knew it. But heck, we got fired all the time. Lamar says Elvis fired him a hundred times, and he quit a hundred-fifty times. Joe got fired two or three times, once on "Follow that Dream," when he and Colonel Parker teamed up to do in Ray Sitton, a three-hundred-pound member of the entourage we called "Chief." We'd all started a big campaign to force Elvis to let Ray go, but it was Joe who really put it to Elvis, and things backfired on him. Joe was hired back, of course. But Ray also stayed.

Part of the reason Elvis was so mercurial was that all the drugs made him moody, and the only people he could take his moods out on were his friends or employees. Sometimes the swings came without warning. That's one reason we often called him "Crazy," instead of Elvis.

One night in Hollywood--I forget the reason--he came in and said, "Every one of you, get out! I don't want to see any of you!" Well, guys started packing. I said, "I'm not leaving." And Elvis said, "What do you mean, you're not leaving?"

"I'm not leaving. I'm staying until somebody else comes. We're not all going to leave you by yourself."

"Well, I don't want to see you."

"Fine," I said. "I'll be in my bedroom."

A couple of the guys left. Even Billy Smith went to the airport. Then about two in the morning, Elvis said, "Where's Billy?" I said, "Well, you fired him. He's at the airport ready to get on a plane." He said, "Call and have that airplane stopped and get him off!" I said, "Oh, you're not firing us now, huh?" He said, "Naw, forget about it."

The irony of Elvis's life at the time was the dichotomy of the sublimely carefree existence he lived on the screen, and the pent-up frustration that marked his private life. He was particularly unhappy around the time he made "Girl Happy" in 1964, something we hoped the change of locale--to Fort Lauderdale, Florida--would help. We hadn't been back to Memphis in eight months, and Elvis was antsy and exhausted. He was also tired of eating one meal a day and depriving himself of his favorite food--bacon, hamburgers, steaks--to keep his weight down for the pictures. Colonel was already screaming that he was too fat and the studios would surely drop him.

From an artistic point of view, "Girl Happy" was one of Elvis's poorest offerings, little more than an excuse to pour curvaceous young women into bikinis. The plot was ridiculous --it had to do with underworld gangsters and Elvis hiring out as the chaperone of a crime boss's daughter. And, as usual,

Elvis fumed about the songs--tripe like "Do the Clam" and "Fort Lauderdale Chamber of Commerce." We were glad the shooting lasted only ten days.

The one good thing about the picture was our relationship with Shelley Fabares, who would go on to make two more movies with Elvis, "Spinout" and "Clambake." Elvis would eventually tell the press that she was his favorite co-star. The truth was he had the hots for her. Shelley didn't want to hear about it--she was going with Lou Adler, who eventually became a big record producer for the Mamas and the Papas. Elvis did everything to get her to come around to his way of thinking, but when she didn't, he consoled himself with Mary Ann Mobley, the Miss America--and future wife of talk show host Gary Collins--who was also in the picture.

When we returned to Memphis after the picture wrapped in late summer 1964, Elvis became reacquainted with a guy named Jerry Schilling during a game of touch football. They'd first met in 1954 at the Dave Wells Community Center, or Guthrie Park. Elvis liked Jerry--he was an all-American Catholic boy who'd won a football scholarship to Arkansas State University --and soon Elvis asked him to join the group. Jerry shared Elvis's growing enthusiasm for martial arts, and Elvis nicknamed him "The Cougar." The Mafia also gained another member in 1964, Mike Keaton, who stayed with us only a short time.

But one of the most controversial members of the entourage had entered the picture several months before. In April 1964, Larry Geller became Elvis's official hairdresser. Sal Orfice had taken care of Elvis's hair for quite a while. That included dying it black, or at least taking it many shades darker than Elvis's natural dirty-blond.

Elvis was a little embarrassed, or at least self-conscious, about the fact that he colored his hair, and so he very seldom talked about it. And nobody in the group ever let on they knew what was happening, just the way they never said anything about his capped teeth or the lifts he wore in his shoes to make him seem six feet tall, instead of his actual 5'11". Every so often, Sal would come to the house, and they'd quietly go to

Elvis's room and do his hair. We'd just pretend we thought he was getting a haircut.

Larry Geller worked at Jay Sebring's Beverly Hills Salon, where he cut Johnny Rivers' hair. One day, Elvis just decided he wanted Larry, and had one of us telephone to see if he'd come out to Bel Air and style for Elvis. The first time he came out, Elvis asked him to become his personal hairdresser.

Of course, Larry ended up being much more to Elvis, becoming, in effect, his primary spiritual adviser. It was Larry who got him into a lot of the occult stuff, the parapsychology, the supernatural, the Eastern religions, reincarnation, and the mystical fascinations. Elvis had a propensity toward hocus-pocus anyway, so he was hardly a reluctant student. He'd sit and listen for days or weeks to anybody who held his interest on the subject, or who could teach him something about a facet he already loved.

Larry got him in deeper than a lot of us liked, though. Elvis called him his "guru." Soon he started building a collection of occult books, many of which Larry got for him, and he read all the time, making us cart all these heavy cases of books with us wherever we went. In a matter of weeks, Elvis began referring to himself as a "divine messenger," occasionally breaking into a rendition of "What a Friend We Have in Elvis."

We never really knew whether he was kidding or not. But clearly he was fascinated with the trappings and the drugs associated with the Eastern religions, and he began keeping company with some pretty far-out folks at the Self-Realization Fellowship Center on Mount Washington in the Hollywood Hills. One was a woman named Fay Wright, who called herself Sri Daya Mata. She looked somewhat like Gladys Presley. Elvis saw her a lot for instruction in meditation and self-control. Some of us thought she was a crock.

Larry, though, I liked. He was a free, loving spirit, a typical Californian of the time, with the sports cars and the newest hairstyles. A lot of people thought he was a con artist. But I think he just wanted to get close to Elvis, and not necessarily to advance his career or his bank account, even if Elvis did buy him a Cadillac convertible. Colonel eventually put an end to the relationship, ordering Elvis's books taken out and burned (a scene right out of "Fahrenheit 451"), and making sure somebody else was present whenever Elvis had Larry over to cut his hair.

What I remember most about that time is that the Memphis Mafia was in some ways becoming almost unrecognizable. Drastic changes were underway. I began to question my place in it.

Elvis wasn't crazy about the term "Memphis Mafia" when the press first started using it in 1960. He told a reporter that he preferred to think of us as "members of a little country club I run." But as time went on, he thought the name conjured up a gangster image, that of a cigar-smoking chieftain, which appealed to him since he *did* like to smoke those little cigars, and at Graceland, sometimes a pipe, with the bowl in the shape of a lion's head.

He'd also begun his obsession with firearms, although he had just a few, like the Derringer, when I was with him. The days of his carrying .38s and automatic rifles and flashlights were still ahead.

The guys thought the term "Memphis Mafia" was pretty funny--a joke, really. I liked the idea of an "inner circle" better than "fraternity," because that was closer to the truth. We weren't college kids. We weren't a "corporation," either, as we were sometimes called. And even though we protected him in the sense that we kept people away from him, we never really considered ourselves bodyguards. Elvis loved to tell the story about how Red and some guy went at it for fifteen minutes one time when Elvis and Red walked out of the Variety Club in Memphis. Elvis watched the whole fight from the curb, and then he got up and finished the guy off with just one punch.

And if we weren't really bodyguards, certainly we were *not* his handlers. More and more, in fact, our main function was to agree with him, something that would lead to my growing dissatisfaction as one of Elvis's employees. Some people say we were buffers, that we removed him from the world. Maybe so, but only because he wanted it that way. At the same time, of course, he removed *us* from the world, or at least the real one.

When the entourage first started, none of us really had specific jobs, because we were living in hotels. There wasn't much for us to do except be companions and have a lot of fun. Nobody made a salary. We were just a bunch of young kids from Memphis out on a lark. We had no idea how big Elvis was, because we were with him all the time, and couldn't really measure his effect and the pervasiveness of his fame. The only real yardstick we had was the way people reacted to us as individuals. People would do almost anything for you if you were traveling with Elvis, but if you weren't with him, they wouldn't give you the time of day. It was amusing to us, because we could see right through them.

People came and went in the Mafia. Sometimes there were only three or four, then during "It Happened at the World's Fair" there were thirteen of us. Sometimes in California there were only five or six, although usually there were eight. I guess there were forty or fifty of us altogether, although certainly never that many at one given time.

Most of us were about the same age as Elvis. Still, there was no real criteria for admission to the Mafia, and no initiation ceremony. If Elvis liked you, you were in.

Sometimes I thought he should have taken more time to see if certain individuals would fit in with the rest of the guys, but Elvis wasn't going to listen to what anybody else had to say. And there were definitely situations other than the Ray Sitton debacle where he'd hire someone that a lot of the guys didn't particularly want to be around, and that had to end in a hurry. It was an unwritten rule that we just had to get along. And so was his expectation that nobody ever talked about him to outsiders. It was like an oath, one that was to be obeyed even if you were no longer in the group.

As the years went on and Elvis had more demanded of him, he needed us to handle a variety of responsibilities for him, not just run errands. That became increasingly necessary when Elvis decided--consciously or not--that all of his real future plans came by the milligram or injectable serum, and he was not altogether physically capable of seeing to many of his needs himself.

For the past three years, then, we'd been receiving a salary of $125 a week. We probably would have gone on working for free, but one day Colonel told him, "You know, it's fine to have these people, but you're paying them 100 percent now. If you put them on salaries, the government will absorb a lot of it." So, soon we started getting little pay envelopes from Vernon.

Granted, it wasn't much, but then again we had almost all of our expenses covered, and we split up the money we earned as extras in the movies. And, of course, we were the frequent recipients of Elvis's famed generosity. Whenever one of us needed something special--such as Lamar's intestinal by-pass operation--Elvis paid for it. He also gave or loaned us the money we needed to make a down payment on a house. And he surprised us with automobiles--I got a new 1964 white Cadillac, and at other times a wallet and a briefcase--and he occasionally rewarded us with small raises and bonuses.

Then there were bonuses from the Colonel. That's a side of Colonel you don't ever hear about. But once when Lamar was down and out, Colonel pressed several hundred-dollar bills in his palm with a handshake. And one day when I drove him to Palm Springs he asked me to take him to a meat market, where he bought $500-worth of meat and divided it up between Elvis and me. Another time, he arranged for me to have a steam bath and massage as a kind of favor for driving him. Colonel could be extremely generous when he was in the right mood. He even handed out big stacks of gambling chips to all the guys when we went to Las Vegas.

By the middle 1960s, it was apparent that we needed more structure to the Mafia. Before, we all had ideas about what each of us was to handle, but the responsibilities were vague and nebulous. I always made sure the cars were clean, repaired and ready to travel at any given time, and drove Colonel and Priscilla in Elvis's Cadillac, since he had the Rolls-Royce auctioned off for charity in 1964. I also still took care of some of his wardrobe. And like Lamar and Gene Smith, I tried hard to keep him amused.

Sometime in 1964, Elvis and Colonel named Marty Lacker

the foreman of the Memphis Mafia. I was his co-foreman. One day, Marty and Elvis sat down and made a list of everyone's duties at Graceland and in California. Each of the guys-- Marty, Joe, Billy, Jerry, Red, Richard, and Mike Keaton, had five or six jobs in each locale. They ranged from something as trivial as "Call Mrs. Pepper of Movie Times (As Early as Possible)," one of Jerry's duties, to "Transact Business and Correspondence with the Colonel's Office for Elvis," one of Marty's tasks.

In addition to what I was already doing, I was to take care of miscellaneous business transactions for Elvis. That included everything from having his sex tapes made, to maintaining a purchase order system for all charges in Elvis's name. One of my Memphis duties was, "Along with Marty, be responsible for Organization, both in good and bad situations." Whatever that meant.

In Los Angeles, I was to oversee the running of the house, including dealing with the maids; receive all of Elvis's correspondence, passing along his personal letters and saving the fan mail; maintain his scrapbook, which was no small job; authorize charge records; drive him to the studio each day; and, my favorite, "be in den with Elvis as much as possible."

On the whole, I took these duties seriously, because making movies was serious business, no matter what anybody thought of their artistic merits. The scripts had to be kept current (there were always changes and new pages added as the shooting unfolded), and Elvis had to know his lines and his schedule for the next day. And if he was supposed to wear part of his own wardrobe in the movie, it had to be there. In addition, someone had to make sure his lunches were prepared the way he liked them, and with low-calorie foods that also satisfied his palate.

That was a real trick, because at home his taste drifted to peanut butter-and-banana sandwiches--and worse. The list of items Elvis demanded be kept at Graceland at all times included:

1. Fresh, lean, unfrozen ground round meat
2. One case regular Pepsis
3. One case orange drinks
4. Rolls (Hot rolls--"Brown and Serve")
5. Biscuits (at least six cans)
6. Hamburger buns
7. Pickles
8. Potatoes and onions
9. Assorted fresh fruits
10. Sauerkraut
11. Wieners
12. Milk and half & half (at least three bottles)
13. Bacon (thin, lean)
14. Mustard
15. Peanut butter
16. Fresh, hand-squeezed, cold orange juice
17. Banana pudding (to be made at night)
18. Ingredients for meatloaf and sauce
19. Brownies (to be made at night)
20. Ice cream (vanilla and chocolate)
21. Shredded coconut
22. Fudge cookies
23. Gum
24. Cigars
25. Cigarettes
26. Dristan
27. Super Anahist
28. Contac
29. Sucrets
30. Feenamint
31. Matches

With a diet made up of staples such as these, it's a wonder Elvis's weight never crept up more than twenty pounds beyond his ideal of 180 pounds in the years I was with him. I was a pretty big boy, with no room to talk, really. But Elvis obviously never met a jelly doughnut he didn't like.

CHAPTER 14

"Crying In The Chapel"

At the end of 1964 I was twenty-eight years old, an age when most young men are either settled down or thinking seriously about it. A lot of my friends were married, especially several of the guys in the group, and I decided that getting married was the thing to do. I was tired of the parade of young girls who spent the night at the house in California. The thrill of the conquest was gone, and I knew a lot of them just stayed overnight because I was associated with Elvis. I wanted someone who cared about *me*.

The woman I chose was Jo Tuneburg. She'd lived in Memphis for years, but she was from a small town in Mississippi, and she'd been married a couple of times before. I'd known her for a long time. She'd dated a friend of mine, and when they broke up, I asked her out. Her petite, blond good looks appealed to me, and I think she liked it that I went to Hollywood pretty often.

Not exactly a great foundation for marriage. But I proposed, and she said yes. We planned a Memphis wedding for the end of December, right after Christmas. By then, production should have wrapped on Elvis's eighteenth film, "Tickle Me," and we weren't scheduled to begin work on "Harum Scarum" until March.

"Tickle Me" was for Allied Artists Studios, a company undergoing financial difficulties. That meant they could pay Elvis only $750,000 instead of his usual million-dollar fee, in addition to 50 percent of the profits. Why Colonel agreed to the arrangement, I don't know, unless he made the money up some other way. The film was budgeted at $1.48 million, which included Elvis's salary. To further pare expenses, no new songs were recruited for the soundtrack, so the musical numbers came from existing Elvis LPs, such as the lackluster "Pot

That's me on the far left as an "extra" in Elvis's eighteenth movie, "Tickle Me," a picture Elvis took a pay cut to make, and the success of which is acknowledged to have bailed Allied Artists out of deep financial trouble.

Luck." The movie was shot entirely on the studio lot in California.

By now, the plots of Elvis's movies were so preposterous that they were downright embarrassing. "Tickle Me" called for Elvis to play an unemployed rodeo cowboy tending the horses at a women's health spa. In the course of the movie, he manages to flee a flock of man-crazy females in exercise attire, fall in love with a shapely instructor, and discover a fortune in hidden gold. I had a tiny part in a fight scene, where Elvis beats up a bully in a bar, played by Red West. Red had to act as if Elvis's punch sent him sailing over a table, and he asked me to break his fall as he came sprawling across the checkered tablecloth.

We retreated back to Memphis that December, and all during Chanukah and Christmas I was as nervous as a nun in a sex shop. Should I go through with the marriage or not? Finally, I decided my anxiety was just typical bachelor's cold feet. On December 29, Jo and I said "I do." That night, we decided to go over to Graceland to tell Elvis we'd actually tied the knot, and on the way, somebody slammed into my '59 Cadillac. The damage was so extensive that the car wouldn't even run. I had to have it towed in.

I told Elvis, "We've got good news and bad news. The good news is we're married, and the bad news is I just wrecked my car."

Elvis looked astonished.

"Congratulations! But how'd you get out here?"

"I rented a car."

"You did what?"

"I rented a car. What was I supposed to do?"

He walked around a minute, and then he asked, "You got a dollar?"

I handed it over.

"Here," he said, leading us out to the drive. "You just bought *this* car." It was Priscilla's little red Corvair, her year-old graduation present.

I kept it for awhile and then sold it. And then Elvis gave me my '64 white Caddy. Sharp as hell. Things were looking up.

Things were also looking up for Elvis, at least on the record charts. In January 1965, the soundtrack from "Roustabout" reached number one on the *Billboard* "Hot LPs" chart, beating out the Beach Boys, the Beatles, and the rest of the British invasion groups. Elvis hadn't had any singles on *Billboard*'s "Top 100 Records of 1964" list, and certainly no single from the album, so he was understandably thrilled.

"Roustabout" would end up being Elvis's last number one album until 1973. But nobody was thinking about how long his record of success would hold, especially since his single, "Crying in the Chapel," recorded years before, hit the number three spot in the spring. It gave the Beatles a real run for the top of the charts, and even became a number one hit in the Beatles' native country. By the end of the year, "Crying in the Chapel" had sold close to two million copies.

The new record success was a tremendous boost to Elvis's ego, especially since he looked down the shooting schedule for the next year and saw nothing but hackneyed shlock movies blurring together--"Harum Scarum," "Frankie and Johnny," "Paradise Hawaiian Style"--after which Colonel would promptly sign him up for another multi-picture run with Hal Wallis. As usual, Colonel demanded so much money for Elvis that the studio had only a tiny budget left over in which to invest in a strong supporting cast, talented directors and cameramen, or even good screenwriters for inventive scripts.

The fact that Elvis wouldn't have been paid a fortune was the reason Colonel nixed Wallis's idea to put Elvis in "The Rainmaker" with Burt Lancaster and Katharine Hepburn, even though Elvis himself would say he changed his mind about the project because he didn't like the "real happy, real jolly, real lovesick" role of Jim Curry, the part Earl Holliman eventually played. Money was also the reason Elvis passed up the opportunity to appear in a John Wayne vehicle, in which Wayne would play the grizzled old gunfighter, and Elvis his eager protege. The tragedy is that appearances in projects such as these just might have changed the course of Elvis's film career.

As it went, it got so that even those of us who were *in* the

Shots of me--one with a playful friend--on location for "Paradise--Hawaiian Style," the third picture Elvis made in Hawaii.

damn pictures couldn't tell them apart, especially if they sounded as similar as "Spinout" and "Speedway," and they were made during the same period. They were just a somnambulistic series of fight scenes, chaste romances, terrible songs, stupid costumes, and flimsy plot lines, placed against so-called exotic locales, usually fudged on the studio lots. Ironically, pop music was becoming increasingly sophisticated, and so were the movies that reflected that culture. And yet Elvis's films looked dated and anachronistic from the day they were released to the theatres.

For example, Elvis invariably played some macho role--a crop duster, a stock car racer, a cowboy, a fisherman, or something of that ilk. It was intrinsic that he remain humble and honest, always seeking to better himself through respectable means. Usually that meant he was cast as someone lost and a little dim, but ingratiating and even a trifle noble.

The formula also called for a sidekick who spent too much money--or was overly interested in the girls--and whose excessive ways landed them in a peck of trouble, usually financial, with some arbiter of authority. Elvis and his pal almost always extricated themselves from this conundrum through Elvis's common sense and ingenuity. And, of course, with the help of the female co-star, whose physical attributes were invariably smeared up against the lens, and whose character was somehow tied in to the troublesome authority figure.

Still, the flights to safety were always too speedy and perfunctory--the audience never actually feared the worst would happen--and nothing was deeply imagined.

In the early years after Elvis made a movie, he'd get a copy of it on 16-mm film, and the guys would slip down to the basement at Graceland and watch it when Elvis was asleep--Elvis didn't ever want to look at his movies himself, and we'd have to turn them off if he awakened. Now though, we didn't care much about seeing them, either. Even *The Elvis Monthly*, the British fan club magazine, called them "puppet shows for not overbright children."

It didn't matter how much Elvis protested to Colonel about wanting to do quality pictures, even though the celebrated director George Cukor visited the set of one of the early 1960s movies and complimented Elvis on his comedic flair, declaring he would be "a dream to direct." Nor did it mean anything to Colonel when Elvis expressed his desire to leave pictures for a while and return full-time to his music. Colonel saw the movies as the best and quickest way to make the most money, and that was that. And publicly, Elvis agreed, citing his limitations as a serious actor, and rhetorically asking, "How can you argue with success?"

But now there was an important difference. Where Elvis formerly chomped at the bit to stretch his acting abilities, now he didn't seem to care. He simply turned increasingly to the pills he carried in his black make-up case to numb his pain, and to keep his resentment and boredom from showing on the screen. The first-run grosses of all thirty-three of Elvis's movies were reportedly $500 million--half a *billion*--dollars, a staggering figure even considering Elvis's share of at least $200 million. But Colonel didn't realize that the movies amounted to an erosion of Elvis's true talents, and that by committing him to another long-term contract he was, in effect, signing his death certificate.

Through the years, Colonel would turn down a number of expressive roles that would have allowed Elvis to find out just what sort of actor he was, among them the part of Hank Williams in "Your Cheating Heart," the lead in "West Side Story," the Paul Newman character in "Sweet Bird of Youth," the Tony Curtis role in "The Defiant Ones," the Jon Voight lead in "Midnight Cowboy," and the Kris Kristofferson role in "A Star is Born," opposite Barbra Streisand.

I don't know the circumstances on the other pictures, but on "A Star is Born," Colonel demanded $2 million, half of the picture, and billing above Streisand, even though she was co-producing. Colonel never weighed how much that role might mean to Elvis's career. He simply said, "Forget it." Maybe Colonel figured that once he landed a decent role, Elvis would find a manager more interested in seeing him realize his artistic dreams.

With his movie career effectively a sealed tomb, then, Elvis ached to make real music again. When Colonel renewed his recording contract with RCA in September of 1965, extending the basic agreement for another ten years, he was jubilant. In 1967, Elvis would win the first of his three Grammy awards from the National Academy of Recording Arts and Sciences, for the album "How Great Thou Art." But that was still down the road, and now, in light of the Beatles' success and the wave of British artists dominating the charts, Elvis had nagging doubts that his old record company would still want to keep him on the roster, except to release his soundtracks--mostly dreadful albums with a lively theme song (usually sung over the opening credits), a slow, sentimental tune delivered to a child or an animal, and some brassy, uptempo tune like "King Creole."

But if Elvis believed that Colonel would have a change of heart--that he would allow him to record *real* songs, songs other than those for which he received a third of the writers' royalties in a publishing kickback--Elvis had another think coming. A couple of times through the years someone would try to circumvent that, or Elvis would specifically ask to cut a terrific piece of material, such as Dolly Parton's "Coat of Many Colors," only to have Colonel veto his plans when Dolly refused to give up part of the publishing.

All that would change in early 1969, with Chips Moman and American Sound Studios. But for now, Colonel stood firm. That's the way they'd started out with Mae Axton and Tommy Durden on "Heartbreak Hotel," and that's the way Colonel wanted it to remain. At first, Elvis received songwriting credits on such songs, even though he'd never written a note or contributed one thought to the lyric. Later, the pretense was dropped, although the financial arrangement stood.

I don't think Elvis was particularly frustrated that he didn't write songs, until he came to be so hamstrung by Colonel's edict on recording only "Elvis Presley Music, Inc.," or "Gladys Music, Inc." published tunes. He then began to think he should have attempted to write songs earlier in his life, so that he might have blossomed into the kind of writers the Beatles were, able to spring hit after hit from their imaginations. He also wished he were more proficient on piano and guitar, so he could be recognized as a true singer-songwriter-instrumentalist, like John Lennon or Paul McCartney.

Those feelings came to a head in 1965, when he showed up to record a soundtrack for one of the movies, and promptly lost his composure when he heard the dreadful songs chosen for the album. Up until then, he'd always recorded with the band. But this time, he threw a temper tantrum and yelled at Colonel that he wasn't in any mood to record. Colonel got mad and screamed that it was costing money to have the musicians there and the studio booked.

"I'll tell you what, man," Elvis retaliated. "Just have 'em cut the tracks of the songs, and I'll come in later and put my voice on 'em!" And that's what he did from then on. He was just so fed up with the routine that he no longer pretended to get psyched up for such material, especially when he was embarrassed about putting out inferior records in the wake of the imaginative music of the British groups.

The Beatles weighed heavier on Elvis's mind as it became increasingly obvious that they would usurp him as the premier icons of popular music, even if *Time* magazine had run an article entitled "Forever Elvis" in May 1965. He began to fantasize about what they were like, even if he didn't particularly like it that Colonel had gotten together with their manager, Brian Epstein, for lunch in September 1964 when the Beatles played Memphis, and that Colonel had extended an invitation for the Beatles to stay at Graceland, something they allegedly declined for security reasons.

As with his aborted meetings with Marlon Brando and Steve McQueen, Elvis perceived any real exchange with the Beatles as some kind of threat, no matter that he was enormously curious about them, and knew that they revered him, John Lennon having once remarked that, "Nothing really affected me until I heard Elvis. If there hadn't been Elvis, there wouldn't have been the Beatles."

We were making "Paradise--Hawaiian Style" in late August 1965 when the two managers arranged for the Beatles to come by the Perugia Way house while they were in Los Angeles on their second American tour. It was weird to hear them introduced to each other, "Elvis Presley...Ringo Starr," and see them shake hands. And at first, it was a little awkward, because everybody was so nervous. They just sat there for the longest time, and finally Elvis broke the ice by saying, "Look, guys, if you're just going to sit there and stare at me, I'm going to bed." Strangely, I don't remember too much about that night. I know that Elvis and the Beatles got into a hell of a jam session that evening, but oddly, it was more instrumentals than singing. I remember, too, that we had the juke box on, and that we got the Beatles into a crap game that went on for quite a while. It was a fun night, one in which we told stories and jokes and watched TV, Elvis drinking Seven-Up and the Beatles downing Scotch and bourbon. They came at ten o'clock and left at two in the morning. And that was that.

The sad part is that in years to come, Elvis would get drugged up and denounce the Beatles as a "subversive group," and the Beatles would put down one of his latest records on British TV. But the Beatles never talked extensively about that night, Paul telling the press only that he thought Elvis was "odd." The respect was still there, though. After Bill Black, Elvis's original bass player, died in October 1965, Paul bought the bass Bill had used on Elvis's historic recordings.

The Beatles' visit to Perugia Way was one of our last big events in the house, for in September 1965, just as we finished production on "Paradise--Hawaiian Style" and were getting ready to come home to Memphis, Elvis rented a modern, ranch-style home at 10550 Rocca Place in Bel Air. It was only about a mile from the Perugia Way house, in Stone Canyon, near the Bel Air Hotel. We'd simply outgrown the Perugia Way house again, and this one was a lot roomier.

Elvis had been thinking a lot about houses lately. In fact, 1965 was also the year he had a Spanish-style house built in Palm Springs. A single-story, white stucco residence, it nestled fifteen rooms and a swimming pool on two acres. Cost: $85,000.

Just why Elvis wanted a house there was never really clear to me. Certainly it wasn't for tax reasons--Elvis and Vernon weren't that savvy, and they had virtually no one to advise them on such matters. Ever since Elvis had been forced to pay an additional $80,000 one year after a tax audit, Vernon just reported Elvis's income each year and let the IRS calculate how much tax was owed.

A more obvious reason might be that he wanted to have a home near Colonel, who also lived in Palm Springs. Except for the fact that Elvis didn't really socialize with Colonel. And as Elvis's drug use wore on and Colonel became less tolerant of it, their relationship began to deteriorate.

Whatever the reason for the house at 845 Chino Canyon Road in Palm Springs, Elvis stayed there only occasionally through the years. I remember Vernon and Dee flying out there to vacation with Elvis in the fall of 1966, in what must have been a strained attempt to quell the uneasiness between Elvis and Dee. And I know Elvis took Cybill Shepherd there when they began a short-lived dalliance some time later. At other times, he and Priscilla invited Joe Esposito and George Klein and their wives out to relax.

Much to Vernon's consternation, Elvis was spending money hand over fist. He could afford it, of course, and he was especially aware of it when RCA sent him a congratulatory letter saying that 1965 was "the biggest of all the ten years" he had been on the label, with more than twenty-eight million records sold in the last two years alone. Somebody figured up that Elvis made about $18 *billion* in his lifetime, but Vernon somehow couldn't see it flowing in at an astonishing rate. In other words, none of this made much of an impression on Vernon, because he figured it could stop at any time.

Anytime Elvis spent any sizable amount of money, then, Vernon had a conniption, and they'd get into a verbal brawl about it. Elvis would start out saying, "It's only money, Daddy. I just have to go out and make more." But then Vernon wouldn't let it drop, and before long Elvis would be throwing things to get him to stop. I'm sure it happened in July 1965 when he bought nine Triumph motorcycles for some of his friends, and then again that October, when Elvis went on another buying spree, starting with a 1966 Oldsmobile Toronado --one of the first front-wheel drive cars--and moving on to yet another new motorcycle and a go-cart, which he delighted in riding around the grounds of Graceland.

Vernon didn't whine when Elvis gave away money to charity. After all, that was great public relations. And 1965 was a banner year for Elvis's contributions to charity, starting that summer, when he donated $50,000 to the Motion Picture Relief Fund in Hollywood, the largest single donation in the history of the fund. Then, in December, he gave another $50,000 to Memphis charities--an annual gift for Elvis.

Poor Vernon figured the gravy train had stopped for a while. But then Elvis read a newspaper story about an old black woman whose wheelchair had all but broken down. Her friends were trying to raise money for a new one. The story touched Elvis, and he went out a bought a new electric wheelchair for her, and delivered it himself, handing her another two hundred dollars as a belated Christmas gift.

Of course, Elvis built a great part of his legend on the fact that he'd give a Cadillac away to strangers at the drop of a hat. I think he did it mostly to see the expression on their face. It tickled him all over to watch a stranger fly out of his mind with joy at the thought of a brand new Cadillac, because he remembered what it was like to want something like that when he had no prospects for ever getting it. He'd say, "Most people work all their lives to buy a brand new Cadillac, and by the time they get it, they're too old to enjoy it. I want 'em to enjoy it now."

All that came to an abrupt halt, though, if Elvis thought you were taking advantage of him. He'd give someone a car, for example, and then they'd sell it. Or he'd give them money and they'd spend it, and still not go to work. But the next time they came back, Elvis would throw up his hands and say, "Hey, man, that's it. There ain't no more."

This happened numerous times with some of his relatives. That's why he'd often stay in his room at Graceland and not come down--the halls were lined with uncles and cousins who wanted money from him. A lot of people got greedy, and it depressed Elvis when he felt people didn't love him for himself. Even if they cared about him, some people lost sight of him as a human being. They thought that since he was so wealthy and famous, he was their chance to amount to something. Or at least to get rich.

Elvis's lavish gift-giving often got into the newspapers, but for a long time nobody knew that Elvis was keeping up a Memphis guy named Gary Pepper. Gary, who was three years older than Elvis, started Elvis's first fan club, which he called the Tankers Fan Club, named after Elvis's army specialty. A victim of cerebral palsy, Gary was confined to a wheelchair. That still didn't stop him from working to get all kinds of things named in Elvis's honor, or from coming down to the gates of Graceland. One day Elvis spotted him and asked somebody why Gary was in a wheelchair. After that, Elvis paid for live-in assistance for him, bought him a specially equipped '66 Chevrolet Impala convertible, and saw to it that he got a weekly check. Vernon nearly went apoplectic when he found out about it, and he stopped Gary's benefits almost the day after Elvis died, even though he'd gotten to know Gary's father, Sterling, whom Elvis had employed as a gate guard.

I'll never forget the Christmas we came home to Memphis and Elvis gave away a quarter of a million dollars worth of gifts to just about anybody he saw--relatives, strangers and employees. I couldn't quite believe it. I said, "Elvis, that would put a dent in anybody's bank account." He said, "Do you know what it really means, Alan? It means that when I go back on the road, instead of doing a thirty-day tour, I've gotta do a thirty-one-day tour."

Looking back over the years, Christmas 1965 is wrapped in a kind of nostalgic glow in my memory. Dozens of people had a special holiday because of Elvis's generosity, and Elvis was greatly relieved to be home for the holidays after such a disappointing run of film projects. He always took refuge at Graceland, of course, but since he loved Christmas with the intensity of a child, he felt particularly safe there during these holy days. The huge tree in the living room, the grounds lit up with hundreds of colored lights, and the large nativity scene out front made Graceland seem like something out of a fairyland.

But things are seldom as they seem. For me, personally, the holidays meant the usual round of parties, including Elvis's bash at the Manhattan Club in Memphis, and our annual fireworks fight at Graceland. But it was also a time of reflection. I'd been married exactly a year, and Jo and I were still working out an understanding of my travel schedule with Elvis. In my heart, I think I already knew the marriage wouldn't last, but I held out hope, and, like Elvis, took more pills when the pressure got bad.

It was Elvis, though, who suffered the crushing load. Priscilla and her father demanded to know exactly what Elvis's plans were regarding marriage, especially since Priscilla was nearing legal age, and Elvis seemed to be spending more and more time away from home. Ann-Margret wanted to know what those plans were, too.

And then there was the ghost of Gladys, who always roamed the rooms of Graceland, but whose face, like Jacob Marley's ghost, appeared almost everywhere this time of year. Elvis saw her staring back from each ornament on the tree, her memory serving as a constant reminder of his inner turmoil, and his decision, patterned after hers, to sublimate his fear and anger in a substance that would eat at the very core of his self-esteem.

Elvis's real tragedy, of course, was not Colonel's ill-conceived plans for his career, but his own inability to confront his enemies one-on-one. It simply was not in him to demand that Colonel and the studio moguls respect his music and nurture his fragile personality, even though that was exactly what he needed to nourish his soul.

How could he possibly cope in the years ahead? Elvis was a praying man, but most certainly he had not asked the heavenly Father for the solutions soon to be placed before him.

CHAPTER 15

"All The King's Horses,
And All The King's Men"

In the early months of 1966, Elvis was home in Memphis when he caught a bad cold. Since he could count the days on his fingers that he'd been sick in his life, he had no family physician in Memphis, just the doctors in Hollywood and Vegas he relied on for "pharmaceuticals." And so he just laid up in his big square bed, self-medicating with traditional over-the-counter cold preparations.

"Man, this is really getting me down," he drawled to George Klein one day. George said he'd see what he could do, and telephoned his girlfriend, Barbara Little, who worked for a local doctors' partnership called the Medical Group. Barbara asked one of the physicians, Dr. George Nichopolous, if he would mind making a house call to the most famous resident of Memphis.

Eight years older than Elvis, "Dr. Nick," as he was called, was the Pennsylvania-born son of Greek immigrants who eventually settled in Alabama. There, the family ran a restaurant in the tradition of their ethnic background, the parents instilling a fierce work ethic in their son and pointing him toward one of the professions. Still, it wasn't until he'd earned a Ph.D from the University of Tennessee that he decided to go into medicine, enrolling in the Vanderbilt University School of Medicine. After his internship, Dr. Nichopolous and his wife, Edna, moved to Memphis.

I had been a patient of Dr. Nick's for some time before Barbara ever steered him to Graceland. He was a grand guy. You could talk to him, and he'd take the time to bullshit with you. Better yet, you didn't have to wait long when you went to see him. And a lot of times, I'd just call him and describe my symptoms, and he'd send a prescription out to me. I may have taken advantage of my relationship with Dr. Nick to get pills sometimes, but I truly believed that he was a good doctor.

It didn't surprise me, then, that Elvis also took a liking to Dr. Nick. After that first meeting, he considered Dr. Nick his personal physician. A lot of people blame Dr. Nick for feeding Elvis's narcotic appetites and contributing to his death. Especially since Dr. Nick prescribed the drugs that eventually destroyed Elvis, dispensing some twelve thousand pills to him in the last twenty months of his life alone.

Dr. Nick says a lot of those were placebos, and that he over-prescribed because he knew Elvis would just go elsewhere for his drugs, and he was trying to keep things under some kind of control. I think he's telling the truth. Poor Elvis, of course, had deluded himself into believing that any drug that came from a doctor was all right--it wasn't something trashy like cocaine. He'd never buy bootleg stuff, or fool with dealers on the street.

My main feeling about Dr. Nick is that like all of the rest of us, he simply found it was very hard to tell Elvis Presley no. Then again, Dr. Nick was very gullible--he believed any story you told him, and I'm sure Elvis, who could charm a rattle-snake, fooled him, at least at first.

But I don't believe there were "two" Dr. Nicks--one who at the beginning tried to keep Elvis on the straight and narrow, and another later on who thought, "To hell with it. I'll just get everything I can out of Elvis." If Elvis gave Dr. Nick a series of expensive presents, loaned him $250,000 interest free, and agreed to go into the syndicated racquetball court business with him, I think it only means that Dr. Nick suffered an error in judgement, particularly in the ethics of the doctor-patient relationship--not that he meant to gouge Elvis for millions.

Still, I know that some of the other guys feel differently about Dr. Nick's culpability. I wasn't with Elvis when Dr. Nick became so entrenched in the organization. That happened in the early seventies. But I can certainly see that Dr. Nick was

Elvis's non-threatening enabler. Elvis "bought" him, just as he'd "bought" a number of other drug suppliers from his army days on.

Unfortunately, as Elvis's drug problem escalated, so did mine. For a couple of years now, I'd been taking two or three pills to stay awake, and two or three to go to sleep, and I was taking them every day. But by 1966, I was taking six to eight pills a day--Dexedrine and Dexamil to stay awake, and Placidyl and Seconal to go to sleep.

I felt that I couldn't function without them, and I probably couldn't have kept up Elvis's schedule on my own, especially when he was making movies and partying all night long. I'd become addicted, although at the time, I would have rejected the idea that I was actually "an addict," because they weren't hard drugs. But anytime you're taking eight pills a day, it's a problem, especially if you have to depend on them to get any rest.

I wasn't the only guy in the entourage to have this problem, of course. Marty was even heavier into the stuff than I was, although again, he did only pills. But Joe Esposito didn't fool with drugs at all, and neither did Jerry Schilling. There were others in the group who did, because it was fun at the time.

On occasion, some of us were so out of it that we neglected our duties. In February 1966, for example, when we went to California to film "Spinout," we committed what Elvis considered to be a grievous error, one that, in fact, might have resulted in a public nightmare.

Elvis normally carried his black make-up case with him at all times, a case that contained his wallet, his combs, and, of course, his stash of stay-awake, sleeping, and pain pills. If Elvis didn't carry it himself, it was up to one of us to keep track of it, and tote it around for him.

We filmed one of the scenes at Dodger Stadium, and, as usual, Elvis brought his case. His dressing room was a small house trailer, and I remembered spotting the case there with Elvis. But when we got home at the end of the day, we froze when Elvis boomed out, "Where's my case?" I looked at Richard, Richard looked at me, and instantly we knew it was still in

Just off the set of "Spinout," March 1966. Beginning on the left, that's Larry Geller, Marty Lacker, me, Joe Esposito, co-star Deborah Walley riding behind Elvis, and Jerry Schilling on the second motorcycle.

the trailer, where a janitor or anyone who had access to the trailer could find it. Of course, Dodger Stadium was locked up for the night, but that cut exactly no ice with Elvis. We had to go back, climb the fence, finagle our way into the trailer, and grab the case.

If Elvis held out any glimmer of hope that the plots of his next movies would get stronger and more believable, "Spinout" finished off that illusion and successfully squelched his ambition. Built, like most of Elvis's sixties pictures, around his carefully orchestrated public persona, the movie cast him as a happy-go-lucky bachelor pursued by three beautiful brides-to-be, Diane McBain, Deborah Walley, and Shelley Fabares--one a millionaire's daughter, one a drummer, and the third a feminist author. As usual, the songs were unremarkable.

The next film on the production schedule, "Double Trouble," was no better. Set in England and Belgium (although filmed on the MGM lot in Culver City), "Double Trouble" took an action cue from the Beatles' two movies, "A Hard Days Night" and "Help," tracking Elvis as he was chased across Europe by mini-skirted dollies, smugglers, and assorted bumbling characters. But alas, director Norman Taurog captured none of the essential wit and charm of Richard Lester's excursions with the Fab Four.

As it turned out, "Spinout" and "Double Trouble" were the last pictures I would work on for quite some time. My father had become ill with cancer, and I was trying to spend as much time at home as I could. By Chanukah 1966, we knew he wouldn't last long. That Christmas Eve, Elvis went over to Baptist Memorial Hospital to see him--something that couldn't have been easy for him, since any hospital visit reminded him of his mother's death.

He never mentioned why he was there, but he'd gone to Harry Levitch, the jeweler, and bought my father a gold pocket watch and had it engraved, "Merry Christmas--God Bless You." It was a touching gesture, and I loved Elvis for doing it, especially since my father died three weeks later. I think it meant a lot to him that Elvis came.

After my father's death, I might have gone back to traveling with Elvis, except for a turn of events in February 1967.

The month before, Elvis went on another spending spree, rounding up seventeen horses to stable and board at Graceland. The horse-buying streak started after he found a four-year-old black quarterhorse, Domino, for Priscilla, who'd loved horses since she was a teen. But Elvis had discovered he enjoyed riding during the making of "Love Me Tender." And so Jerry Schilling found a beautiful Palomino named Rising Sun for him so he and Priscilla could ride together. The horse wasn't all that expensive--$3,500. But after that, to Vernon's great displeasure, Elvis hauled off and bought horses and western gear for everybody at Graceland, whether they could stay in the saddle or not.

The day he marched me out to look at my horse, a kind of drab, non-descript animal, I took one look at it and stopped in my tracks.

"What's wrong with him, Hog Ears?"

"Well, nothing."

"What is it?"

"Elvis, it looks like a mule. I want one like Rising Sun, a Palomino."

"I'm not sure we can get you one of those, Alan."

"Well, then, let's just forget it. I'm not sure I really want a horse, to tell you the truth."

The Memphis Mafia were unlikely cowboys, but in Elvis's opinion, I had to have a horse. He looked all over, and finally, he found a Palomino named Model that he thought I'd like. But damned if my horse didn't kick his horse and raise a big knot on his leg the first day he brought him out to Graceland. The veterinarian bill must have been $5,000, and I don't think the mark ever went away. After that, Elvis kept Rising Sun separated from the other horses in his own barn. We jokingly called it "House of the Rising Sun," after the old black blues tune. Elvis never liked to do anything half-way, of course, and the next month, he further indulged his new craze for all things western by buying a 163-acre cattle ranch near Walls, Mississippi, just over the state line and only about ten miles from Graceland. Priscilla had spotted it one day while driving along Horn Lake Road in De Soto County, and she thought it would make a great get-away for Elvis and herself.

Then one evening, she and Elvis and I were out driving in one of Elvis's convertibles, when I saw the ranch for the first time. It was like something out of a movie. The grass was absolutely immaculate, like a golf course, and everything was painted and polished like a country club. "Golly, that place is beautiful," I said. "I know it," Elvis replied. "I ride down here all the time." We kept on driving, and then I said, "You know, Elvis, it has a 'For Sale' sign on it."

Elvis turned sharply. "Really?" he gushed, the excitement in his voice. We turned around and went back to read the sign. The contact was Jack Adams, an airplane salesman at Twinkletown Airport. Elvis wasn't really in the market for more property--he'd just bought the Palm Springs house--but it *was* an incredible place. And Elvis liked the huge, fifty-foot-high concrete white cross on the ranch. It had a practical purpose as a marker for approaching planes, but Elvis took it as a mystic sign that he was meant to have it.

When we got to the airport, Elvis told me to go in and ask Adams his asking price, since he was afraid Adams would jack the price up if he knew Elvis Presley was his buyer. I was just into the conversation when I turned around and saw Elvis walking in the door. Adams, who called his ranch Twinkletown Farm, was a smooth operator and a good salesman. After we'd talked for a little while, he turned to Elvis and said, "Mr. Presley, let's not discuss buying and selling just now. I want you to go over there and stay as long as you want to. Take all your people, use the house, ride the horses, and treat everything just as if it were yours. Then if you like it, we'll talk about it."

Elvis was like a little kid, he was so happy. We went back to Graceland and loaded all the horses and took everybody down there and stayed a couple of nights. The first morning Elvis declared, "I've never slept so good in all my life!" That was it. We went over and asked Adams how much he wanted for it. Adams said $300,000 would get it, which was far and above what the land was really worth, even with the eighteen head of Santa Gertrudis cattle that grazed there.

Vernon, who practically walked around with an adding machine all the time, never stopped moaning from the minute Elvis told him about the place. Elvis immediately told Adams he'd take it, even as I was nudging him and saying, "Elvis, you don't quite do things like that." With the right negotiations, he could have gotten it a lot cheaper. But he said, "I like it, I'm happy, and I want it." He even called Colonel and told him.

And to appease Vernon, who loved to fancy himself as a gentleman farmer, Elvis kept the cattle, with the idea of moving most of the residents of the Graceland stables down there, too, since Graceland wasn't really big enough for a horse farm. The first thing he did was rename the place the Circle G Ranch, the "G" for Graceland.

Elvis needed a ranch like he needed a third eye, but it was a great new toy. He had a pilot fly him over it for an aerial view, and he played the role of "ranch baron" to the hilt. Vernon grew purple in the face as he watched his son order eight new house trailers for the entourage to stay in, since there was only an existing white, one-bedroom home, and a three-bedroom trailer with a king-size bed and brick fireplace that Elvis and Priscilla planned to share. Like Vernon, Priscilla was furious that Elvis planned to bring all the guys down. In her view, the ranch was a perfect romantic getaway.

Priscilla didn't complain nearly as loud as Vernon, though. I thought he was going to have a stroke when Elvis turned to me and said, "Call the Ford dealer and have six trucks sent out here, and then call the Chevy dealer and order eight more." By the time he was finished, he'd bought twenty-five or thirty Ford Ranchero and Chevrolet El Camino trucks, at a collective pop of about $100,000. Everybody got one, whether they wanted one or not. Elvis thought, "This is a ranch. You've got to have a pick-up!"

After that, he stocked the property's small lake with expensive fish, and threw up a ten-foot fence to keep out the curious. He was spending money like an Arab sheik. Even at the beginning, we knew the ranch would be a constant drain on

Elvis's bank account, since it didn't produce any income.

But for now, Elvis didn't want to hear about it. I suppose he saw it as reward for the grind and the frustration of his career--a new retreat. The Jordanaires said they'd never seen him so exuberant, Ray Walker remembering that after a while down there, Elvis let his hair go back to its natural blond, and eventually bought a suit to match: "He looked like a million dollars."

Jack Adams had a fella by the name of Ralph Boucher running the place, and Elvis kept him on. But he also wanted one of his own down there, and so he approached his uncle Earl Pritchett about it, who'd been the head groundskeeper at Graceland. Earl gladly accepted. Then Elvis announced he had someone else in mind for ranch foreman.

Me.

I didn't know beans about running a ranch. I knew even less about cattle. And I rode horses only when I had to. But I think the main reason Elvis asked me to manage the ranch was so I could get off the road and enjoy some time with my new wife, and still be a part of the entourage. It was a generous and gracious offer.

Some of my friends said they knew I'd miss going out to Hollywood all the time. But in many ways, I was only too glad to be out of the Elvis mainstream. A lot of things had changed in the past couple of years, and I was one of them. The pills had altered my personality to a greater extent than I realized. Bill Leaptrott, a photographer for the Memphis *Press-Scimitar* who'd gone to high school with Elvis, came down to the ranch one day, and I lost my temper and snapped at him something fierce. I wouldn't have done that had I not been in a pharmaceutical fog, trying to be a big-shot bodyguard, pushing people around.

The real truth was that being part of Elvis's entourage wasn't that great anymore. Since Elvis had formally proposed to Priscilla and given her an engagement ring the size of Plymouth Rock--a 3 1/2-carat diamond surrounded by a ring of smaller diamonds--I knew that things were bound to change. Where Priscilla had once been meek and retiring, she had been trying to assert some control for several years now, and as Elvis's wife, she would enjoy considerably more power.

The guys and I knew that she deeply resented the time that Elvis spent with us, and while I could see her point, we were Elvis's employees. Still, she wanted more time with him alone, without being interrupted by his having to make a movie, rent out the fairgrounds, or indulge the whims of eight guys who had nothing more pressing to do. "We never have any privacy!" she told me once. And it was true. Just as she couldn't believe Elvis would want to take all of us and our wives down to the ranch, I found it odd that Elvis often circumvented her plans to be alone with him by inviting an entire herd of people to come along.

Quietly, then, she began conspiring with Vernon to find a way to get rid of us, or at least reduce our numbers. It wasn't that she didn't like us as individuals. She just felt threatened by our presence. I think she had a fantasy of a normal home life with him, one in which he went to work like other husbands, came home in the evening, helped her cook dinner, and then sat around with her at night. But Elvis had never been average, and he surely wasn't going to be.

Vernon was only too happy to listen to Priscilla's complaints about the Mafia, since he always thought we were just after Elvis's money. He hated it when Elvis bought us presents, and he particularly resented the salaries--tiny as they were--that Elvis paid us. He'd been trying to figure a way to cut back the payroll for a long time, especially after his sister, Delta Mae Biggs, moved into Graceland after her husband died in 1966, and Vernon had been forced to pay her a salary as housekeeper and companion to Minnie Mae. Aunt Delta Mae proved to be another source of irritation to the guys, since she had a tongue that could split a board in two, and she seemed to delight in picking fights with us.

I believe that Priscilla and I had a better relationship than she had with most of the other guys, in part because I had chauffeured her around so much in California. But I also understood how she cringed to see several guys in the group change from simple yes-men into submissive zombies through the years. I hated it, too, and I shared her observation that some of the guys waited to see if Elvis laughed before they reacted to a joke. In other words, they seldom laughed and cut up unless he did, and then they mimicked his actions to stay on his good side.

I wasn't sure what was happening to us, but it filled me with feelings I didn't like. And so for now, while I was wrestling with a number of personal things--my father's death, my wobbly marriage, my escalating drug use--I was content to stay home and take care of the ranch.

The tension between Elvis and Colonel had built steadily in the last months, too. When the guys went to California early in 1967 to make "Clambake" for United Artists, Elvis was furious that Colonel had sent his minions to the set to check out how much weight he had gained while he was down on the ranch.

Colonel was right--Elvis *had* gained a considerable amount of weight, relaxing and having fun for the first time in a long time. For weeks, he'd gobbled down hamburgers, cheeseburgers, bacon sandwiches, pork chops, and of course, his favorite breakfast food, the famous deep-fried peanut butter sandwiches, prepared with a full stick of butter.

Usually before a film, Elvis would diet by eating only one meal a day, and he could lose fifteen or twenty pounds in two weeks. He had fantastic will power. He wouldn't eat any sweets or breads, and he'd drink plenty of water--he liked the Mountain Valley bottled variety--to flush the fat out of his system. This time, he'd just let himself go hog wild, and he was up to two hundred pounds, a weight gain of twenty or twenty-five pounds. The director, Arthur Nadel, was furious, and ordered the wardrobe department to whip up a dozen jackets that would help conceal Elvis's girth.

Colonel had first gotten wind of Elvis's condition not through the movie people, but through some of us, particularly Joe Esposito. Colonel had marshaled a couple of "spies" within our ranks for some time now, and Joe was certainly Colonel's man, as was Charlie Hodge. The guys suspected it, and it caused us to break down into separate camps within the ranks.

When I first went to work for Elvis, there had been a certain feeling of camaraderie. We didn't knife each other in the back, and we didn't try to be Elvis's main man. Now things had changed to where some of the guys were trying to say, "I'm the closest one to Elvis," or "Elvis gave me this and that." And when they weren't jockeying for position with Elvis, they were rubbing up next to Colonel.

Many times when I'd drive Colonel to Palm Springs he'd ask me questions about what Elvis was up to. He was crafty, of course. He phrased them as polite conversation, like, "Is so-and-so still around?" But I knew that he really wanted me to rat on Elvis's most personal habits, especially his drug use ("Have Elvis's eyes been looking a little cloudy lately?"), and I wasn't going to be a party to it. I just said, "I don't know, Colonel. I don't know nothin'." And after awhile, he quit asking. If it had leaked to Elvis that I'd told Colonel something I shouldn't have, Elvis would have fired me.

Things came to a head between Elvis and Colonel in 1967, shortly into production on "Clambake," with an incident that would forever change not only the relationship between the two men, but the financial course of Elvis's life. One night at Rocca Place, Elvis, stoked full of pills and woozy, got up to use the bathroom, when he lost his balance and hit his head on the side of the tub. He lay there motionless for hours before anyone knew what had happened.

When Elvis was finally discovered, all hell broke loose. Joe hurriedly got Colonel on the phone, and somebody else called one of Elvis's private doctors, who carted portable X-ray equipment to the house. Elvis had suffered only a mild concussion, but it meant that filming had to be postponed on the movie for at least a week or two, and that one of the guys had to follow behind Elvis at every step, in case he pitched and fell again.

As the doctor delivered his instructions, Colonel walked out into the hallway and exploded in rage. He lashed out at the other guys, berating them for allowing Elvis to get into such a state, and then ranted about how angry United Artists was going to be about the delay in filming: "They could tear up the contract! This could cost us millions!" Finally, he collected himself, and told the guys to take care of Elvis and to let him know when Elvis was feeling better--they needed to have a talk.

It was certainly time that Colonel had a good talk with Elvis, but it was also time that somebody had a stern lecture for most of the rest of us. Because by 1967, all the guys who did drugs had virtually lost control of their habits. We were taking a lot of pills. How many, I don't know. Hundreds. Thousands, I suppose. None of us were really into psychedelics, which were the fad drugs of the moment, even though Elvis had some of us try acid--LSD--one time to see what it was like. He was too scared to try it himself, and we were stupid enough to be his guinea pigs.

When Colonel came back to the house in a few days, then, the guys expected him to chew Elvis out a little bit--try to scare him into curtailing his habits. What happened, though, threw everybody for a loop: Colonel told Elvis that if he didn't stop doing drugs, he would not only drop him as his client, but ruin Elvis's career. Furthermore, he was setting up new guidelines for everyone. Marty Lacker would no longer be the foreman of the Mafia, and the new foreman would take orders from Colonel, not Elvis.

And then the kicker. Instead of taking 25 percent of Elvis's gross--already an astronomical fee--Colonel informed Elvis that he would now siphon off exactly half of every dollar that came in. Before expenses, before anything. Colonel was now demanding 50 percent of Elvis Presley's gross. And Elvis, who sat there like a whipped dog, merely nodded his head. That was that. In many ways, it was one of the bleakest days of Elvis's life. Not because of the money, so much. But because Elvis had become a total puppet, silently jumping in any direction that Colonel pulled the strings.

CHAPTER 16

"A Flare-Up Of Genius"
New Beginnings

Colonel always said that the lines were strictly drawn in his relationship with Elvis. "I'll take care of business matters," he'd puff with the fatigue of repetition, "and Elvis will take care of the rest." That supposedly meant that Elvis could do anything he wanted in his private life, even swallow every pill ever made. But the decisions he made about Elvis's business affairs--particularly his movie career--made a huge impact on how Elvis lived his life, and about how Elvis felt about himself.

Of course, though Colonel was no psychiatrist, he was shrewd enough to know that Elvis was chronically depressed--that he was bored and restless to the point that he'd turned those feelings into self-loathing and a kind of slow suicide. And as the "Clambake" incident proved, Colonel very skillfully knew how to manipulate Elvis's private life for his personal gain. Maybe he thought that taking half of Elvis's income would force Elvis to pull himself together and go for treatment. But it certainly looked to most of the guys that Colonel viewed Elvis's addiction as a weakness he could exploit in the most shameful way possible.

Colonel's insidious grasp into Elvis's life became even more apparent when it came to Elvis's engagement to Priscilla. The pair were supposed to marry in the early days of 1967, but Elvis had postponed it so he could finish "Clambake." Now as the new date, May 1, loomed closer on the calendar, Elvis desperately began trying to find some way out. He cared about Priscilla, of course, but he wasn't on fire about her the way he had been in the early days, and he wasn't sure he could ever settle down with one woman. He felt more responsible for her than anything. And to complicate things, Elvis had *two* women picking out their wedding gowns, since Ann-Margret was still expecting him to marry *her*.

With hindsight, I see that Colonel had a lot of reasons for wanting to see Elvis settled down and married, not the least of which was Elvis's increasing fetish for spiritualism, his eating binges, and the speculation among some of the show business community that Elvis was homosexual, latent or otherwise. Colonel rationalized that marriage might cost Elvis some of his sillier female fans, who fantasized they had a chance to win him themselves. But he figured that was the smaller price to pay. And so Colonel laid down the law, telling Elvis he had to go through with the ceremony. Otherwise, Captain Beaulieu would raise a stink smelled 'round the world. Priscilla was now twenty-one and a full-fledged woman, not just some underage plaything. The air force officer had no intention of letting Elvis toss aside his step-daughter with a stain on her reputation.

In recent years, writer Albert Goldman, and Elvis's step-brother David Stanley, have asserted that Elvis was so distraught about the impending wedding that he intentionally downed a fatal overdose of barbiturates one night after a violent fight with Priscilla. David says somebody found Elvis unconscious in his bedroom, and telephoned Vernon, who hung up the phone and hysterically blurted, "My son tried to kill himself!"

With that, Vernon supposedly rounded up the family and sped over to Graceland, where he ran up the stairs crying, "Son, please don't die! Don't die!" According to David, Elvis was laid out on the bed, with paramedics working frantically to administer oxygen and revive him.

I wasn't there, because I was running the ranch. But Marty and Billy insist that nothing like that ever happened, and I believe them. First of all, Elvis wasn't even home in Memphis at the time, since the delay with "Clambake" meant he filmed right up until three days before the wedding. Furthermore, the wedding took place in Las Vegas after a gathering at Elvis's new Palm Springs house of Priscilla's mother and step-father, Vernon and Dee, Colonel, Joe, Marty, Jerry Schilling, George Klein and their wives or girlfriends. Elvis hadn't been at Graceland in months.

Aside from that, the main reason I refuse to believe that Elvis tried to kill himself rather than marry Priscilla is that he was too big of a ham. If he'd meant to kill himself, he would have done it on national TV, because pardner, he was a show horse!

Besides, his religious beliefs strictly forbade it. Elvis may have hastened his death every time he popped a pill, but he viewed intentional suicide as a cop-out. And while he certainly wasn't in the strongest frame of mind around this time, he would have rationalized that if he married Priscilla and he felt the need to play around--he honestly believed it was "in his blood"--he would simply be discreet about his extramarital activities.

I always thought that if Elvis ever got married, he'd wed at home in Memphis. I was surprised, then, when Elvis said he and Priscilla were tying the knot in Las Vegas. But Vegas was where Frank Sinatra had married Mia Farrow the year before, a detail not lost on Colonel, who went out of his way to position Elvis as the Sinatra of his generation. In fact, Sinatra offered Elvis the use of his Learjet, "The Christina," to transport the newlyweds back to Palm Springs for their honeymoon.

That was Colonel's doing, no doubt, since he handled all the arrangements for the wedding, and since he was the only one in a position to notify Sinatra that Elvis was getting married. Still, Elvis didn't really want to get married in Las Vegas, but aside from the fact that it was easier for Colonel to maneuver in Las Vegas than Memphis, I'm sure he thought he could better control the privacy and press there. That way, Elvis and Priscilla could simply sneak in and out of town. Nobody lingered, that's for sure--the ceremony, held at the Aladdin Hotel, lasted exactly eight minutes.

Priscilla, who picked her wedding gown off the rack in Los Angeles, wore enough black eyeliner to keep the Avon lady, who regularly called on her at Graceland, in business for a year. Her thirteen-year-old sister, Michelle, graciously served as her maid of honor, and Joanie Esposito as her matron. And Elvis, whose black locks were piled in an unusually high helmet of hair--by now, it seemed his desire was to look more like Priscilla, with *her* looming architectural tower of hair, rather than have her look more like him--had two best men, Joe and Marty.

Most grooms scrape by with only one best man, of course, but the guys believed that Joe was hand-picked by Colonel, and that Elvis had asked Marty to stand up for him as a "consolation prize" after they'd had a knock-down, drag-out fight at Graceland several months earlier.

After the ceremony, Colonel announced the big news with great fanfare at a press conference in one of hotel's banquet rooms. Then Elvis introduced his bride, and mouthed the words that would have reporters scribbling down the makings of a storybook romance. "Priscilla was one of the few girls who was interested in me, for me alone," Elvis enthused in a mushy tone, his eyes snapping. "We never discussed marriage in Germany. We just met at her father's house, went to the movies, and did a lot of driving--that's all. I waited for her to grow up. We'll continue to live in Memphis, and we hope to spend a lot of time on my new horse farm in Mississippi."

Even at that moment, Elvis must have held his breath in fear that someone would uncover the fact that Priscilla had essentially been Elvis's jail-bait paramour--or so it would have appeared--but nobody did, and that was that. The press then adjourned to mingle with the tiny clot of guests in the Aladdin Room, which was all decked out for a $100,000 reception--a pretty fancy affair considering how short the guest list was. Harry Levitch, the jeweler, who'd made the wedding bands, was there, as was George Klein and his girlfriend, Barbara, and Gary Pepper, from the fan club. The rest of the abbreviated party were family--Patsy Presley Gambill, Elvis's cousin, and her husband, Gee Gee, who sometimes acted as Elvis's chauffeur, and Priscilla's parents and brother. Fourteen in all.

When the news hit the AP and UPI wire, girls all over the world flew into a frenzy of grief. Presumably, that included

Ann-Margret, whom Elvis had cut off without any explanation, more out of cowardice than cruelty. He'd simply stopped taking her calls, although in time, he would send her flowers on her opening nights in a gesture of friendship. If she was bitter about the way Elvis had dumped her like a common dog, she kept it to herself. She was a lady. Ten years later, when Elvis died, she and James Brown were two of the first people to come to Memphis.

Priscilla, who'd insisted that the word "obey" be stricken from her marriage vows--she would promise only to "love, honor and comfort" her husband--must have thought that those eight minutes before a justice of the Nevada Supreme Court ensured her a lengthy Palm Springs honeymoon, or at least some stretch of time in which she would finally be alone with her man. But once again she was fooled. The day after the wedding, Elvis went to Hollywood to complete some last-minute dubbing on "Clambake," leaving Priscilla to enjoy at least one day of her honeymoon by herself.

Surely Priscilla voiced hurt feelings over the situation, but when the couple returned to Memphis two days later, Elvis learned that she wasn't the only one miffed about how the wedding plans were handled. The secrecy and far-away location had prevented a number of Elvis's family and close friends, including Red West, from attending, and they felt shut out of what was supposed to have been one of the biggest days of Elvis's life. I never questioned not having been invited, because I realized Elvis couldn't include forty people in everything he did, and I knew he and Colonel didn't want the information to leak out.

My attitude was definitely not shared by most of the rest of the guys. To appease them, Elvis and Priscilla held yet a second reception, this one at Graceland, at the end of May. Priscilla climbed back into her wedding gown, and Elvis donned the same black, brocaded jacket and vest he had worn for the ceremony in Las Vegas. We all ate, drank and had a big time, even pretended to like the strolling accordion player. No one enjoyed the day more than Vernon, who for once didn't seem to be totaling up the expenses on a calculator in his head.

At the time, some of the guys speculated that the reason Vernon so whole-heartedly endorsed Elvis's marriage was because Priscilla was as much of a penny-pincher as he was. Now that she and Elvis were married, Priscilla was in a better position to assert financial influence over him, and to try to curtail his incessant spending.

All the same, they hadn't been married but a week when Elvis bought a split-level, French regency-style house at 1174 Hillcrest Road in L.A.'s affluent Trousdale Estates. Six years old and fully furnished, the house boasted four bedrooms, six bathrooms, an Olympic-size swimming pool, and a guest house. Until now, Elvis had merely rented the houses he and the guys lived in while he was making movies. But now he plunked down $400,000 for his first real home in the Los Angeles area. The reason given at the time was that the house, in a relatively private and secluded area--Danny Thomas lived at the end of the street--offered better security than the Rocca Place home.

Elvis was said to be concerned that some of his more ardent fans, upset over his marriage, might seek revenge by threatening to harm his new wife. As further protection, he installed one of the first Sony video cameras at the front gate, a camera he would later move to his bedroom to make sex tapes.

His real estate holdings now included Graceland, the Palm Springs home, the ranch in Mississippi, and the house in Trousdale Estates. He'd borrowed money to finance the newer properties, putting Graceland up as collateral. Vernon could hardly sleep at night, worrying about it all, and by November 1967, we'd be auctioning off some of the Circle G inventory, including most of the house trailers Elvis had bought for the guys. Elvis seemed to have gotten bored with the ranch, and he was tired of hearing how much money it cost. Little by little, we began closing it down.

I had been away from Elvis and the guys for some time, then, when Elvis invited me to California to see the Trousdale house, which was really just an excuse to see if I wanted to come back on the road. When I got out there, I was distressed to see that since Priscilla had taken a stronger stand with Elvis in the event of their marriage, some of the guys now fawned over both Elvis and Priscilla in the hope that she wouldn't single them out when she decided to reduce the size of the entourage.

In the old days, we used to put on a show for people who seemed mystified that Elvis kept a pack of guys around for the express purpose of granting his every wish. Whenever we found somebody like that, Elvis would play it to the hilt. If he sat in front of a yellow table, for example, he'd say, "Boys, that table looks red to me, right?" And everybody would say, "Right, Boss!" in unison.

It was funny at the time. But when I went back out to California for my visit, I found that the entourage had deteriorated into an "Emperor's New Clothes" situation.

I remember one night when Elvis stood looking at the stars. All of a sudden he turned to one of the guys and said, "You see that star? Well, keep watching, because I'm going to move it." The guy looked and looked, and then Elvis got excited and said, "Did you see that? Did you see it?" And the guy said, "Yeah, Elvis, I saw it! I saw it move!" On the way back to the car, Elvis leaned over to me and whispered, "Aw, he's full of bullshit. I was just testing him."

Elvis himself might have turned into a puppet where Colonel was concerned, but he didn't respect any of the guys who put their own strings in his hands, even if he also demanded loyalty to the extreme. The paradox was that he wanted the people around him to be stronger, but he couldn't take it if they were. It was a terrible "Catch-22." Elvis was in a situation where he got bored with everything, including the people he kept under his thumb. But he wouldn't risk the growth that came from self-examination or truth.

If the guys were already nervous that Priscilla would boot them out, their discomfort increased in mid-July, when Elvis announced on the set of "Speedway" that Priscilla had conceived on their honeymoon, and that they'd welcome a baby into the world the following February--exactly nine months from the day of the wedding. For years, Priscilla would cling to that convenient piece of timing as proof of her declaration that Elvis never physically consummated the relationship until after they were married.

I was concerned that Priscilla's pregnancy would have a negative effect on Elvis, that he would feel trapped by his new commitment and imminent fatherhood, and become even more self-destructive. But when I went out to the Sedona, Arizona, set of "Stay Away, Joe" in October 1967 to get some ponies to bring back to the ranch--we hadn't shut it down completely yet--it was obvious to me that Elvis beamed whenever he talked about the baby. The news seemed to be one of the few bright spots in his life.

And yet there was another spectacular event looming in Elvis's future. For quite awhile, now, Colonel had been hard at work trying to pull off what would eventually be regarded as the high point of Elvis's post-army career.

In January 1968, Colonel held a press conference to announce that NBC-TV would produce a one-hour Elvis special to be shown later that year during Christmas. The news was a total surprise to most of the guys, since Colonel had Elvis locked into the movie mill to such an extent that he hadn't appeared live on stage since he did the benefit for the U.S.S. Arizona in 1961. Furthermore, he hadn't made a TV appearance since Frank Sinatra's "Welcome Home, Elvis" special in 1960.

Why, then, did Colonel go to the network and propose offering Elvis for a television special that couldn't hope to pay as much as one of Elvis's formula movies, even if it took half the time? It was years before we would learn the real dollar figure--the Singer Sewing Machine Company paid $400,000 to sponsor the program, and another $275,000 for a rebroadcast-- but there probably wasn't additional money in the soundtrack, since it was released as part of Elvis's deal with RCA. We heard, though, that Colonel had cut a deal that allowed the special to be released as a movie sometime down the line, which would have allowed him to reap Elvis's customary million-dollar fee.

Yet perhaps an additional incentive was Colonel's tardy realization of just how miserable Elvis was in grinding out his romantic travelogues. Elvis told Colonel that he simply wasn't going to do any more of them once the contracts ran out, and where Colonel could have forced him to do just about anything he wanted, Colonel also saw the writing on the wall. The movies weren't losing money, but the grosses were leaner than they'd been in a long time, and there weren't any big pictures like "Blue Hawaii" on the schedule. Maybe a television special was just the thing to lure new fans and viewers, and to keep the Hollywood producers standing in line to get a piece of Elvis.

Colonel's philosophy had always been, "The more you keep them away, the more they'll want you." That's why he hadn't wanted Elvis to do much TV. Ricky Nelson had discovered that people figured they could turn on the television once a week and watch him perform on "The Adventures of Ozzie and Harriet," so they didn't need to shell out hard-earned money to see him in the movies. Conversely, Elvis had made so few television appearances that NBC was as happy as a speckled pup in a little red wagon to get him. The show quickly became the most anticipated event of the 1968-69 television season.

Elvis was scared out of his mind at the prospect of performing for television cameras after such a long time on the sound stages of Hollywood, where any mistake could easily be corrected. But he didn't have to face them until June. In the meantime, there was another matter vying for his attention-- the delivery of his child on or about February 1.

Elvis and the guys knew that the arrival of the foremost rock 'n' roll baby would be front page news in Memphis, and that reporters would want to be there when it happened. So they worked out an elaborate plan by which Elvis and Priscilla would go to the hospital when she began to feel her early labor pains. They rehearsed it over and over like a movie scene. First, several decoy cars would shoot out of the driveway to lead the press to Methodist Hospital--the wrong facility. Then Charlie would drive Elvis and Priscilla to Baptist Memorial Hospital, and Joe would follow in a back-up car in case Charlie's car broke down.

The funny thing is that on the morning of February 1, when Priscilla woke Elvis and told him it was time to go to the hospital, Charlie forgot the game plan, and, in a haze, began driving the route to Methodist! They must have looked like something out of the Keystone Cops, all these cars rushing around, with this woman in the back seat, ready to pop with child.

Actually, Priscilla was in labor a long time, and Elvis was out of his mind with worry. In addition to Vernon and Dee, Joe, Charlie, and a lot of the other guys showed up to keep him company--Richard, Jerry, Marty, George, and even Lamar, who'd just been on the fringes of the group since 1962. Finally, at five o'clock in the afternoon, Elvis learned he was the father of a 6 lb., 14 oz. girl. As soon as the nurse gave her permission, he slipped into Priscilla's room and whispered in her ear. "Nungen," he said, "us has a baby girl." He grinned like a guy who'd just jumped over the Empire State Building and hadn't torn his pants.

"Oh, man," he later told reporters, his voice filled with emotion. "She's just great. I'm still a little shaky. She's a doll. I felt all along that she'd be a girl." Elvis and Priscilla agreed to call her Lisa Marie, the second name in honor of Colonel's wife. Privately, Elvis would call his infant daughter "Buttonhead."

Elvis got to stay home with the baby for a little more than three weeks. Then he had to go to California to start work on "Live a Little, Love a Little," for MGM. Like "Stay Away, Joe," the movie updated Elvis's image a tad by allowing his screen character to intimate he'd just bedded down the leading starlet. But for once Elvis didn't have sex on his mind. Three days after he got to California, he missed Priscilla and the baby so much he asked Joe to bring them out west.

The baby made a tremendous difference in Elvis's attitude toward life in general. I think he was surprised at how much love she brought out in him, a love that spilled over to Priscilla. During a break in filming, Elvis drove her over to Las Vegas to catch Tom Jones at the Flamingo Hotel.

Much to Priscilla's wonder, Elvis now seemed to want to spend more time with her, and at the end of May, when filming wrapped on the movie, he took her to Hawaii for vacation. While they were there, they attended the Karate Tournament

of Champions, where Chuck Norris and a man named Mike Stone--later an infamous name in the Elvis saga as a man who could win Priscilla's affection--competed for the mainland against the islands.

Elvis used the trip as an opportunity to trim down his excess weight, since rehearsals for his NBC special, "Elvis"--today commonly referred to as the " '68 Comeback Special" or the "Singer Special"--were scheduled to begin in mid-June. Some of the guys say he tried to wean himself off of prescription drugs, too--although more out of his new sense of parental responsibility than for the TV special--and that he succeeded to a greater extent than anyone hoped.

The director of the show was Steve Binder. Binder knew that if the show were simply a Christmas special, as Colonel planned, it would be a hokey and sanctimonious hour of television. Early in the planning, Binder sat down with Elvis and learned that he was a lot more hip than the movies made him out to be, but that he still needed a jolt of reality. To that end, Binder did something that on the surface seemed cruel--he took Elvis out for a walk on the Sunset Strip, where not one soul recognized the King of Rock 'n' Roll. It shattered Elvis's illusions about not being able to go out in public, and I think it embarrassed him that Joe was along to see it. But it also drove home the truth about the ephemeral nature of fame like nothing else in this world. Binder wanted to restore Elvis to his former glory--and then some.

When the director told Colonel what he had in mind--a live performance of Elvis's old material, rebuilt for speed and guaranteed to strip the bark off the trees, Colonel put his foot down. "You want to do a Christmas special, don't you Elvis," Colonel prompted, staring at his charge across the room.

Elvis, smoking Dutch cigars and guzzling Pepsi, nodded affirmative. But then when Colonel turned away, Elvis looked at Binder and shook his head no. From then on, with the Sunset Strip stroll fresh in their minds, the two were in cahoots to do the show of Elvis's career.

Still, Elvis was scared shitless. He worried constantly about the fact that at thirty-three, he was a decade older than the newer rock acts, and that he was regarded by some as an "elder statesman." As such, he bolstered his shaky ego by bedding a number of young women Joe procured for him during rehearsals. Already, his new-found bliss with Priscilla was over, and now he was refusing to go home at night. After one or two o'clock in the morning, Joe and I would run girls in and out of the NBC dressing rooms as if the place were equipped with conveyers. I don't know how he did it. As for me, I was tired--those were long days--and I wanted to go home.

Binder's choice of settings--the casual guitar-pulling in the "living room" and the black-leather stand-up performance in front of a live audience--were nothing short of inspired, the exact arenas for Elvis to display what one writer called "a flare up of genius."

I don't know if Elvis had in mind Jim Morrison's recent black-leather slither, or the Tom Jones performance he had just seen in Vegas, but he knew that his fifties gyrations--the quivering pelvis, the frenetic shake of the leg--now seemed tame. Whether Binder prompted him or not, he realized how important it was for him to move with the fire and grace that was now all but gone from his screen performance--that it was imperative he sustain the old erotic tensions his movies had effectively sanitized.

He was lucky in that Binder, executive producer Bob Finkel, and musical director Bones Howe knew better than to haul in an orchestra made up of sixty-year-old men waiting to collect their retirement benefits. Some of the music was pre-taped with a large string section, but the tape was augmented by a terrific set of young rock musicians--Don Randi, piano, Mike Deasy and Tommy Tedesco on guitars, Larry Knechtel (later of Bread) on bass, and Hal Blaine, drums--who kept things raw and honking.

Colonel didn't like it one bit that he was being overruled about a Christmas theme. Yet, after he calmed down and quit griping that the music wasn't coming out of publishing companies that Elvis controlled, he accepted the premise of the show, even embracing the idea of Elvis closing the hour not with a traditional Christmas song, but with "If I Can Dream," a rhythm-and-blues tune with a kind of humanistic theme that Earl Brown had written especially for the show. Elvis loved the piece, since it gave him an opportunity to sing something of real depth, and allowed him to show off his range, suppressed too long in the three-note span of movie songs.

But Colonel finally drew the line when Binder shot his Boy in a bordello sequence. It wasn't anything terribly suggestive, really, because Elvis was supposed to be leaving home and taking to the road--an innocent making his way in the world-- when his path inevitably led to a whorehouse. He sang a song called "Let Yourself Go," and the way Binder filmed it, the girls, dressed in harem pants, came out of the background and danced over to him, letting him know by their gyrations what they had in mind. But before any transaction took place, police raided the house and Elvis was back out on the road. In 1968, some people might have thought it slightly risque. Today they wouldn't look twice. Still, Colonel said, "Definitely not!" even though it was the best thing in the show.

When we finished production on the special, everybody knew we had something extraordinary. That December, it earned a 32 rating and a 42 share, which made it the highest rated program of the week. Eventually, somebody figured out that more women aged eighteen to forty-nine watched it than they did any other special of the entire year. Bob Finkel even won a Peabody Award for it. And it essentially made Steve Binder's career.

But for Elvis, it meant something far greater. He had faced a challenge and triumphed in ways he didn't think possible. And even though he still had some film obligations, in a way, the "Comeback Special" signified the end to the long and largely barren movie years. In the coming months, Elvis would tackle the one performance arena that had closed him out years ago-- Las Vegas.

For me, the "Comeback Special" was surely the most exciting and important moment of my dozen years with Elvis. But I also thought of it as my swan song, something I reacted to with a mixture of fear and relief.

CHAPTER 17

"Shutters Set To Banging"

In retrospect, 1968 was a turning point for several of us who'd spent the better part of our lives around Elvis--it was the grey-black moment that the clouds rolled in before the storm.

Billy Smith, Elvis's first cousin, decided to leave the group just before the "Comeback Special." His father was seriously ill, and just as I had taken a leave of absence when my father was dying, Billy wanted to spend more time with his family. After that, he opted to go to work for the railroad rather than come back with us, in part so he could make a decent wage instead of the paltry salary we earned with Elvis.

Marty Lacker, too, left the entourage in late '68. Married with a family, he was weary of being away from home so much, and thought he'd give the local music business a try. He also found the situation with Priscilla, who was flexing more muscle than most of the guys liked, too uncomfortable. And he hated the way some of the guys, particularly Charlie--who was a hangnail away from one of his several nervous breakdowns-- gloated whenever any of the guys in the group defected. Later, in the seventies, Marty and Billy would return, although things would never be as they had before.

With Billy and Marty now gone, the brotherhood, for me at least, had fallen apart. I realized that I was largely without allies. I also saw that the dissatisfaction had been building up in me longer than I realized, that I hated the way I'd be home on Sundays and the guys would call and say, "Be here, be there." I was getting tired of traveling, and I was bored with it, too. And with Billy and Marty earning adult wages at their new jobs, I started thinking that one day it was all going to end. If Elvis decided to retire--I never even thought he might die--he wasn't going to need twenty or thirty people working for him.

I was now thirty-two, almost thirty-three, and I knew that if I were going to find a career, I'd better start exploring the possibilities. I always thought I'd go home and take over my father's scrapyard, but now he was gone, and somebody else was running things, and doing a good job of it. If I'd had some singing or songwriting talent of my own, or been involved on the music side of things with Elvis--working in publishing, playing an instrument, or booking his tours--it would have been different. But I could just see myself at forty-five, going for a job interview and having them say, "So, what have you done?"

"I traveled with Elvis Presley for twenty-five years."

"Well, that's wonderful, but we don't need anybody to travel around here."

I'd had a lot of fun, and I'd learned a lot, but it was all part of growing up. Now I was grown, and I needed to prove it. I didn't want to sit back and be a bum and live off of Elvis's name for the rest of my life, talking Elvis twenty-four hours a day. The trouble was, despite my boredom, the glamour had never worn off, and I was torn between staying and going.

For now, I did what I thought was the best, if not exactly the most mature thing--nothing. I figured something would happen to determine my fate. As far as my wife was concerned, it had better happen soon. She was growing increasingly restless with a part-time husband, a husband who was often too drugged up to be attentive to her.

Right after we filmed the "Comeback Special," Elvis went to his house in Palm Springs, where he seemed to spend more time. He had about a month to learn his lines for "Charro!" It was a western period piece set in 1870, to be shot in Arizona. I don't know why I felt that Elvis had retreated more into himself, but I did. Maybe it was because his Trousdale house had only four bedrooms, which meant that only a couple of the guys could stay there with Elvis and Priscilla and the baby, and the rest of us either got apartments or checked into hotels. Or maybe it was because Marty and Billy--who were really Elvis's best friends--had left. Whatever the reason, things just

Elvis as Jess Wade completing takes for "Charro!", the first movie he made without singing a song in the course of the film (although he sings the title song over the credits).

Elvis gets a dusting-off and studies the script between takes for "Charro!". Elvis had to grow a beard for the movie (the heat precluded the use of makeup to simulate a beard), so most of the rest of us grew beards, too--including Colonel!

didn't feel right. The old camaraderie seemed like history.

In July 1968, Elvis and the guys traveled to Apache Junction, Arizona, to begin location work on "Charro!" for National General Pictures. The movie was a rarity for Elvis--a dramatic role in which he never sang or played a guitar (except in the title tune over the opening credits), something he'd hungered to do for years. He played a character (Jess Wade) on the run from both American and Mexican officials, trying to prove his innocence on a trumped-up charge levied during the Mexican revolution. He was Clint Eastwood via Memphis, replete with squint, dirty serape, and a hat that obscured his eyes more often than not.

The lobby card advertised "Charro!" as, "A different kind of role. A different kind of man...On his neck he wore the brand of a killer. On his hip he wore vengeance." He also wore a real beard, or rather an authentic growth of stubble, since the Arizona heat precluded a fake one.

Elvis discovered that life at the ranch had finally paid off, since he was able to do a lot of his own riding in this film. I took my camera to the set, where I snapped a lot of pictures of him looking confident on a rearing horse. Unfortunately, I took a greater interest in the picture than a lot of Elvis's fans, who acted as if Elvis had just phoned in his performance. "Charro!" was one of the worst-received of his movies, a change of image apparently only Elvis appreciated.

In the next few months, Elvis would go on to make his last two films, "The Trouble with Girls (and How to Get into It)"-- another period piece set in the Roaring Twenties--and "Change of Habit," in which he was cast as a ghetto doctor, Dr. John Carpenter. Mary Tyler Moore co-starred, as a nun.

"Charro!" was my first film back on the set, but it would also be my last. I was tired of traveling. And too many bad omens were popping up. Elvis had a terrible bout with tonsillitis right after the film wrapped, and the same month, his cousin, twenty-six-year-old Bobby Smith, died of a heart attack. Dewey Phillips, the Memphis disc jockey who'd been the first person to play Elvis's "That's All Right (Mama)" on the air, also died that fall, of pneumonia. And barely a week later,

Elvis's uncle, Johnny Smith, one of the Graceland gate guards and the man who gave Elvis his real instruction on the guitar, likewise succumbed. It was enough to make me paranoid.

But while so many eras were ending in Elvis's private life, his professional life began to soar with the December broadcast of the TV special. A single from the show, "If I Can Dream," reached number twelve on the *Billboard* charts, the highest position any Elvis single had attained in three years. And the soundtrack also peaked high, staying on the charts for thirty-two weeks. Elvis was being taken seriously again. In England, a poll by the prestigious rock paper *New Musical Express* named him the "Outstanding Male Singer" of the year.

The "Comeback Special" gave Elvis a new shot of confidence about his live performance capabilities, and now he was eager to show what he could do in the recording studio, if serviced with the right kind of material. "I want to see if I can do it again," he said.

He got his chance at the American Sound Studios in Memphis in January 1969, in what would prove to be the most important recording sessions of the last half of his career. The twelve-day marathon sessions ran from eight at night until five in the morning on January 13-16, and stopped only because Elvis again came down with tonsillitis and a hundred-degree temperature. They resumed on January 20-23 and ran for another week beginning February 17.

Out of them came some of his most enduring work, including "Suspicious Minds," "In the Ghetto," and "Kentucky Rain," three singles which sold in excess of a million copies each. All in all, the thirty-six sides resulted in two gold albums, and signified that Elvis was a real presence again on radio. "Suspicious Minds," written by Mark James, became a double milestone, as Elvis's first number one record since the early part of the decade, and the last number one record of his career.

The sessions, which marked the first time Elvis had recorded in his hometown since his Sun Records days, came about largely because of a talk Elvis had with Marty, who never stopped being Elvis's friend, even though he was no longer his employee.

Marty was now making his living representing a number of music publishers, including Screen Gems. He knew there were great songs out there for Elvis to cut--they just weren't being published by companies willing to give up a third of a tune, as Colonel demanded. In no uncertain language, Marty told Elvis that that's the way it was. He could go outside of Hill and Range, who oversaw Elvis's publishing companies, and find some first-rate material to keep him on the top of the charts, or he could enjoy his new short-lived flurry of radio activity, and stay with the same old junky tunes. If he chose the latter, he'd look like an over-the-hill joke who just happened to hit a nostalgic winning streak.

Elvis said he didn't care who published them, but he wanted some good tunes, songs that would satisfy him as a creative artist, no matter if they sold a million records or not. And so Marty went looking for them, and he brought him some great stuff--not all of which Marty made money on. It was also Marty who lined up producer Chips Moman, who was red-hot at the time, and a completely new set of young pickers--the kind who know that one note with the right tone beats out a thousand weak notes--including Reggie Young, guitar; Tommy Cogbill, bass and guitar; Mike Leech, bass; Bobby Wood, piano; Bobby Emmons, organ; and Ronnie Milsap, piano and vocal on "Don't Cry Daddy." Some of the tracks were later overdubbed with the Memphis Horns.

Today, the mix on those sessions, particularly on the "From Elvis in Memphis" album, seems terribly unbalanced, with the bass guitar often more prominent than the rhythm or lead. But the soul is the very essence of what made Elvis Presley so great, a voice for the ages.

I went over to the studio for some of the sessions, and I remember how happy I was to see Elvis really back in his element again. The only hitch came when they played a demo tape of "Suspicious Minds," and Elvis said, "Yeah, man, I like it. I want to record it."

Colonel spoke up and said, "Just wait a minute. Let me work out the publishing first," meaning, of course, that he wanted a piece of it or Elvis wouldn't cut it. He went to Chips and began, "We'll do the song if you give us...," and Chips, who knew what was coming, just cut him off. He said, "No way, man. If he wants to do the song, he can do it. If he doesn't, we go on to the next."

Of course, Chips was kind of hard-headed, but he was right. And Elvis stood up for himself, for once. He turned to Colonel and said, "I don't care, Colonel. I like this song." And Colonel finally said, "Fine. We'll do it." I was shocked as hell. And I think Elvis was, too.

At the end of January, and before the sessions resumed in February, Elvis, Priscilla and Lisa Marie flew to Aspen, Colorado, for a couple of weeks. There, Elvis would relax, learn to ski, and he and Priscilla would celebrate Lisa Marie's first birthday. When they came back in the middle of February, Elvis was on top of the world, talking about how much he'd loved it there, and how he wanted to take all of us and our wives back the following week, after his sessions were finished with Chips. "We're gonna do it up right," he announced excitedly. "We're even gonna go to Beverly Hills and buy ski equipment."

Going to Colorado sounded all right to me, but I also knew that Elvis was moody enough to travel all that way, get to Aspen, and then not be able to find his favorite TV show, and say, "All right. Let's go back to Los Angeles." So I didn't take it all that seriously.

Sure enough, though, we went to California, and the next day, one of the guys said, "We're all gonna go down to the sporting goods store on Wilshire Boulevard and buy ski equipment. Be at the house at midnight. The store's gonna open up especially for us." I said, "Great." My wife and I went over to the house, Elvis came out, and we all went to the store.

When we got there, everybody started buying sweaters and vests and ski equipment, but my wife and I picked out only the bare necessities of what we thought we needed for the trip, because we figured we might not ever need it again. The total came to something like five or six hundred dollars for the two of us.

Normally when Elvis did something like that, he picked up

the tab. I thought it was fair, because we sure weren't making a lot of money, and I was keeping two apartments--one in Los Angeles and one in Memphis.

The clerk was settling up everybody's bill, then, and I saw all the guys taking out their credit cards. I went over to Elvis and said, "Look, I don't have any credit cards, but I don't owe anybody. Would you mind if I charged it to you? You could just take it out of my check."

Elvis said, "No, problem, man. Just get what you need."

So I told the clerk to charge the stuff to Elvis, and then I told Elvis I'd done it. I said, "I'll call your father and get it straight with him."

Later, we went over to Elvis's house, and as it so happened, Joe put a call in to Vernon. Joe turned to me and said, "I've got Vernon on the phone. How much do you want me to tell him to take out of your check?" I was surprised we were getting around to this so quickly. I said, "I don't know, Joe." I was making only about eight hundred a month, but I said, "Tell him to take out a hundred a week." Joe relayed the message in a kind of low voice that I didn't particularly like, and then he turned back and said, "Vernon wants to know if he can take out more."

I felt my anger spread like a rash across my face. Hell, I didn't owe anybody. Hell, I'd borrowed money from Elvis only once, when I bought a motorcycle in California, and I'd paid him back as soon as we got home to Memphis. Everybody else had borrowed money from him and never paid him back. So I said, "I'll tell you what, Joe. I'll go home and figure out my bills, and then I'll call you back and tell you how much to take out, okay?"

With that, my wife and I left. Driving home, it was all I could think about. I thought, "Man, isn't this some shit? Here I am making two hundred dollars a week, I'm keeping two apartments, I'm traveling back and forth, jumping every time Elvis snaps his fingers, and a hundred a week isn't going to be enough on a six-hundred-dollar tab."

As soon as I got back to the apartment, I called up Joe. I said, "I've been thinking, Joe. If it's such a big deal charging

the clothes to Elvis, why don't I just take the clothes back? I
don't need any ski clothes, and I don't need any damn sweaters. Tell Elvis I'll just go with what I have. If that's gonna put
Vernon in a bind, then I don't want to do it."

Joe was silent for a minute, like I'd knocked the wind out of
him. Finally, he spoke.

"Are you serious? Do you really want me to tell him that?"

"Sure, tell him that."

Five minutes later, the phone rang again. Joe sounded
strange.

"Alan?"

"What?"

"Elvis said you don't have to go to Aspen."

"Okay," I said. "That's great." I was steamed.

"And he said to tell you you've got four weeks' notice."

For a second, I couldn't say anything. I couldn't even think
of any of the words in the English language. I was completely
stunned. For nearly a year, I'd figured I wouldn't be an Elvis
employee that much longer. But I always thought I'd quit--I
never thought it would happen like this. After what seemed
like an hour, I managed to say, "I'll talk to you later," and hung
up. That was it.

In the years that I've had to think about it, I've concluded
that it wasn't Elvis who made the decision. It was Vernon. I
never held anything against Priscilla at all. It was only natural that she thought there were too many guys around her
husband. But I knew Vernon didn't like Jews, and that he was
jealous of their success, although he seemed to trust them
more after Elvis went to Hollywood and dealt with so many
Jewish producers and directors. He seemed to figure out that
he had to look past the religion to the individual.

In the next weeks and months, I fell into a deep depression.
Traveling with Elvis meant that I'd never had much time for
my wife, Jo. We never should have gotten married to start
with, and during the time I was on the road, the gulf between
us had grown wider. At the same time, her interests changed.
Even when I was in town, or I could take her with me on the
out-of-town trips, I'd be gone all day, and then I'd come home

and take sleeping pills just to be able to relax. I was still popping six or eight pills a day, mostly Dexedrine and Dexamil to stay awake, and Seconal and Placidyl to go to sleep. I also drank more than I should have, and I did a lot more of it when I got fired.

Jo just couldn't take it, and one day she announced she was leaving if I didn't shape up. Now I was more despondent than ever. Pretty soon I was drinking a lot more and taking more pills, and I'd wake up and not know if I'd taken a sleeping pill or not. As a result, one night I took too many.

The only thing that saved me was that I was smoking a cigarette, and the cigarette fell on the bed and the mattress started smoldering. Jo smelled smoke and called Red West, who ran over and called the ambulance. Red said I wasn't breathing, and that I was already black. They took me to UCLA Medical Center. For the next few days, I was apparently delirious, because they said I was biting and kicking the nurses, and tearing the equipment up. I have a vague recollection of being strapped to a table in the emergency room, and having my stomach pumped. Pills just came up whole, they said. That's probably what saved me. The pills didn't have time to dissolve.

All I really remember is waking up five days later tied to the bed. I was going through withdrawal, and the doctor offered to give me something to help ease me off the drugs. I said, "Uh-uh, I don't need anything. I'm getting out of here, and I'll promise you, you'll never see me back on drugs again."

When I got out, I started hallucinating. I thought I saw people staring at me over the fence. I thought I'd robbed a liquor store. I could feel the house breathing on me. The doctor said, "You've just been doing them so long that they've slowly been eating you away. You've got to give yourself time to rebuild." All the guys came to see me. Elvis, whom I also thought I saw through a groggy haze, although I might have been dreaming, paid my hospital bill.

Some of the guys thought it was a suicide attempt. Now, I might have killed my wife, but I wouldn't have killed myself. Even so, I almost died because of my stupidity, trying to cure my sorrows with a bottle of pills and a bottle of whiskey. You always think you're the smart one, that you can do it, and it's not going to control you. The next thing you know, you wake up dead, or pretty close to it. I was lucky.

For the next few months, I stayed in California working as an extra in the movies. I worked almost every day, because of the contacts of casting directors and assistant directors I made with Elvis. I'd remembered that old adage about being nice to people on your way up, because they're the same people you'll see on the way down.

The irony was that I made more money per week as an extra than I'd ever made with Elvis, working regular days plus overtime. I worked on the sequel to "Planet of the Apes," called "Beneath the Planet of the Apes," with James Franciscus and Charlton Heston, in which I wore--what else?--an ape mask. Then I was in a crowd scene in "They Shoot Horses, Don't They?" with Jane Fonda and Gig Young, who'd been in "Kid Galahad." And I was in "Rachel, Rachel," which Paul Newman directed for his wife, Joanne Woodward, and in "Suppose They Gave a War and Nobody Came," with Tony Curtis and Ernest Borgnine. I was also in some Elizabeth Taylor vehicle, the title of which I've forgotten.

I never had to worry about working as long as people I knew stayed in the business, and I'm sure I could have worked in television with Gary Lockwood in "The Lieutenant" series if I'd tried. Or with Kent McCord on "Route 66," since I used to let him work in Elvis's movies as an extra when he was still using his real name of McWhorter. But I could also see that a lot of people worked for six months, and then waited tables for two years. If I'd been a decent actor, it might have been a different story. But I knew I was an extra, and that I'd always be an extra.

After three or four months out there, I got tired of the rat race and decided to come home. California wasn't really my cup of tea, and it wasn't where I really wanted to live. The first thing I did when I got home was file for a divorce. The next thing I did was see about a job. Before I left California, I'd called a guy in Memphis that I'd been friends with since I was

ten years old. His name was Herb O'Mell. We'd gone every-where together as kids, and now Herbie owned the hottest club in Memphis, T.J.'s, where Ronnie Milsap, still a relative un-known, led the house band.

I'd told Herb how unhappy I was, that I didn't think I wanted to stay out in California for the rest of my life, but that I didn't know what to do. Herb said, "Come on home, Alan. You can work at the club and live with me." I packed up and left the next day.

I was Herb's manager and bartender at T.J.'s for about a year and a half, making $125 a week. Bartending wasn't as complicated then as it is now, since there weren't that many different kinds of drinks. Even so, I wasn't the greatest at it, but Herbie trained me, and I did all right. After a while, Richard Davis started working there, too.

When I first got back to Memphis, I was still a little miffed at Elvis. I was grateful that he'd paid my hospital bill, but never once had he picked up the phone to say he was sorry for the way the firing came down, or to explain why he didn't intervene. And that hurt. Then one day, I thought, "What the hell?" and I went on out to Graceland. In a 'round-about way, he apologized. Well, not really, but I could tell he was sorry. He asked why I hadn't come to see him sooner. I told him that I didn't get along that well with the guys he had working for him then, that I felt they were sycophants and not strong enough to be their own men. Besides, I just didn't go out a lot. I was surprised, then, when Elvis asked me if I'd start coming back out to the house on a regular basis.

As the holidays approached, I drove out to Graceland and told Elvis that Richard was working at the club now, and that we'd love to have him come out for New Year's Eve. It was December 1969, and I thought we should give the sixties a big send-off--welcome a new decade.

For years, Elvis had thrown a New Year's Eve party at the Manhattan Club. But now I said, "T.J.'s is the best club in Memphis, Elvis. We'll just sell it out until you lock the doors." And Elvis said yes. Flash and the Board of Directors played that night, with Ronnie Milsap and Mark James, who wrote "Suspicious Minds," as special guests. Everyone had a great time. It was good to see Elvis enjoying himself like the old days.

But it was also time for me to have some happiness of my own. The day after my divorce became final, I got married again, to a pretty, dark-haired woman named Marian Stokes. Marian was originally from the Carolinas and had lived with her grandparents growing up. Her mother was from Memphis. As with Jo, Marian had dated a friend of mine, and when I came back in town and learned that she and my friend had broken up, we started dating. She used to come into T.J.'s, and I told her that the only reason I'd get married was to have kids. Nine or ten months after the ceremony, our son, Miles, was born. I was happier than I'd ever been in my life.

Not too long after the wedding, I began looking closely at some of T.J.'s clientele, and at my own future. I saw a lot of young guys and girls coming in wearing silk suits and gold jewelry, and driving Cadillacs and Lincolns. A lot of them came in every night and spent anywhere from twenty-five to a hundred dollars a pop, which was a considerable amount of money to blow in a Memphis bar in those days, especially every day.

Finally, I asked Herbie, "What do these guys do?" He explained to me that they were in the bond business. I didn't know from bonds. I said, "Bail bonds?" He said, "No, tax free municipal bonds. It's the latest craze in Memphis."

I asked a couple of these guys if they were in the bond business, and sure enough, they were. One in particular used to talk to me a lot, and one day he said, "You know, Alan, I like you. I'm getting ready to enlarge my company, and when I do, I want you to come to work for me." I told him that I appreciated it, but that I didn't know anything about that business.

"Don't worry," he said. "We'll teach you. You can even keep your job here and work for me in the daytime. I'll pay you two hundred a week while you're learning."

What could I lose? I thought I'd do it for a couple of weeks and make some money, and that would be the end of it.

As expected, the first day on the job, I felt as if I were in a foreign country. They were talking about New York City G.O.s (general obligations), and Puerto Rican telephone revs--and I didn't even know that "revs" meant "revenues." I went home and told Marian, "I don't know. It's all Greek to me. I don't think I'm going back."

Marian said, "Yes, you are. It's one thing if you don't make it, but you're not going to be a quitter. If you're going to be one of those, you might as well take your clothes and move out." I didn't feel like living with Herbie again, so I told her I'd go back. I've been in the municipal bonds business ever since.

Once I began working regular hours, I didn't have much time to go out to Graceland anymore. I took Marian out there a few times, and she and I went to one of Elvis's Nashville concerts in 1973. But that was about it. In my business, you have to be in the office between seven and half past seven in the morning, because it's an hour later in New York than in Memphis, and our market opens on New York time. We make more money from seven to nine than we do the rest of the day combined.

All the same, I'd run into Elvis from time to time, and even though I hadn't seen him that much, we were still friends. I knew it, and he knew it. We had too much history together for our friendship to fade away. Right after Priscilla left him in 1972, I sent him my regards. My marriage to Marian was just about bust, too, and I could commiserate. Elvis joked that he always said, "I came, I saw, I conquered," but that Priscilla said, "I came, I saw, I left."

But Elvis couldn't just keep Priscilla chained to the house, doing nothing all day long. She was no longer fourteen years old and content to wait around while Elvis and the guys sprinted off to Palm Springs or Las Vegas, leaving her alone in L.A. or Memphis. He still insisted he was going to be Elvis, of course, which meant that if he saw a good-looking girl, he was going to have to talk with her. And Priscilla, who complained of a lack of intimate relations with her husband, just said, "I'm not gonna sit here and wait until I'm forty years old and he decides to leave. I'm going to do something about it."

A lot of the fans felt that Priscilla betrayed Elvis when she left, but I can't say that I blame her. Elvis probably wanted to be intimate with her, but if you don't have much private self left anymore, that's hard to do. Elvis could have kept Priscilla if he'd wanted her to stay. The trouble was, he wanted it all, and that included his freedom.

As the years wore on, I saw Elvis less and less. But since Marty and Lamar and Billy were back with him in the last years, I heard plenty about his deteriorating health and his escalating drug use. If the stories had come from anybody but those three, I wouldn't have believed them. Even still, they were horror stories--tales that on a typical night Elvis would consume thirty-three sleeping pills and nine shots of Demerol, and that he regularly ingested large doses of Quaalude, Morphine, and Codeine, in addition to the old pills we used to eat like candy.

That meant that his internal organs were like those of a ninety-year-old man, his heart enlarged and clogged. And, never fond of bathing, he would now go for such long periods without a shower that he developed a series of bacterial skin infections.

It broke my heart to hear this. But although he'd entered Baptist Hospital on occasion to detox, he'd stay clean only until he met his challenge--like the "Elvis: Aloha, From Hawaii" TV special in 1973--or until he felt pressured. Then he'd go right back to his old habits. Since Priscilla's pleas for him to enter a California drug treatment center fell on closed ears, I knew it was fruitless for me to try to talk him into checking into a hospital. Nobody can get you off of drugs. You have to want to get off of them first. And Elvis was too egotistical, and too hooked, with his tolerance for amphetamines and barbiturates at a frightening level, to stop.

Neither the efforts of Dr. Nick nor Vernon--who must have freaked at paying all the bills that came in from the prescription houses--would sway him. He'd built up such immunities that he needed more and more drugs to reach the same effect, and he was always looking for something new.

I doubt if Elvis would have done anything about his habit,

even if Lisa Marie had pleaded with the angels of his soul. Certainly Red, Sonny, and Dave Hebler's book, *Elvis: What Happened?*, which he read in galleys just before his death, did nothing to jar him into cancelling his tour and entering treatment, although Billy says he worried about how his fans would react to the knowledge of his extensive drug use. In the end, though, nothing really mattered much to him. He was simply, as he told producer Felton Jarvis in 1977, "tired of being Elvis Presley." And he was slowly, systematically doing something toward eradicating that problem, consciously or not.

If only Colonel had found more challenges for him! Elvis was like a kid who looks forward to Christmas. And then Christmas finally comes, and it's over within five minutes. He was a victim of circumstances, a man who had conquered every mountain he had tried to climb. There wasn't anything left for him to achieve, the way Colonel structured things, and he got bored. Bored literally to death. He needed something to work for--a good movie role, maybe--and he didn't have it. At one point, he told Priscilla, "Good old Colonel. We've come a long way. He's still puttin' out that same old stuff. It's a wonder people are still buying it."

And it was a wonder Elvis didn't self-destruct earlier than he did, with his hopes and dreams dissipated like puffs of smoke. He had as much money as he needed, even if he did experience a cash flow problem in the latter years, something Colonel tried to cover by having RCA transfer a million dollars to Elvis's checking account when he died. And he had as many women as he wanted, including a real sweetheart in Linda Thompson, who truly cared for him. He could have been a much better husband and father, of course. But what did he have to *work* for in those latter years? Nothing, the way he looked at it. Pity the man who sees no purpose in life. And cry for Elvis Presley.

The last time I saw Elvis alive was six or eight months before his death. I'd stayed in touch with Joe, Richard, and Red, and one night, they told me Elvis was going to go throw one of his ritual, all-night movie-watching sessions at the Memphian Theatre. I couldn't go--I had to get up early in the morning to go to work. But I promised I'd drop by on my way in.

I was flabbergasted at how bloated Elvis was, and how he seemed like some grotesque caricature of the long-ago King of Rock 'n' Roll. There was an unnaturalness about his size, just as there had been about his mother's. Something was radically wrong. At 255 pounds, he looked as if he might burst open before me, like some kind of overripe fruit. It scared me.

We chatted for what I'd guess was thirty minutes. Elvis asked me how I was doing, and how my son, Miles, was. But he didn't ask me to come back to work for him. He knew I wouldn't. He hated to see people he loved leave the group, but he liked to see them go out on their own and make a success of themselves, too. When Jerry Schilling, with whom Elvis had had several bitter arguments, got into film editing at Paramount, Elvis loved it. He rarely asked people to come back to work unless he knew they weren't doing too well. I felt we were good friends again, and that it might just be better to leave it that way.

Several times during the last two years of Elvis's life, I heard rumors that he was dead or dying, that he suffered from a terminal illness, such as bone cancer or advanced cancer of the colon. I didn't know what to think. But I always checked the rumors out.

Then on August 16, 1977, the earth stopped spinning. It started as a day of anticipation--the day the workmen would pour concrete for my swimming pool--but it quickly turned chaotic. I was into a busy morning at the office when the concrete man called and asked me to come home to see how much extra surface I wanted. Then while we were standing there, my son, Miles, came running down the street with his arm cut open like a watermelon. I rushed him to the hospital, where the doctor's needle and thread took twenty-five stitches.

When I got back to the office and settled down after lunch, I got a phone call from someone who said, "Hey, man, there's a rumor that Elvis is dead." I said, "Aw, man, cut that stuff." Then five more calls came in quick succession, all saying the same thing. Finally, I thought, "I'd better look into this."

I hung up and dialed George Klein at his office. George was out of the office on an emergency. I felt a terrible stab of pain in my stomach, and a pasty taste in my mouth. My breathing grew labored. I quickly called Graceland, and one of the maids answered, crying. I said, "This is Alan." And she said, "Oh, Mr. Alan...," and I knew it was no rumor this time. "I'll be right over," I rasped. When I got there, it was really spooky. Elvis was supposed to have left for Portland, Maine, that night for the first show of the tour. All his luggage and costumes were setting in the hallway, packed and ready to be put on the plane.

A day passed of numbing pain and sadness. Telephone calls. Random memories. Good times. Pharmaceutical nightmares. Flashes of Elvis riding the deserted downtown streets of Memphis in the small, thin hours of the morning, when the citizenry were asleep and the town belonged only to him. "My boy, my boy, my boy." How in God's name could this have happened? Why in hell had I not tried to help?

It was a mighty lonely feeling. I empathized with John Filiatreau, a reporter for the Louisville *Courier-Journal* who covered the funeral, and who had written about his own mother's death only a couple of years before: "She who could not have died was dead so quick, the years of dread were shutters set to banging."

The galaxy had emptied by half.

Going back to Graceland to say good-bye was one of the hardest things I've ever had to do. I couldn't get over the way he was laid out, in a white business suit his father had given him for Christmas, his hair styled--by Larry Geller, no less--in a lubricious pompadour. I kept thinking of one of the songs he'd cut with Chips, "Long Black Limousine." Of course, Vernon had arranged for a white hearse to carry the coffin, but the sadness and the irony of that song just hit home. Elvis hadn't died in a car crash, as the lyric went, but one part of the verse was certainly true: "My heart and my dreams are with you in that long...limousine."

When it came time to carry Elvis's body out to Forest Hill, Lamar and I, and George and Charlie Hodge stood out in the

Elvis's gravesite at Graceland, between those of Minnie Mae and Vernon.
(Photo: Alanna Nash)

yard, waiting to get in one of the Cadillacs to go to the cemetery. It was one of those August days hot enough to turn milk into cheese, and just eerily still, with not enough wind stirring to blow dandelion dust. We were watching as the coffin was being carried out the front door, when a huge limb fell off one of the trees in front of Graceland with a terrific crash.

The tree had been standing there for thirty years, but for some reason, it just decided to dump a limb on the very day Elvis's body was being hauled out of the house. Everybody immediately thought of all of Elvis's mystical shit, but nobody dared move a muscle.

Finally, Lamar looked up and turned about fifty shades. "We believed you'd be back, Elvis," he said with his usual dry wit, "but not this soon." Still, Colonel had the best line: "Elvis isn't dead," he said. "Just his body is gone."

I couldn't believe the sheer numbers of floral arrangements--everything from the stately to the unbelievably tacky. ("Jesus Called," said one banner, wrapped around a telephone and a spread of chrysanthemums.) But the pandemonium--the awesome mourning and hysteria--on the street in front of Graceland was unlike anything I had ever witnessed. Women fainted from the grief and the heat, and men cried as if they'd lost a member of their family.

In a way, of course, they had. In a few short years, almost single-handedly, Elvis had changed the attitudes of the world. Not only about sexuality and "race music," but about class barriers, taste, and Southerners themselves. To those who never knew or who had forgotten, Elvis proved that to be poor and Southern did not mean you didn't count.

When he died, country music, once the voice of the Southern working class and the illiterate, was well on its way to mass acceptance all around the world. And a peanut farmer from Georgia was living in the White House. They owed Elvis no small vote of thanks. The surprise was that his death was a catharsis not just for the poor or the working class of the South, but also for the middle class of the East, the West, the North.

And the irony was that for all of his millions and mansions,

Elvis still had "too many rough edges for anyone ever to smooth away," as rock chronicler Greil Marcus wrote. He was no longer of the class that produced him, but he would never be of the class whose income bracket he shared. To everyone but Elvis, of course, that mattered not at all. He had taught them that himself.

Since then, thousands of articles and some one hundred books have been written about him, many of them a disgraceful waste of trees. I do not believe that Elvis is alive and living in Michigan--or anywhere else, for that matter. Nor do I believe that any of the so-called illegitimate offspring are indeed the children of Elvis Presley. He was far too careful for that, and if he knew that he had sired a child, he would have certainly provided for his welfare. And Dr. Nick's assertion that Elvis was murdered is too preposterous for words. I can only think that Dr. Nick somehow got pressured into saying that before he had a chance to think it out.

Furthermore, no matter what odd or kinky habits Elvis might have indulged in his latter years, including visits to the morgue and local funeral homes--stories which are inherently true, but which have been wildly exaggerated--Elvis was not the wacko freak a couple of the Elvis biographers have tried to make him out to be.

He was simply an immensely talented, intensely troubled man. No saint. No satyr. "The pure products of America go crazy," the poet William Carlos Williams once wrote. Elvis's life was a dream with no way out but the end.

Yet, for me, it will never be over. I don't think about him constantly the way I used to, and I've quit castigating myself about what happened. But it is impossible to separate my life with Elvis from my life, period. It just goes on. At Dr. Nichopolous's hearing in 1980, I was a subpoenaed witness. The Tennessee state health department had decided I was one of the patients Dr. Nichopolous had over-medicated, along with Elvis. Dr. Howard Foreman of Nashville took a look at my prescription records and found sizable quantities of Placidyl, Eskatrol, and Quaalude.

"Are you abusing medicine?" he asked me.

A photo of me with ex-Memphis Mafia buddy Charlie Hodge,
taken at Memphis State University in the mid-1980s.
(Photo: Alanna Nash)

"I'm still alive," I said.

And so I am, despite a recent bout with cancer.

Like everybody else, I still miss him. But for better or worse, I also have a part of Elvis inside of me. Everybody wants a touch of Elvis. And nobody wants to let go.

###

"My boy, my boy, my boy. . . ."
Elvis the way I want to remember him--sitting on a beach, looking out to sea,
his arm around a pretty girl's waist.

General Index